THE ELECTIONS
OF 1992

THE ELECTIONS
OF 1992

Edited by
Michael Nelson
Rhodes College

PRESS

A Division of Congressional Quarterly Inc.
Washington, D.C.

Cover design: Ed Atkeson, Berg Design, Albany, New York

Printed in the United States of America
Second Printing

Library of Congress
Cataloging-in-Publication Data

The Elections of 1992 / Michael Nelson, editor.
p.   cm.
Includes bibliographical references.
ISBN 0-87187-937-9 : ISBN 0-87187-657-4 (pbk.)
1. Presidents--United States--Election--1992.   2. United States. Congress--
Elections, 1992.   3. Elections--United States.
I. Nelson, Michael, 1949-.
JK1968   1992b
324.973'0928--dc20   93-2783
                                                         CIP

Soli Deo Gloria

Contents

Preface

How, and for what, will the elections of 1992 be remembered? Will they be remembered mainly, as the authors of one chapter suggest, as "one of the most surprising and significant elections of the twentieth century"? Or, as another author argues, will they enter history mostly in familiar form, perhaps as the latest in a century-long series of elections that constitute "a recurring cycle of electoral politics and governmental response"?

A variety of answers to these questions are offered in this book, and I have made no effort as editor and coauthor to shoehorn my colleagues' views into a single, cramped perspective. My approach in designing *The Elections of 1992* was the same as for its predecessors, *The Elections of 1984* and *The Elections of 1988:* first, to assemble, more than a year before election day, a team of authors with well-established expertise and a demonstrated ability to write clearly and engagingly, and, second, to commission them to describe and analyze the elections both as a set of distinct events and in broader historical and theoretical context. This charge they have fulfilled. In the course of doing so, they have uncovered much that was new and much that was familiar about the 1992 presidential and congressional elections.

Among the new elements in 1992 (new, that is, to the modern political era) were these: the generational change in executive leadership brought about by the election of baby boomers Bill Clinton and Albert Gore, Jr.; the election, for the first time in sixteen years, of a Democrat as president; the improved quality of the presidential campaign; a number of innovative campaign roles for the media, both as a tool for and monitor of the candidates; the independent candidacy of Ross Perot, who won a larger share of popular votes than any independent candidate since Theodore Roosevelt in 1912; the rapid change in the demographic makeup of Congress, as many new women, African Americans, and Latinos were elected; and the end (or interruption) of the quarter-century era of divided government, during which the Republicans dominated the presidency and the Democrats controlled Congress.

Not everything about the elections was new, however. The familiar aspects of the elections included the century-long cycle of politics and policy into which Clinton's election fell; the structured workings of the once novel but now established presidential nominating process; the role of the modern vice presidency in the campaign; and the mix of "valence politics" and cultural politics that constitutes the substance of modern elections.

The contributors to this book are more than qualified to make sense of the unusually interesting elections of 1992. Donald E. Stokes and John J. DiIulio, Jr., of Princeton University describe the historical and political setting of the elections in Chapter 1. Ryan J. Barilleaux and Randall E. Adkins of Miami University of Ohio analyze the Republican and Democratic presidential nominating contests in Chapter 2. In Chapter 3, Paul J. Quirk and Jon K. Dalager of the University of Illinois at Urbana-Champaign sort out the general election campaign and results. Philip Meyer of the University of North Carolina at Chapel Hill assesses the media's roles in the election in Chapter 4. Jean Bethke Elshtain of Vanderbilt University interprets the campaign's issues and themes in Chapter 5. I analyze the consequences of the elections for the presidency in Chapter 6; Gary C. Jacobson of the University of California, San Diego, does so for Congress in Chapter 7. And Chapter 8, the concluding chapter, summarizes and synthesizes the various authors' findings.

Many hands, not least of them the authors', have labored long and hard to make this book, like its predecessors, the first and best volume on the elections. My thanks are longstanding to David Tarr, director of the Book Department, and Nancy Lammers, assistant director, who have worked with me on this series of postelection books from the beginning. Thanks are also gratefully extended to those with whom I worked for the first time on this book but whose assurance, skill, and warmth quickly made them seem like old friends and colleagues: developmental editor, Shana Wagger, and senior editor, Ann Davies. Steven B. Kennedy, Nola Healy Lynch, and Jon Preimesberger brought their considerable talents to the editorial process. And my beloved family Linda E. Nelson, Michael C. L. Nelson, Jr., and Samuel M. L. Nelson sustained me as husband and father even when I edited manuscripts under the Christmas tree.

Michael Nelson

Contributors

Randall E. Adkins is a doctoral candidate in political science at Miami University of Ohio. His research interests include the presidency, electoral politics, and American foreign policy.

Ryan J. Barilleaux is associate professor of political science at Miami University of Ohio. He is the author of *The President and Foreign Affairs* (1985) and *The Post-Modern Presidency* (1988) and the coeditor of *Leadership and the Bush Presidency* (1992).

Jon K. Dalager, an attorney, is a doctoral candidate in political science at the University of Illinois at Urbana-Champaign. His dissertation research concerns the effect of the mass media on presidential elections.

John J. DiIulio, Jr., is professor of politics and public affairs at Princeton University and nonresident senior fellow at the Brookings Institution. He is the author of *Governing Prisons* (1987) and *No Escape* (1991) and the editor of *Courts, Corrections, and the Constitution* (1990). The founding director of Princeton's Center of Domestic and Comparative Policy Studies, he is a member of the National Commission on State and Local Public Service.

Jean Bethke Elshtain is the Centennial Professor of Political Science and professor of philosophy at Vanderbilt University, where she directs the program in social and political thought. She is the author of *Women and War* (1987) and *Power Trips and Other Journeys* (1991) and editor of *Just War Theory* (1992). A second edition of her book *Public Man, Private Woman* will appear this year.

Gary C. Jacobson is professor of political science at the University of California, San Diego. He is the author of *Money in Congressional Elections* (1980), *The Electoral Origins of Divided Government* (1990), and *The Politics of Congressional Elections* (3d ed., 1991), and the coauthor of *Strategy and Choice in Congressional Elections* (2d ed., 1983).

Philip Meyer is Knight Professor of Journalism at the University of North Carolina at Chapel Hill and president of the World Association for Public Opinion Research. His most recent books include *The Newspaper Survival Book* (1985), *Ethical Journalism* (1987), and *The New Precision Journalism* (1992).

Michael Nelson is professor of political science at Rhodes College. A former editor of the *Washington Monthly*, he has written articles that have appeared in numerous scholarly publications and popular magazines. He is the author, coauthor, or editor of fourteen books on the presidency, including *Presidents, Politics, and Policy* (1984), *The Elections of 1984* (1985), *The Elections of 1988* (1989), *The Presidency and the Political System* (3d ed., 1990), and *The American Presidency: Origins and Development, 1776-1990* with Sidney M. Milkis (1990), which won the Benjamin Franklin Award for History, Politics, and Philosophy.

Paul J. Quirk is associate professor of political science at the University of Illinois at Urbana-Champaign. He is the author of *Industry Influence in Federal Regulatory Agencies* (1981) and the coauthor of *The Politics of Deregulation* (1985). He is currently writing a book about the president and public policy making.

Donald E. Stokes is Class of 1943 University Professor of Politics and Public Affairs at Princeton University and former dean of Princeton's Woodrow Wilson School of Public and International Affairs. He is the coauthor of *The American Voter* (1960), *Elections and the Political Order* (1966), and *Political Change in Britain* (1974), winner of the Woodrow Wilson Award.

1

The Setting:
Valence Politics in Modern Elections

Donald E. Stokes and John J. DiIulio, Jr.

According to the civics book model of democracy, the job of the presidential candidates is to take opposing positions on the issues confronting the nation, and the job of the voters is to study those positions and vote accordingly. Political scientists have invested enormous energy in efforts to discern how well the candidates and, especially, the voters fulfill their responsibilities in this model of "position politics." The results of their labors have been, at best, mixed.

In this chapter, Donald E. Stokes and John J. DiIulio, Jr., offer a different model of issues campaigning and voting in recent U.S. elections, with particular attention to the 1992 contest between the Republican incumbent, George Bush, the Democratic challenger, Gov. Bill Clinton, and independent candidate Ross Perot. They find that most modern elections are dominated by "valence issues"—that is, issues on which the voters distinguish parties and candidates not by their real or perceived differences on position issues but by the degree to which they are linked in the voters' minds with conditions, symbols, or goals that are almost universally approved or disapproved by the electorate, such as economic prosperity, public corruption, and resolute leadership. The authors go on to explain the origins and the consequences of valence politics in the United States.

Two transitions stand out in the presidential election of 1992. The election marked first of all a transition in party control. America's parties were born in Thomas Jefferson's time, reborn in Andrew Jackson's, and took their modern form in Abraham Lincoln's day as a means to capture the great prize of our politics, the presidency. Only once since Richard Nixon's accession to the presidency in 1968 had the Republican hold on this prize been broken, and then only by Jimmy Carter's single term. The first, signal transition in 1992 was therefore the return of a Democrat to the White House.

The second was the passing of leadership to a new generation. George Bush was not only of the generation that fought World War II; in the course of the campaign he repeatedly disclosed how deeply his view of the world and the imperatives of leadership were shaped by that war. Bill Clinton was, by contrast, not only of the generation that experienced the dilemmas of the Vietnam War; in the course of the campaign he repeatedly showed how deeply these dilemmas had touched his life. The succession of generations is also part of what gives significance to the election.

These changes were so visible as to partially conceal a third transition of great significance, one that has been building through a series of elections: the transition to a newer, more fluid politics, far less constrained than in the past by party alignments rooted in issues of great power and durability. We address ourselves mainly to this third signal change, to a revolution that also seems to us of lasting significance, as we analyze the meaning of the 1992 election. Nowhere are its marks more evident than in the recent volatility of popular support.

The Extent of Volatility

The fluidity of public attitudes can be suggested by a few remarkable facts. In March 1991, 88 percent of a sample of the American public told the CBS News/*New York Times* poll that they approved of the way George Bush was handling his job as president. Only 8 percent disapproved. Only fifteen months later, in July 1992, a mere 34 percent told this poll that they approved of the way the president was handling his job, and fully 56 percent disapproved. In little more than a year, George Bush's triumph had turned to dust, and the balance of positive and negative opinion had shifted more than 100 percentage points against him.

President Bush's awesome ratings in early 1991 discouraged a number of leading Democratic hopefuls, including Sens. Bill Bradley of New Jersey and Al Gore of Tennessee and Missouri representative Richard Gephardt, from entering the Democratic presidential primaries. A fairly typical preelection year analysis in this period read as follows:

> It can never properly be said, a year prior to an election, that an American president is "unbeatable." The public thinks and cares about the presidency too much for that. . . . Still, it's evident to everyone, including most Republican and Democratic strategists, that a president who more than 30 months into his tenure has the support of 70 percent of the public occupies a commanding if not unassailable position.[1]

In the absence of the Democratic party's "first team," it was left to distinctly secondary candidates—former Massachusetts senator Paul Tsongas, Sens. Tom Harkin of Iowa and Bob Kerrey of Nebraska, Gov. Bill Clinton of Arkansas, Gov. Douglas Wilder of Virginia, and former California governor Jerry Brown—to fulfill Woody Allen's dictum that 80 percent of life is showing up. Governor Clinton, the early favorite, emerged the wounded victor from a series of punishing primaries in which he took devastating hits on charges of marital infidelity and draft evasion. Evidence of his weakness as a candidate could be found in every poll. A May cover story in the *New*

Republic, "Why Clinton Can't Win," pointed out that he trailed Bush by 47 percent to 41 percent in a recent Gallup poll. The article went on to say, "The negative poll numbers are staggering, and they've dogged Clinton since the New Hampshire primary in February. . . . Absent a scandal [for the Republicans] or economic catastrophe, Clinton's a goner." [2] In a few short weeks, however, Governor Clinton chose a popular running mate (Gore), choreographed an astonishingly successful nominating convention, and immediately put his show on the road in a bus tour that delighted the public as well as the media. During these few weeks he went from dead last in the polls to a 20-point favorite. Suddenly, Clinton the "goner" became Clinton the "reanointed." [3]

If we needed further evidence of the fluidity of popular support, it was supplied by the public's response to the diminutive, jug-eared Texas businessman whose one-liners matched the country's antipolitical mood and whose personal fortune was an order of magnitude greater than anyone needed to finance a race for the presidency. Ross Perot was launched into independent orbit from the unlikely pad of a television talk show in February. Twelve weeks later he was favored by a third of the electorate. A May cover story in *Time,* "President Perot?," reported that Perot led with 33 percent, followed by Bush with 28 percent and Clinton with 24 percent. "Make no mistake," the story advised, Perot could "well be the next President. . . . No independent candidate in 80 years has attracted anything like this kind of support. . . . Perot would not be a spoiler but the front runner in the popular vote for President." [4]

Two of the polls still declared Perot to be the front-runner in June. But he lost two-fifths of his support by mid-July and abruptly removed himself from the race, only to reverse that decision in late September. With both the Democratic and Republican parties paying him court and inviting him to participate in the presidential debates, Perot once again began to ascend like a rocket. In early October, before the debates, most national polls showed Perot with about 10 percent of the vote. But before the end of the month, following his participation in the three debates, he had doubled his support in most polls.[5] That support flagged soon after, however, when Perot failed to substantiate his sensational allegation that agents of the Republican National Committee had earlier forced him out of the race by threatening to make public compromising information about his daughter shortly before her summer wedding.

In view of this volatility among the voters, we may well ask what is going on. Here was an incumbent president who during much of his tenure was as well known and highly honored by the American people as any chief executive in the past quarter-century, one whose favorable ratings soared to unprecedented heights after the triumph of the American-led coalition in the Persian Gulf war. Yet the meltdown of President Bush's strength in less than a year and a half left him one of the weakest presidents to seek reelection in this century; no incumbent since 1912 won so small a percentage of the popular vote as did Bush. What can help us to understand this degree of fluidity and to learn what it tells us about the transformation in presidential politics?

The Lens of History

We are indebted to George Bush for a historical marker in our inquiry. The inspiration he found during the 1992 campaign in Harry Truman's come-from-behind victory in 1948 reminds us of the quite different politics of an earlier time. President Truman was no stranger to volatility. He universally endeared himself to his country by the simple grace with which he accepted the mantle of his fallen chief, Franklin D. Roosevelt, as World War II neared its end. Yet much of Truman's support evaporated as he seemed ill-equipped to deal with the domestic dislocations of the postwar world, and the Democrats were swept from power in both branches of Congress in the elections of 1946. But Truman's predecessor left him a priceless asset. Despite the interruptions of war, the electoral alignment forged by the Great Depression and Roosevelt's New Deal was still intact. Harry Truman came from behind in 1948 by rallying to his cause enough of the Roosevelt coalition to win.

President Bush's revisionist historical enthusiasm therefore was anachronistic; it reached back to a time when, far more than today, the electorate was constrained by party loyalties rooted in issues of sufficient power that they had altered the partisan alignments of millions of voters and recruited to the parties millions of new or previously inactive voters. Such a lasting party alignment has been created three times in our history since the mid-nineteenth century.[6] (See Table 1-1.) The deepest of these alignments was forged by the issues that led to the Civil War. Slavery and the other controversies that divided North and South acted so strongly on the electorate as to break apart the antebellum party system, displacing the Whig party with the newly formed Republicans in 1856 and sundering the Democratic party into northern and southern wings that had to piece themselves together after Reconstruction. This alignment was held in place by the continued grip of the issues that created it, as the Republicans "waved the bloody shirt" to invoke memories of Democratic perfidy and the Democrats responded in kind in successive elections after the Civil War. The division of the vote between the parties, charted over succeeding decades, shows almost no variation, so taut were the voters stretched by their experience with the issues and events that produced the post-Civil War alignment.

But as the decades passed and the Great Reaper reaped the harvest of souls, these voters eventually were gone. The weakening alignment was held in place not by the passions of those who had lived through the Civil War but by the secondary processes that transmit party loyalties from generation to generation in the childhood home. The alignment was therefore ripe to be displaced by a new, sectional alignment in the 1890s. The great new storms

Table 1-1   Three Major Political Realignments

Period	Realignment	Issue
1856-1864	Whig party collapses and Lincoln Republicans rise	Slavery
1896-1900	Republicans defeat William Jennings Bryan Democrats	Regional interests [a]
1932-1936	Democrats with Roosevelt and New Deal coalition defeat Republicans	Haves versus have nots [b]

[a] The realignment was preceded by depressions during the 1880s and 1890s. The Republicans stood for industry, business, hard money, protective tariffs, and urban interests; the Democrats stood for farmers, small towns, low tariffs, and rural interests. The former championed the interests of the Northeast and Midwest; the latter favored the South and West.

[b] The realignment was preceded by the Great Depression. Democrats, isolated since 1896 as a southern and midwestern sectional party, attracted urban workers, blacks, and Jewish voters away from the Republican party. Regional party politics gave way to a politics of haves versus have nots.

that swirled about William Jennings Bryan and his opponents pitted the Republicans, as champions of the modernizing industrial Northeast and Midwest, against the Democrats, as champions of the traditional, agrarian South and West, fighting savagely over cheap money and the tariff. Should the tariff be high to protect the rising industries of the Northeast and Midwest or low to allow southern and western farmers to buy cheap farm implements from abroad?

This second alignment, which produced a larger Republican majority than had the Civil War, was interrupted only by the Woodrow Wilson era before being overwhelmed by the political forces unleashed by the Great Depression of the 1930s. The New Deal alignment produced a substantial Democratic majority and came closer to a class-based alignment than the country had witnessed since the age of Jackson. One difference: the Democrats now wanted to use the power of government actively to help the less advantaged, not just to block the use of government power in the interest of the privileged and well-to-do. Despite World War II and what Roosevelt described as the displacement of "Dr. New Deal" by "Dr. Win-the-War," the Roosevelt alignment was very much in place in 1948, the year of the first postwar presidential election. Opinion polls and academic surveys repeatedly showed a large standing Democratic majority.

In subsequent decades new issues have chipped away at the Roosevelt coalition. Civil rights and the Vietnam War allowed the Republican party to mount a "southern strategy" that aligned the South with the Republicans in presidential politics, even as the Voting Rights Act's enfranchisement of southern blacks in 1965 added a "liberal" wing to the constituency of southern Democratic governors and senators. Vietnam, crime, and race detached from the Roosevelt coalition many white ethnic voters in the North, who voted with lesser enthusiasm for Richard Nixon and greater enthusiasm for Ronald Reagan. But none of these "wedge" issues has had anything like the force of the issues and events that created the three past alignments, each of which lasted for many years.

It is therefore tempting to say that the Roosevelt alignment is still intact, although very old and very weak. Certainly, it has not been displaced by a new alignment as strong as those of the 1860s, 1890s, or 1930s. In the absence of such a realignment, it is probably more accurate to say that we have experienced a long period of *de*alignment. There is survey evidence of this: a declining fraction of respondents in polls describe themselves as *strongly* identified with the Republican or Democratic party. In 1952 about 22 percent of voters described themselves as "strong" Democrats and 13 percent described themselves as "strong" Republicans; by 1980 the figures had dropped to 18 percent and 9 percent, respectively. Likewise, in 1952, 22 percent of voters described themselves as "independent"; by 1988 that figure had risen to about 38 percent.[7]

There is also evidence of a weakening alignment in three aspects of the actual voting returns. One is the marked rise in split-ticket voting. In the elections of 1984, for example, Ronald Reagan attracted the support of two out of every three voters in the state of New Jersey as the Republican candidate for president, while Bill Bradley attracted the support of two out of every three voters as the Democratic candidate for the Senate. Another is the long-term decline in turnout. The old-time party loyalties, rooted in powerful issues, had helped get voters to the polls; the weakening of these loyalties has caused many to stay home. Yet another is the greater amplitude of party swings, with a more weakly aligned electorate moving freely between the parties from election to election.

Here, surely, is part of the reason for the fluidity of party support in the current period: with the progressive weakening of the party identifications that were so strongly held by the electorate in the wake of each major realignment since the Civil War, today's voters are far more promiscuous in supporting particular parties and leaders than were the voters of earlier eras. But to leave the explanation there would be to overlook a parallel change in the structure of the issues that move the electorate, a change visible in the election of 1992 that gives further significance to the weakening of the alignments that have organized most contests for the presidency since 1860.

Position Politics and Valence Politics

We can understand the weakening of these alignments only by drawing a distinction between two kinds of issues, a distinction that has yet to enter our general understanding of the workings of American democracy. The two kinds of issues that matter in presidential elections are position issues and valence issues. A *position issue* is one on which the rival parties or candidates reach out for the support of the electorate by taking different positions on a policy question that divides the electorate. Position issues have punctuated the history of presidential elections. For example, the party alignment that emerged from the Civil War was formed from a position issue of extraordinary power—the Negro, slave or free? Each of the three great alignments of our electoral past has been rooted in position issues. In the regional realignment of the 1890s the Republicans drew support from those who favored high rather than low tariffs on manufactured goods. In the 1930s the Democrats drew support from those who wanted to protect the interests of the poor and working class rather than those of the more affluent in American society. In the 1960s the New Deal coalition began to unravel around another position issue that divided the electorate along racial and regional lines—civil rights laws, for or against? And in the 1980s rivals for the presidency reached out for the support of the electorate in part by staking out different positions on an issue that sharply polarized voters—abortion, prochoice or prolife?

When political pundits intone that the voters are disenchanted because the rival parties or candidates are not discussing "the issues," they normally mean that most voters perceive no clear differences between the parties or candidates on the position issues of the moment. When Alabama governor George Wallace bellowed as an independent presidential candidate in 1968 that "there's not a dime's worth of difference" between the Democrats and the Republicans, he was seeking public support on the basis of his positions on issues, such as civil rights and welfare, that divided the electorate more than they (at the time) divided the parties.

The familiar liberal-conservative or left-right spectrum is a position issue in a somewhat more abstract and finely differentiated form. In many press and academic accounts the rival parties or candidates are thought to place themselves at different points along such a spectrum as they appeal for the support of an electorate that is also assumed to be spread out along this continuum.[8] Similarly, the issue of the size or role of government presents a position continuum from large to small, along which parties or candidates are thought to place themselves as they appeal to an electorate that supposedly is divided as to the proper size or responsibility of government. The same could be said for other position issues that present a set of ordered alternatives, such as gasoline taxes or deficit reduction.

But some of the issues that powerfully move the electorate do not present even two alternative positions that divide the parties and candidates on the one hand and the electorate on the other. These are issues on which voters distinguish parties and candidates not by their real or perceived difference in position on policy questions but by the degree to which they are linked in the voters' minds with conditions, goals, or symbols that are almost universally approved or disapproved by the electorate.

The economy is a prime example of a *valence issue* with this radically different structure. We do not have one party advocating economic prosperity and the other advocating economic bad times. There is no constituency for economic distress. In the United States and the other liberal democracies, all parties and the whole of the electorate endorse good times. The issue of economic prosperity acquires its power from the fact that the parties or candidates may be very unequally linked in the public's mind with the universally approved condition of good times and the universally disapproved condition of bad times. The difference between electoral success and disaster may turn on each party's ability to strengthen or weaken these perceptual bonds, or valences, in the public's mind.

Examples abound of valence issues that have powerfully moved the electorate. Corruption is such an issue with a deep historical resonance in the United States. Many times in American political history—indeed, as recently as the House of Representatives' check-kiting scandal in 1992—there have been calls to "throw the rascals out." It should be obvious, however, that the impact of the corruption issue could not depend on what position the parties or candidates advocated along a continuum extending from honesty to dishonesty: no party is avowedly propeculation. It depends rather on how closely the rival parties or candidates are linked in the public's mind with the universally approved symbol of honesty and the universally disapproved symbol of corruption. There is as little constituency for corruption as there is for economic bad times—or for a variety of other negative symbols that are staples of "valence politics," such as irresolute leadership, unpatriotic beliefs, weak national defense, wasted tax dollars, and failure itself.

It follows that the electoral politics of valence issues differs markedly from the electoral politics of position issues. In *position politics*, parties and candidates see their essential strategic problem as one of finding the electorate's center of gravity within a space defined by a series of ordered policy dimensions. By contrast, in *valence politics*, parties and candidates mount their appeals by choosing from a large set of potential valence issues those on which their identification with positive symbols and their opponents' identification with negative symbols will be most to their advantage.

There are innumerable examples of valence politics in modern presidential elections. In 1964 the Democratic campaign was largely a valence campaign in which voters were encouraged to link a vote for the Republican nominee, Arizona senator Barry Goldwater with negative symbols, such as nuclear annihilation, and a vote for President Lyndon B. Johnson with positive symbols, such as carrying on the work of a beloved fallen president, John F. Kennedy. Four years later Richard Nixon made law and order a valence issue. In the shadow of Watergate, Jimmy Carter made honesty in government a valence issue in 1976. In 1980 Carter was the victim of a valence campaign that linked a vote for him with symbols of abject failure, from the long gas lines to his inability to rescue our hostages in Teheran. Ronald Reagan's campaign in 1984 was carefully designed to encourage voters to link the president with such positive symbols as patriotism, peace, and prosperity—"morning in America." Likewise, in 1988 the Bush campaign encouraged voters to link Bush with positive symbols, such as respect for the flag, and his rival, Michael S. Dukakis, with negative symbols, such as disrespect for the flag, water pollution, and the fawning treatment of violent and remorseless criminals.

Presidential elections have always been a mix of position and valence politics. The valence issue of economic prosperity cost Martin Van Buren the presidency in 1840, when the electorate held him responsible for the misery that followed the panic of 1837. But the importance of valence politics has risen as party alignments rooted in the powerful position issues of the past have weakened. This trend is one of the most important, if largely unrecognized, shifts in our current politics, one that supplies a further key to understanding the recent fluidity of presidential politics. Let us see how the structure of valence issues adds to the volatility of public support.

Valence Politics and the Amplitude of Swing

One reason that party managers are so drawn to valence politics is that there is no ceiling—short of 100 percent—to the heights to which a candidate can soar in an ideally crafted valence campaign, whereas there *is* such a ceiling in a campaign focused on position issues that genuinely divide the electorate. The leaders who once reached out for the country's support by saying that the western territories should be free could expect to lose the votes of those who believed the western territories should be slave. Similarly, those who today reach out for the voters' support by arguing the prochoice position on abortion can expect to lose the votes of those who believe in the prolife position. But a party that reaches out for support on the basis of the strength or effectiveness of its leaders cannot lose the votes of those who believe in weak or ineffective leaders. Hence, a skilled campaigner can develop a persona that is overwhelmingly positive by stringing together a series of valence issues that "unite" the country—as Jimmy Carter did by promising honesty, efficiency, and prosperity in his quest for the presidential nomination in 1976—without bumping up against the ceiling that is built into a position issue that divides the country.

The structural difference between valence and position issues has a darker side for those who become linked to the negative symbols of valence politics. If there is no ceiling over the heights to which candidates can soar in ideally crafted valence campaigns, there is also no floor—short of 0 percent—under the depths to which they may fall if they become strongly linked to negative conditions or symbols on which the electorate is also united. In earlier eras, when long-term party alignments were rooted in position issues of great durability, presidential candidates could count on a base of support from party loyalists whose cause their parties championed on the overriding position issues of the time. But this base is smaller and softer in the current era, when party loyalties are weaker and less rooted in strong and enduring position issues.

The example of Jimmy Carter (this time in 1980) is again illuminating. President Carter lacked the secure base of Democratic loyalists cemented to the party for reasons of class that carried Harry Truman through his darkest days in 1948. When Carter was confronted at home by the oil shocks and "stagflation" of the 1970s and abroad by a string of reverses, culminating in his failure to win the release of U.S. hostages in Teheran, there was no political safety net under his free fall in public esteem. The brilliant valence campaigner of the 1976 nominating contest became the hapless victim of valence politics in the 1980 election. Ronald Reagan rammed home the negative Carter valences when he summed up a television debate by asking the national audience "whether you are better off today than you were four years ago, whether this country is more respected in the world today than it was four years ago."

We now have a deeper insight into the reasons for the fluidity of electoral support in the current period, including the extraordinary swings of the electorate in 1991 and 1992. George Bush's honeymoon after his 1988 victory was graced by the revolutions of 1989 in Eastern Europe and by the end of the Soviet empire and the Cold War, events that provided symbolic content for valence issues of great potency, namely, peace and strength. Moreover, his presidency began in the late stages of the longest peacetime economic expansion of the postwar era. There were some negative symbols, especially the perception of Bush as a weak leader—a "wimp," in his critics' phrase. He had been tormented by the build-up of this image during his long vice presidential apprenticeship to Ronald Reagan and by his inability to shake it even when he invaded Panama and seized its leader, Manuel Noriega. But he did indeed shake the wimp image in the graver circumstances of the Gulf war. Few would doubt that his strong valences with the highly positive symbols of strength and resolve would have returned the president to office in a landslide if the election had been held soon after the victory in Desert Storm.

With Saddam Hussein still in power and with the mounting suspicion that he was coddled by the United States before he invaded Kuwait, the electorate took a more mixed view of this victory as the months passed. More serious politically, with the end of the Cold War and a recession in full swing by 1990, the country turned inward and was increasingly critical of Bush's failure to attend to domestic issues. The positive valences that linked the president to the collapse of the Soviet bloc and the end of the Cold War soon gave way to negative valences linking him with economic distress at home. He quickly discovered what Martin Van Buren had learned a century and a half before—that past glories count for little if the country is hurting economically. Indeed, Bush made matters worse by showing a Herbert Hoover-like ability to see recovery just around the corner. The displacement of one set of valence issues, on which Bush was judged almost completely favorably, by another, on which he was judged very unfavorably, produced the extraordinary fifteen-month swing against him and cost him his office. His free fall was cushioned only a little near the end of the campaign by linking Governor Clinton with the negative symbols of indecisiveness, untrustworthiness, and lack of patriotism.

An exercise in the hypothetical can illuminate how little these swings in public support were constrained by the kind of overriding position issues that once anchored voters to the parties. For the sake of argument let us assume what is not wholly unimaginable—that abortion had become so powerful an issue as to produce the distinctive marks of each of the great realignments of the past: the shift of millions of voters from one party to the other so that they could support the party endorsing their position on abortion, the recruitment of millions of new or previously inactive voters to one or the other of the parties on the basis of their stands on abortion, and the subsequent constraint on the parties to put forward candidates who placed their party's distinctive stand on abortion at the center of their campaigns.

If abortion had realigned our politics in this way, President Bush would neither have soared so high in the aftermath of Desert Storm, since the bulk of prochoice voters would have continued to oppose him for his stand on abortion, nor would he have sunk so low during the recession, since the bulk of prolife voters would have remained steadfastly loyal in view of his party's stand on abortion. But abortion does not in fact play such an aligning role in our politics. Neither it nor any other position issue constrained Bush's rise in popularity or put a safety net under his free fall during the months between his victory in Desert Storm and his defeat in the election.

It is impossible, then, to understand what Bush described as the "screwy" 1992 presidential election without thinking mainly in terms of valence politics. But the 1992 election is only the latest in a series of presidential contests that have turned increasingly on valence issues. Our central thesis is that valence issues and politics have been, and continue to be, far more important in shaping the behavior of parties, candidates, and voters than is commonly recognized. Although the importance of position issues and politics in presidential elections has often been wildly exaggerated, the importance of valence issues and politics has been almost completely neglected.

The rising importance of valence politics leads to two further questions. First, what factors have so weakened the old-time party loyalties as to produce the valence politics of today? The answer will give us a clearer view of whether this shift is likely to continue or could be reversed. Second, what is to be made of a politics organized more in valence than position terms? The answer will give us a clearer view of the dynamics of democratic government in today's world.

The Sources of Valence Politics

It is tempting to say that the rise of valence politics has been fueled primarily by the changing technology of mass communication. In an hour-long speech to an old-time political meeting it was difficult to avoid position issues altogether. But it is easy to do so in a thirty-second television spot. Indeed, the electronic media seem ideally suited to the needs of valence campaigning. Certainly, television lends itself all too well to the negative valences that are so conspicuous an element of modern campaigns. This point has hardly been lost on the political commentators, even if the more general nature of valence politics remains largely unexplored.

It is equally true that the erosion of the old-time party loyalties is in part due to the demise of the partisan press. In an older politics millions of Americans subscribed to newspapers that corresponded to their party loyalties. A city's papers differentiated themselves by the party stands they took and thereby reinforced the party alignment by feeding their readers a continuing diet of angled information in their editorial pages and news columns. All of this has been dramatically changed by the concentration of the press. Today, one newspaper typically survives in each metropolitan market. Its problem is not how to attract readers with biased reporting but how to keep from repelling readers who will disagree with a partisan pitch and thus be lost to the newspaper's real competitors, local television. Faced with these realities, the modern dailies neutrally convey the appeals of each of the parties and their candidates rather than seeking to reinforce readers' identifications with a particular party.

What concentration has done to the press, custom and the law have required of the electronic media. Since the rise of radio in the 1930s and of television in the 1950s and 1960s, the electronic media have kept their political coverage neutral. Right-wing complaints about network anchors notwithstanding, it takes a much finer caliper to detect bias in television's political coverage than it did in the time of the partisan press. Even more than the surviving metropolitan dailies, the electronic media feel constrained to convey the appeals of each of the parties and their candidates for president and to keep their political content free of bias. They also have earned a great deal of revenue by carrying television spots, and now half-hour "infomercials," for whichever party or candidate buys the time. There are signs that "talk radio," and perhaps the television talk shows as well, feel a new freedom to angle their content. But (Rush Limbaugh excepted) they do so primarily by opening a channel for the expression of citizens' views rather than by supplying an angle of their own, as the old-time party press did. Hence, the electronic media, too, have failed to reinforce the party loyalties that once were rooted in enduring position issues.

The key to understanding the transition from a position politics expressed in long-time party alignments to a valence politics expressed in political volatility lies in the transformation of the world of public affairs. In the simpler, slower paced world of the nineteenth century, it was easier for long-developing, well-understood, deeply felt, and highly durable position issues to organize the dialogue of leaders and led. But in the world of the late twentieth century, presidents deal with a far broader range of problems and issues that arise and change at a far brisker pace than in the past. In this kaleidoscopic world presidents often are required to act on issues that were scarcely visible when they sought their electoral mandate; worse, they have little chance of building up a deep and stable base of public understanding of the policies they adopt. Almost inevitably, then, presidents are held account-able by the voters for past or retrospective results of presidential action or inaction. It is inevitable, therefore, that the fate of presidents and rival candi-dates should rest on the valences in the public's mind.

Foreign policy issues illustrate this difference. It may be that the dia-logue of leaders and led was last organized by a position dimension during the prolonged period between the two world wars, when the isolationist-internationalist dimension dominated American politics. Woodrow Wilson's dream of a new international order in which America would play a leading role foundered on the Senate's rejection of the League of Nations covenant at the close of World War I. Although the great economic expansion of the 1920s and the Great Depression of the 1930s turned America inward, the isolationist-internationalist dimension reemerged as the clouds of a new war gathered over Europe and Asia in the late 1930s. Franklin Roosevelt's duel with the isolationist "America firsters" was part of his third bid for the presi-dency, and his reelection in 1940 was in part a mandate to help the belea-guered democracies—although it was not really as clear as the mandate he later received when the Japanese bombed Pearl Harbor. America's experi-ence in the ensuing war, as close to a "great patriotic war" as we ever have fought, laid the foundation for the postwar consensus on the Soviet threat and led to national security arrangements on which the parties basically agreed. If the Cold War worked to the advantage of one party or the other over the subsequent decades, it was largely in valence terms—which party was more anticommunist and propeace than the other.

In contrast, the public's need in the late twentieth century to judge its leaders in valence terms is evident in its response to the two regional con-flicts that have been strongly controversial in the postwar world. The Korean War burst on the country two years after President Truman's 1948 victory. An explicit commitment to resist communist expansion on the Korean penin-sula could not have been part of his mandate because no one anticipated this attack. Although the country backed Truman's response in the early stages, support rapidly drained away when General Douglas MacArthur pushed to the Manchurian border, the Chinese entered the war, and American casual-ties mounted. MacArthur was dismissed for disagreeing with his commander in chief over how limited a war to fight. He then sought to rally the country to his side of the quarrel. Both Truman's response to the invasion of South Korea and MacArthur's stand that cost him his command suggest that the critical issue of the war was a position issue—with bombing Manchuria, perhaps with atomic weapons, at one pole and pulling back to Japan at the other.

Despite this appearance, the public saw the issue of the war in the simpler valence terms of success and failure. Truman's policies had failed. But so in a sense had MacArthur's, and the country now wanted as president Dwight Eisenhower, the victorious European commander from World War II who was nominated by the Republicans in 1952 and was expected to deal successfully with the problem. During the campaign Eisenhower gave not the slightest hint of where he would come down on the policy dimension that divided General MacArthur from President Truman; he simply proclaimed, "I shall go to Korea." The scent of prospective success helped elect Eisenhower president and strip the Democrats of the White House for the first time in twenty years.

The Vietnam War is a still more revealing example of the postwar dominance of valence issues in foreign policy. Here again, a full-scale regional war burst on the country too late for U.S. resistance to have been an explicit part of President Johnson's mandate in 1964. Indeed, Johnson had pictured his opponent, Barry Goldwater, as more likely to involve the country in war. As the conflict in Vietnam escalated, the controversy it engendered was widely thought to be structured by the hawk-dove dimension that was a staple of media coverage and elite debate. But once again the public saw the war largely in the simpler, valence terms of failure and success. By 1968 a majority of Americans had concluded that Johnson's policies had failed. They wanted the problem fixed. In the Democratic presidential primaries that year the wounded president was dealt a mortal blow by Minnesota senator Eugene McCarthy, the quintessential dove, who persuaded a huge bloc of Democratic voters in New Hampshire and Wisconsin to give him their support. The polling organizations found to their astonishment that McCarthy's supporters had responded to the Vietnam issue not in the position terms of the hawk-dove dimension; indeed, almost as many McCarthy voters believed that McCarthy wanted to bomb North Vietnam as believed (correctly) that he wanted to pull out of the war. They simply wanted a terrible failure to be ended, whether by hawkish or dovish means. In the general election of 1968 Richard Nixon also exploited the war in valence terms, linking the Democrats with the failed war and with the violence of the demonstrators who opposed it.

What of the future? We would not expect a reversal of the trend toward valence politics if our historical analysis is broadly correct. A transition driven by the spreading and rapidly changing responsibilities of government—and of the chief executive who holds so much of the initiative in dealing with the country's problems—is unlikely to occur as we approach a new century. Since the time of Wilson and the two Roosevelts, presidential candidates have needed to set out a vision, often articulated and understood in valence terms, from a remarkable array of swiftly changing problems and issues that face the country.[9] So ineluctable are these parameters of our modern political life that the valence framework will continue to capture an essential part of the dialogue of leaders and led.

Certainly, the valence strategy, tactics, and tempo of the Clinton campaign were entirely consistent with the trend. The Clinton campaign was battered with charges of marital infidelity, draft dodging, and pot smoking. At their convention the Republicans depicted Clinton as "Slick Willie" and his wife as a power-hungry radical feminist who equated marriage with slavery, encouraged children to sue their parents, and eschewed "family values." In the debates and up to election day, the Bush campaign attempted to make Slick Willie into the unpatriotic, indecisive, fast-talking, failed governor of a small and insignificant state.

But, as the *New York Times* reported a week after the election, Clinton's campaign strategists took a public relations hose to these valence fires. While continuing to stress the positive valences of "change" and better economic times, the Clinton campaign responded with "one of the most ambitious campaigns of political rehabilitation ever attempted. They proposed the construction of a new image for Mr. and Mrs. Clinton: an honest, plain-folks idealist and his warm and loving wife." As the paper explained, "Retooling the image of a couple who had been already in the public eye for five battering months required a campaign of behavior modification and media manipulation so elaborate its outline ran to 14 single-spaced pages." [10]

Known within the Clinton campaign as the General Election Project, the plan called for the candidate to depict himself as the "agent of change." The message was to be delivered in town-hall style forums, on live talk television, and in a series of speeches challenging specific special interests. The candidate was to appear on television to play the saxophone and poke fun at himself for saying that he had tried marijuana but "didn't inhale." The plan also orchestrated events where the Clintons would "seem more warm and cuddly: 'events where Bill and Hillary can go on dates with the American people.' " It even called for staging an event where "Bill and Chelsea surprise Hillary on Mother's Day," and "joint appearances with her friends where Hillary can laugh, cry, do her mimicry." [11]

None of this involved a position politics in which candidate Clinton staked out positions for which President Clinton would be held accountable. As president, Clinton will need to make a number of difficult position choices on new issues as well as difficult choices in managing the economy before he returns to the electorate in 1996. But he almost certainly will be judged in valence terms—by the apparent success or failure of his choices on these issues—rather than on the choices themselves.

Valence Voters Are Not Fools

Is valence politics good or bad for American democracy? If, as we have argued, the 1992 election was a valence election par excellence, is this something to be celebrated or lamented?

Our view of the sources of valence politics suggests in part the normative judgment we would make of it. As we spell out this judgment, we are keenly aware of how easy it is to mock valence politics, so drastically does it depart from the civics book ideal of the electorate as an informed kibitzer to the decisions of government, looking over the shoulders of the players in the policy game and periodically awarding the deal to some rather than to others.

But it has long been recognized that this ideal requires the electorate to possess a level of information it could never attain. Far removed from a complex world of public affairs issues capable of baffling and dividing the policy experts, the public is bound to look for ways to simplify the choices it is periodically asked to make. From the 1950s to the present two flourishing branches of the academic literature have sought to identify what these simplifying devices are and to justify them in terms of democratic theory.

One branch consists of so-called spatial models of elections. As many analysts have noted, plurality and majority-rule electoral systems "create pressures on candidates to take similar stands on any position issue that is foremost in the minds of most voters." [12] In 1957 the intellectual architect of spatial models of elections, Anthony Downs, argued that candidates who want to win tend to espouse the position favored by the so-called median voter, meaning the voter who has equal numbers of voters to the left and the right of his or her position.[13] As Barry Goldwater learned in 1964, and George McGovern in 1972, candidates who ignore the median voter and appeal to the extremes often do so at their electoral peril.

The idea that political conflict can be summarized, and hence simplified, in terms of a left-right or liberal-conservative spectrum is as old as the French Revolution. There is a great deal to be learned from the formal and empirical literatures within political science that have been built on this idea. But the spatial image of the dialogue between leaders and led may obscure more than it reveals, because it requires a level of information and capacity for abstraction in political matters that the electorate cannot meet. It is one thing to use this framework to model the competition of firms for the consuming public, where the spaces are real and given. It is quite another to use this framework to model the competition of parties or leaders, where the spaces will need to be abstracted and commonly perceived by the "consuming" electorate.

Moreover, we wonder whether the normative bias implicit in spatial models of elections is not akin to that of classical democratic theory itself— namely, that elections in a democracy can and should be mainly about position issues, with candidates articulating distinct and detailed policy alternatives on health care, crime, the environment, foreign trade, and other issues, and most voters taking pains to become highly informed about these issues, to relate the candidates' positions to their own beliefs and interests, and to vote accordingly. But, as many students of elections have pointed out since the 1950s, the classic requirements of democratic citizenship (interest, discussion, motivation, knowledge, principle, rationality) are not met by most American voters, and American democracy is none the worse because of it.[14] We would not go as far as Bernard Berelson and his colleagues once did in celebrating the "implicit division of labor" within the electorate between the weakly interested many and the highly motivated, knowledgeable, and caring few.[15] But we would agree that the dialogue between leaders and led can be democratically legitimate and satisfying, even if it is not centered squarely on position issues and politics.

Some of the limits of the spatial-model framework are evident in Norman Nie, Sidney Verba, and John Petrocik's prize-winning book, *The Changing American Voter*, published in 1979, which heralded the "rise of issue voting." [16] The spatial conceptions of these writers led them virtually to rule out the possibility that a right-wing Republican could capture the presidency because such a candidate would be too distant from the positions of most voters on most issues. This prediction left the authors ill-prepared to explain the success of Ronald Reagan's valence appeals within a year of the book's publication.

Another branch of the literature begins in 1960 with *The American Voter*, continues in V. O. Key's posthumously published work, *The Responsible Electorate* (1966), is refined in Morris Fiorina's book *Retrospective Voting in American National Elections* (1981), and is further refined in several works published in the early 1990s. A central message of this literature is that most voters, whether they are moved by what we have termed position issues, valence issues, or both, are perfectly capable of figuring out their central beliefs and interests in relation to politics and elections, and voting accordingly. As the concluding chapter of *The American Voter* explained:

> The importance of the public's concern with certain broad objectives of government is quite clear in our studies.... [T]he electoral decision results from a comparison of the total image of one of the candidate-party alternatives with the image of the other. A good deal of the public response to these political actors simply expresses feeling, or affect. Many people see this party or that candidate as "honest," "dependable," "capable," or, more generally, as just "good." ... But our examination of public attitude shows that certain generalized goals of government action enter the [voter's] image of the parties and candidates and that these goals play a major role in electoral change.[17]

In *The Responsible Electorate*, Key analyzed voters who switched parties from one presidential election to another and found that most of them switched in a direction consistent with their own beliefs and interests. "The perverse and unorthodox argument of this book," wrote Key, "is that voters are not fools." He set out the crux of his argument in these words:

> In American presidential campaigns of recent decades the portrait of the American electorate that develops from the data is not one of an electorate straightjacketed by social determinants or moved by subconscious urges triggered by devilishly clever propagandists. It is rather one of an electorate moved by concern about central and relevant questions of public policy, of governmental performance, and of executive personality. Propositions so uncompromisingly stated inevitably represent overstatements. Yet to the extent that they can be shown to resemble the reality, they are propositions of basic importance for both the theory and the practice of democracy.[18]

In *Retrospective Voting*, Morris Fiorina emphasized Key's insight that the electorate could learn a good deal of what it needed to know to reach an informed decision simply by monitoring the performance of the parties or leaders in power.[19] Whereas prospective voting imposes on the electorate the classic requirements of democratic citizenship, demanding that the voter closely examine the views of the rival parties and candidates on the position issues of the day and forecast what they would do if elected, Fiorina argued that retrospective voting involves a simpler calculus. He therefore posed the empirical question, how far can it be said that in presidential elections the voters look at how things have gone in the recent past, voting for the party that controls the White House if they like what happened and against it if they do not. Fiorina found a good deal of evidence that this is exactly what many voters do, although he also found evidence of prospective voting and reached a mixed empirical judgment.

A number of recent books on voting have extended the tradition of seeking a "reasoning voter" and a "rational public." [20] Our observations are firmly in this tradition. In particular, Key's portrait of an American electorate "moved by concern about central and relevant questions of public policy, of governmental performance, and of executive personality" can be seen as a rough sketch of valence politics: valence voters are not fools.

The valence framework adds two things that are missing from the Key-Fiorina analysis. On the one hand, the structure of valence issues, which allows successful valence candidates to soar to great heights and unsuccessful ones to plummet to great depths, explains the fluidity of contemporary politics. On the other, the valence framework shows why the electorate can sometimes make prospective as easily as retrospective judgments and judgments on those who seek office as easily as judgments on those who hold office. The power of valence politics to simplify the electorate's choices in both respects was evident in General Eisenhower's victory in the 1952 election.[21]

Conclusion: Valence Politics and Presidential Trustees

We may better appreciate the positive democratic potential of valence politics by noting that the difference between position and valence politics parallels the most famous distinction in the normative theory of representation: Edmund Burke's contrast between the representative as instructed delegate and the representative as trustee.

Without unduly distorting either Burke's concepts or our own, we can think of Burke's instructed delegate as a leader who seeks the electorate's support by taking stands on position issues that the leader will later translate into government action. Likewise, we can think of his trustee as a leader who seeks the electorate's support in valence terms, using his or her own best judgment as to the best means for achieving universally approved goals.

We note this parallelism without endorsing Burke's blanket rejection of instructions to the representative by the electorate. In our view, it is right for the majority of the people to seek to bind a president when it has a strongly held view on a well-defined position issue. But it is also right for the electorate, when it is without the resources of information to instruct a president in policy terms, to affirm the priority of certain conditions or values or goals and to leave to the president-as-trustee the question of how these are to be achieved. Bounded rationality, limited voter interest and information about position issues, and the constant stir of valence issues are facts of electoral life that in no way diminish the value of the ongoing dialogue between leaders and led that is at the core of democratic politics.

In the 1992 presidential campaign the electorate above all else decided that its deep concern about the economy was not adequately shared by the president and gave its support instead to the challenger who had posted "The Economy, Stupid" on the wall of his Little Rock campaign headquarters. It was, in other words, a campaign in which American democracy was alive and well as the electorate used the means of valence politics to elect a new trustee to achieve its goals.

Notes

1. Carl Everett Ladd, *The Ladd Report*, 4th ed., vol. 1, 1991, 10.
2. Fred Barnes, "Why Clinton Can't Win," *New Republic*, May 4, 1992, 19, 21.
3. Sidney Blumenthal, "The Reanointed," *New Republic*, July 27, 1992, 10-14.
4. Walter Shapiro, "President Perot?" *Time*, May 25, 1992, 27.
5. *Public Perspective* 4 (November-December 1992): 100-101.
6. William Nisbet Chambers and Walter Dean Burnham, eds., *The American Party Systems: Stages of Political Development*, 2d ed. (New York: Oxford University Press, 1975).
7. James Q. Wilson, *American Government*, 5th ed. (Lexington, Mass.: D. C. Heath, 1992), 138-139.
8. The classic statement of this view is Anthony Downs, *An Economic Theory of Democracy* (New York: Harper, 1957).
9. It is no surprise that the rise of valence politics corresponds broadly with the rise of what Jeffrey Tulis has termed the "rhetorical presidency"; see Tulis, *The Rhetorical Presidency* (Princeton: Princeton University Press, 1988).
10. Michael Kelly, "The Making of a First Family: A Blueprint," *New York Times*, Nov. 14, 1992, 1.
11. Ibid., 1, 10.
12. Jack H. Nagel, *Participation* (Englewood Cliffs, N.J.: Prentice Hall, 1987), 111.
13. Downs, *Economic Theory of Democracy*.
14. Bernard R. Berelson, Paul F. Lazarsfeld, and William N. McPhee, *Voting* (Chicago: University of Chicago Press, 1954), esp. chap. 14.
15. Ibid.
16. Norman Nie, Sidney Verba, and John Petrocik, *The Changing American Voter*, enlarged ed. (Cambridge, Mass.: Harvard University Press, 1979), chap. 10.
17. Angus Campbell, Phillip E. Converse, Warren E. Miller, and Donald E. Stokes, *The American Voter*, abridged ed. (New York: Wiley, 1964), 283.
18. V. O. Key, *The Responsible Electorate* (Cambridge, Mass.: Belknap Press of Harvard University Press, 1966), 8.

19. Morris P. Fiorina, *Retrospective Voting in American National Elections* (New Haven: Yale University Press, 1981).
20. Two influential works are Samuel L. Popkin, *The Reasoning Voter: Communication and Persuasion in Presidential Campaigns* (Chicago: University of Chicago Press, 1991); and Benjamin I. Page and Robert Y. Shapiro, *The Rational Public: Fifty Years of Trends in Americans' Policy Preferences* (Chicago: University of Chicago Press, 1991).
21. For a fuller treatment of the structure of valence issues and a discussion of other aspects of contemporary American politics that are best understood in terms of the valence framework, see Donald E. Stokes, "Valence Politics," in *Electoral Politics*, ed. Dennis Kavanagh (Oxford: Clarendon Press, 1992), 141-164.

2

The Nominations:
Process and Patterns

Ryan J. Barilleaux and Randall E. Adkins

The process by which political parties in the United States nominate their candidates for president is endlessly complex. Formally, nominations are conferred by the national nominating conventions of the Republican and Democratic parties in the summer of the election year. Realistically, the process begins as much as four years earlier and culminates in a series of more than fifty (times two, one for each party) state and territorial primaries and caucuses strung out over a four-month period. In 1992 the process was complicated by the self-nomination of an independent candidate, Ross Perot.

Ryan J. Barilleaux and Randall E. Adkins bring order to the apparent chaos of nomination politics. They begin by describing the "nominating environment" within which Bill Clinton and George Bush competed with party rivals for their respective nominations, an environment dominated by features such as the media's role as intermediary and the importance of fund raising. From there, the authors go on to describe a five-stage process of competition between the "out party" candidates, beginning with an "exhibition season" and ending with the conventions, and the less elaborate process employed by the party of the incumbent president.

Political observers invariably find something that makes each American presidential election unique and somewhat surprising. The 1992 contest was full of such surprises. George Bush, despite his tremendous popularity following the Persian Gulf war, found himself struggling to protect his presidency from six relatively weak Democrats, a conservative Republican journalist, and a politically independent billionaire businessman. The Democrats avoided the protracted contest many party leaders feared and nominated two New South politicians in their effort to win back the White House. The year will also be remembered for Ross Perot's idiosyncratic challenge to the two major parties.

At first glance, the central feature of both parties' nomination process seems to be almost continual surprise. In every election since 1968 the rules have been somewhat different from those before. As Rhodes Cook, a veteran observer, has commented, "The constant is change." [1]

The fluidity of the nomination process is real, but it can be overrated. Although the specific rules used to select the two parties' nominees in each election may change, the underlying characteristics of the nominating environment have remained stable since the early 1980s. Indeed, understanding the nominating environment is central to interpreting the events of 1992. The primary victories of Bill Clinton and George Bush did not occur in a vacuum but represented each candidate's ability to survive and triumph in that environment.

The Nominating Environment

The Democrats have been tinkering with their nominating system for more than two decades. Because Democratic-dominated state legislatures have altered election laws affecting both political parties, the Republicans have been dragged along on the tide of those changes.[2]

The 1968 election marked a turning point in the nomination process. For most of the twentieth century, nominations were decided at party conventions dominated by state and local party leaders. Many of these leaders were "bosses" of political machines that controlled votes and patronage in places such as Cook County, Illinois, and Duval County, Texas. Before 1968 candidates for president won their party's endorsement by appealing to these elites and by entering a limited number of presidential primaries to demonstrate their potential electability. For example, in 1960 John F. Kennedy entered only three primaries, most notably the one in the predominantly Protestant state of West Virginia, in order to show the bosses that a young Catholic senator could win votes nationally.

In 1968 President Lyndon Johnson, battered from all sides for the failure of his Vietnam War, chose not to run for reelection after being embarrassed in the New Hampshire primary by the "peace candidate," Sen. Eugene McCarthy of Minnesota. Even though Johnson received 49 percent of the vote in the Granite State as a write-in candidate, McCarthy's 42 percent showing was interpreted by the press as a defeat for the president. Vice President Hubert Humphrey won the Democratic nomination at a convention in Chicago that was marked by violence in the streets and rancor in the hall. Humphrey had entered no primaries, but because the process was dominated by party leaders he managed to capture the nomination. This outcome was unacceptable to the reform elements in the party who had supported McCarthy or the late senator Robert Kennedy. In consequence, Humphrey and other regular Democrats had to agree that a commission would be created to reconstruct the party's nominating process to enhance democracy and improve the representation of various groups in the party. After Humphrey lost the election to Republican Richard Nixon, the process of reform was set in motion.[3]

The reform era replaced the old system of selecting party nominees with a new one in which national convention delegates are selected through state primaries and caucuses over a five-month period. As a result, the balance of power in the parties has shifted from the bosses to the activists and the voters who participate in the primaries and caucuses. But there is more to the system than just a long, hard struggle. The underlying environment of presidential nominations has four characteristics: (1) the methods and timing of delegate selection, (2) the media's role as intermediary in the nomination process, (3) the importance of fund raising to winning the nomination, and (4) the entrepreneurial nature of a presidential candidacy.

What shapes the nomination races in each election are not only these characteristics but the responses that candidates develop to deal with them. As we shall see, certain strategies and tactics of campaigning are better suited to the new nominating environment than others, thus affecting who runs and how they conduct their campaigns.

The Methods and Timing of Delegate Selection

A candidate's chief object in the nomination campaign is to acquire delegates who will lend their support at the party convention. The Democratic and Republican parties do not so much select delegates as organize and conduct the process by which the voters select them. Delegates are chosen in primaries or caucuses held in each state according to a mix of national party rules (in the case of the Democrats) and state rules and laws (both parties). Forty states hold Democratic primaries, and the delegates chosen in those contests occupy about 70 percent of the convention's seats.[4] Thirty-nine state primaries account for the majority of the delegates to the Republican convention.

Delegate selection rules. During the 1970s many states awarded delegates to the victor in their primary or caucuses by the rule of *winner take all.* This system corresponded to the way electoral votes are allocated in the general election. Since 1980 the Democrats have shifted toward proportional representation as the means of awarding delegates. In 1992 delegates in all Democratic primaries were assigned to the candidates roughly on the basis of their proportion of the popular vote. Additionally, there were some special benefits for first-place finishers and penalties for candidates with poor showings. Several states employed a "bonus system," in which the top vote getter is awarded additional delegates. Democratic party rules also required candidates to win at least 15 percent of the primary vote to receive any delegates, thus punishing those candidates who could not attract large percentages.[5]

Professional politicians have seen their influence modified in recent years. In the 1970s and early 1980s party leaders and elected officials virtually were excluded from the Democratic National Convention by a process that put issue and candidate activists in charge of the nomination. Since 1984 the former groups have returned to the hall as "superdelegates." In 1992

approximately one-fifth of the Democratic delegates were awarded their
seats by virtue of their status as party or elected leaders. The stated purpose
of superdelegates is to leaven the ideological influence of activists with the
hard-headed, victory-oriented outlook of political professionals. But it is not
yet clear that the superdelegates have any real influence on the outcome of
Democratic presidential nominations, because the eventual nominee usually
secures victory long before the convention meets.[6]

Republicans, in contrast, have not left behind the winner-take-all system. They still use it in most states, guaranteeing a big prize in delegates to
the candidate who comes in first. Only fourteen states and the District of
Columbia allocate Republican delegates in proportion to the popular primary
vote. Unlike the Democrats, who require that half of each delegation be
women and that minorities be represented, Republicans impose no specific
rules concerning what kinds of people constitute a state's delegation.[7] The
two parties also differ in the size and composition of their conventions. The
1992 Democratic convention consisted of 4,287 delegates. The 1992 Republican convention was composed of 2,209 delegates.

Candidate response. Candidates who understand and can take advantage
of the rules have a decided advantage in seeking the nomination. In 1972
Sen. George McGovern of South Dakota, who had been the chief author of
the Democrats' reforms, used his knowledge of the process to help him win
his party's standard. Today, all serious candidates become masters of the
process.

Because of proportional representation, candidates in the Democratic
party benefit from entering all primaries. By winning even 15 percent of the
vote in a state, the contender will be awarded some delegates. Moreover, a
reasonably strong showing in an early primary such as New Hampshire can
win a candidate valuable name recognition and momentum that may be
important in later, more delegate rich states. On the other hand, as with Ohio
senator John Glenn in 1984, a poor showing in early contests effectively can
end a candidacy.

Timing. States generally decide for themselves when they will hold their
delegate-selection events. The Democrats have a national "window" for
these contests, which extends from the first Tuesday in March to the second
Tuesday in June, but they allow exceptions for four states (Iowa, New
Hampshire, Maine, and South Dakota) that have traditionally conducted
their contests earlier. Republicans impose no window but generally follow
the Democratic calendar because of state laws governing primaries and
caucuses.

There is considerable front loading of the delegate-selection process.[8]
For example, the second Tuesday in March is known as Super Tuesday,
because a large number of states hold their contests on that day. The original
impetus for this event was a desire by southern Democratic leaders to give
their region a larger role in influencing the party's eventual nominee. Their
strategy was to require candidates to be tested in the more conservative

Figure 2-1 Proportion of Delegates to the 1992 Democratic Convention

Percent chosen

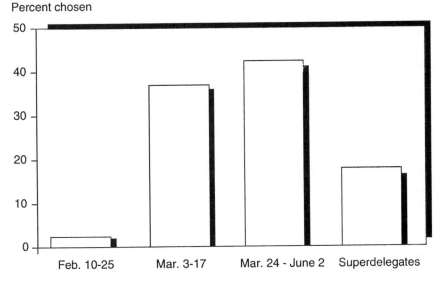

Source: *New York Times,* Feb. 19, 1992, A17.

South so that liberal voters in Iowa, New Hampshire, and other northern states with early primaries and caucuses could not determine who dropped out and who stayed in the race. Liberal candidates such as George McGovern were favored in these early contests, but they had proven unelectable in the fall. Since 1980 Alabama, Florida, and Georgia have held simultaneous primaries. By 1988 Super Tuesday had become a regional fixture of the nominating process, even if it did include a few states from outside the South, such as Massachusetts.

In 1992 a new wrinkle was added to the nomination calendar. Several states moved their primaries and caucuses to Junior Tuesday, one week before the big event. They hoped to blunt the influence of the South and at the same time share in the effort to narrow the field. This group consists of states from several regions but has a decided western orientation; it includes Colorado, Utah, Idaho, and Washington.

The effect of front loading is substantial. In 1992 approximately one-third of all Democratic delegates were selected during the eight-day period bounded by Junior Tuesday on March 3 and Super Tuesday on March 10. (See Figure 2-1.) At this point in the process, a clear front-runner usually emerges and gains momentum from the array of primaries and caucuses that are held during this short span of time.

Several large industrial states do not hold their nomination contests until later in the season. New York, Ohio, and Pennsylvania, for example, hold primaries in May, and Californians do not vote until early June. Indeed, voters in a number of these late states frequently complain that they have been effectively disenfranchised by the timing of their state's event, because the most important decisions have already been made and most candidates have withdrawn from the race. Because the front-runner is by this time often unstoppable, voters in industrial states are faced with the choice of either endorsing the presumed nominee or casting what amounts to a protest vote for someone else. Although there have been proposals in Ohio, California, and elsewhere to reschedule primaries, local consider-ations (especially primaries for state and local offices) and disagreements on alternative dates keep these potentially powerful states from having more influence.

Candidate response. Those who contend for the presidential nomination are keenly aware that they must start early if they want to win. Indeed, some even begin their quest four years early, during the preceding presidential election, hoping to gain name recognition and identify potential financial supporters. Candidates also know that the media pay exhaustive attention to the results of the two earliest contests in Iowa and New Hampshire, looking for signs of the potential nominee. Because journalists tend to view the process in terms of a horse race, they are eager to assign front-runner status to one candidate.

Although Iowa has been holding presidential caucuses for about a cen-tury, the intensive media focus on that state began after Jimmy Carter cam-paigned tirelessly and successfully there in 1976 and emerged from its cau-cuses as the surprise front-runner in the New Hampshire primary two weeks later. Carter's New Hampshire victory propelled his nomination forward and made possible his eventual election. The New Hampshire primary gets at-tention because it is the first in the nation and because it is regarded as a bellwether. The superstitious and not-so-superstitious know that all modern presidents except Bill Clinton have won that state's primary before winning the White House.

Candidates seeking the nomination must work hard to gain momentum or wrest it from the hands of others. Larry Bartels argues in *Presidential Primaries and the Dynamics of Public Choice* that momentum plays a decisive role in shaping the outcome of the nomination race.[9] Momentum, or "big mo," as George Bush once called it, gains the candidate who has it media attention, money, and voter interest. "Free media" (that is, news that candi-dates do not have to buy) tend to follow those who do well or who are exceeding expectations. This kind of assistance helps a candidate to reach more voters than personal appearances or even paid advertising allow. Fur-thermore, potential contributors and banks who might lend campaign money are impressed by momentum because it suggests success. The experience of candidates such as Al Gore in 1988 is instructive: Gore sat out Iowa and New Hampshire, hoping to "jump start" his candidacy in the South on Super Tuesday. By the time he entered the race, however, Michael S. Dukakis already had established himself as the front-runner. Dukakis had the money, momentum, and organization that went with that status, and Gore's candidacy stalled.

The short time (just two weeks) between New Hampshire and the Junior and Super Tuesday events puts a premium on starting campaigns early. Candidates must organize well ahead of the actual contests in each state and raise money in advance of the highly compressed events of March. Otherwise, they will be unable to put together an effective campaign in the South and West even if they emerge from Iowa and New Hampshire with considerable momentum. This describes the problem faced by Sen. Paul Simon of Illinois and House majority leader Richard Gephardt of Missouri in 1988. Although Gephardt won Iowa, he could not take advantage of his momentum in New Hampshire because he had concentrated all his efforts on the first state and had few resources available for the second.

Candidates who seek the nomination must do two things: they must consider how they will appeal to voters at the ballot box and how they can win support in the right places at the right time. The nomination process unfolds in a particular order, and successful nominees are those who can navigate from Iowa to New Hampshire to the West, the South, and beyond. As we shall see, Bill Clinton was able to meet these challenges more effectively than were his opponents.

The Media as Intermediary

Although they engage in a laborious process of handshaking, "town hall" meetings, rallies, and other kinds of personal appearances during the nomination race, candidates ultimately rely on the media to communicate with the masses of people they must reach to win delegates. As the chief intermediary between the candidates and the public, the media perform three central functions in the campaign: (1) as a "gatekeeper" for news, (2) as an investigator and watchdog, and (3) as interpreter of political events.[10]

The Media as gatekeeper. Journalists and their editors determine what stories are newsworthy and which deserve more or less attention from the public. This gatekeeping function has a powerful effect on what the public sees and learns about the candidates. The stories that lead a television newscast or win major headlines in newspapers and magazines will draw more attention and interest from the voters. Because candidates (except a billionaire like Ross Perot) generally cannot afford to buy all the air time or print space they need to reach voters, they depend on free media to communicate with the public.

Candidate response. To maximize their newsworthiness, candidates work to develop a clear, coherent message for each day's news coverage. Much of the recent emphasis on "sound bites" by candidates arises from their desire to win media attention. If a candidate can say something memorable or pithy, it is more likely to be reported. (So are gaffes, which means that saying the wrong thing can gain the wrong kind of attention.) In the crowded field of an early nomination race, the ability to gain media attention may be important for candidates seeking to distinguish themselves from the pack of relatively unknown contestants. In 1984 Sen. Gary Hart, D-Colo., kept repeating the phrase "new ideas" as a way to stand out from the group of candidates who were challenging former vice president Walter Mondale's front-runner status. Mondale, in turn, borrowed the sound bite "Where's the beef?" from a fast-food commercial to beat Hart at his own game and win journalistic and public attention.

In recent elections, candidates also have learned to employ technological advances to their own benefit, from cellular phones for talking to journalists to laptop computers and other devices. In the 1992 campaign, facsimile machines were important weapons used by campaigns to send their messages immediately to news organizations. Press releases were faxed to reporters from campaign staffers, who often carried laptop computers to produce these announcements as events developed.

The media as investigator and watchdog. In the prereform era, the candidates' suitability for office was scrutinized by the professional politicians who determined the nomination. Candidates with personal "baggage" might pass the test of electability if their peers judged them to be otherwise substantial contenders. This was the case with John Kennedy, whom the professionals came to regard as a promising and effective candidate despite a reputation in Washington for womanizing. But in the era of reform, peer evaluation is lacking because the great mass of primary and caucus participants (few of whom know the candidates personally) determine who will win the party's endorsement.

In this environment, the media have assumed part of the role previously played by the professional politicians. They investigate and expose the background, record, and personal lives of contenders but leave it to the voters to determine what is relevant in deciding who will make a suitable nominee. This approach, compounded by journalists' experiences in uncovering governmental scandals such as Watergate and the Iran-contra affair, has led to intensive searches into the lives and characters of presidential candidates.

Candidate response. In an environment of media scrutiny, the conventional wisdom is that candidates with excessive personal baggage are discouraged from entering the race. This may be true, but it is impossible to prove: no potential candidate has yet pointed to personal problems as a reason for not running. In 1987 Gary Hart tried to behave as if the media did not matter when he was dogged by allegations of marital infidelity. When initially questioned about the charges, he denied them and challenged disbelieving reporters to follow him. The *Miami Herald* took up the challenge, staking out Hart's townhouse in Washington and photographing him with model Donna Rice. Hart offered excuses, but he ultimately withdrew from the race for the nomination because he could not get past this issue.

The media as chief interpreter of political events. Journalists continually monitor the progress of the nomination race and tend to focus on its "horse race" aspects: who is ahead, who is behind, and so on. Not only do the media report on and interpret the outcome of each event in the process, but they do so through the lens of expectations.

Expectations of candidate performance are crucial to interpreting the evolution of the race. Primary and caucus results are reported not just as raw data but in terms of how the candidates performed against what was expected of them. As Bartels has noted,

> the media tend to give substantial attention to some candidates who do "better than expected." As with any horse race, prerace handicapping, a source of interest in its own right, serves as a bench mark against which actual results are measured. The history of primary campaigns is dotted with famous examples of losers treated like winners (Eugene McCarthy in New Hampshire in 1968) and winners treated like losers (Edmund Muskie in New Hampshire in 1972).[11]

Candidate response. Because they run as much against media-made expectations as they do against other contenders, candidates and their staffs undertake a variety of activities designed to influence journalistic evaluations of the progress of the race. These activities are grouped under the collective term "spin control," a relatively new addition to the arsenal of presidential candidates. One aspect of spin, as it is now called in political shorthand, is to lower expectations by pointing out to reporters the obstacles to a candidate doing well in the next nomination contest. Staffers, acting as "spin doctors," will comment on opponents' strengths, particular constituencies that must be satisfied, and other formidable challenges their candidate faces. The goal is to make any showing in a primary, caucus, or group of events look "better than expected."[12]

Another kind of spin is to try to put the best face on the outcome of an event that has already occurred. Immediately after primaries, caucuses, or debates, candidates' staffers assault journalists to explain why their contender is pleased with the outcome. A candidate who is effective at spin control may receive better press coverage than the objective performance might warrant.

Ultimately, the media are not a neutral force in the nomination process. They are an active part of the environment, and candidates must deal with them as they do the rules and calendar of the delegate-selection process. As we shall see, the way Bill Clinton dealt with the media in 1992 helps to explain why he won the nomination.

The Need for Fund Raising

Candidates need money even to begin a campaign for the nomination. The existence of early high-visibility events in Iowa and New Hampshire, combined with the heavy front loading of the primary and caucus schedule, means that contenders must enter the nomination race with money already in hand. During the months that precede the start of the primary season, a

sort of "money primary" takes place. Candidates seek funds from large contributors and political action committees. Those who are able to amass large
"war chests" are better positioned to endure the tortuous, fast-paced, and
expensive campaign to follow. Moreover, as Stephen Wayne has noted, "Another advantage of having money up front is that the news media interpret it
as a sign of strength in the prenomination period prior to caucuses and
primaries." [13]

Candidates also need money to keep their campaigns alive during the
long weeks of the unfolding nomination process. Early success gives a candidate not a free ride but only the opportunity to continue contesting future
events. As Wayne has observed, "To take advantage of any boost that Iowa
or New Hampshire may provide, it is necessary to fund simultaneous media
campaigns in a number of states." [14] Victory does not reduce the need for
money; on the contrary, the need increases.

Potential candidates who anticipate a run for their party's nomination
must plan far ahead to raise money during the money primary and must be
able to continue raising it as the primary season progresses. Governors often
raise seed money from friends in their home states, while senators look for
funds from interest groups, large contributors, and other traditional sources.
Candidates must also learn to exploit federal matching funds, which can
nearly double their fund-raising efforts, especially in the crucial early weeks
of the campaign when each contender is trying to emerge from the pack of
challengers.

The Entrepreneurial Nature of Candidacy

In a nominating environment dominated by primaries, caucuses, and
the media, a presidential candidacy is essentially entrepreneurial in nature.
Prospective presidential candidates select themselves to run for office; build
their own campaign organizations, strategies, and circles of advisers; raise
money for themselves; and seek nomination and then election on their own.
They win the White House by "selling" themselves to voters, the media, and
their parties. [15]

Because nominees in the reform era are not selected by party leaders,
candidates decide for themselves whether they will run for president. An
early start is indicated for those who need to build name recognition. Jimmy
Carter used his December 1974 start in the 1976 campaign to build a base
of support in Iowa. In the prereform era, an early start was a sign of weakness
because seasoned contenders did not need a long time to establish their
credibility among those who would choose the nominee. As LBJ's heir apparent, Hubert Humphrey did not even enter primaries in 1968 but still managed to win the Democratic nomination. Incumbents still can wait longer
than unknowns before declaring their candidacy.

Ever since Jimmy Carter emerged from nowhere (figuratively speaking)
to win the Democratic nomination and the presidency in 1976, the media

have come to describe repeated primary victories in terms of a candidate winning the horse race. Bartels quotes Hamilton Jordan, Carter's campaign manager, on the importance of momentum to winning nomination:

> The press shows an exaggerated interest in the early primaries as they represent the first confrontation between candidates, their contrasting strategies and styles, which the press has been writing and speculating about for two years. Good or poor showings can have a profound and irrevocable impact on succeeding primaries and a campaign's ability to raise funds and recruit workers.[16]

The strategic response of candidates is simple: try to build their own momentum and stop or block everyone else's. For the candidate who is seen as the front-runner, all efforts are directed toward making the nomination seem inevitable. Ronald Reagan took this approach in 1980, by behaving as if all the other contenders were guests at his party.

For candidates who are behind the front-runner, the object is clear: gang up on the leader. In 1988, once he took the lead, Michael Dukakis became the target of all his opponents in the candidate debates that he and other contenders took part in during the primary season.

In the end, successful candidates for nomination are those who can perform best in this complex but relatively stable nominating environment. As we shall see, Bill Clinton's victory in 1992 was the product of a campaign strategy that combined early fund raising and organization to build momentum over the course of the spring.

The Rhythm of the Race

Just as there is a relatively stable nomination environment, so there is a recurring rhythm to the nomination race: an elaborate five-stage process through which the "out party" chooses its candidate; the renomination of an incumbent president through consistent primary victories over any challenger; and the occasional and somewhat idiosyncratic emergence of a major independent challenger.

The Outs: A Five-Stage Affair

If a party does not control the White House or if its president is leaving office, a sizable field of contenders will form for the presidential nomination. The progress from the many to the one evolves over several months, and perhaps even years, in five stages: (1) an exhibition season, (2) a winnowing stage, (3) a breakaway stage, (4) a mop-up stage, and (5) the convention.

The exhibition season. Before the process formally begins, there is a period in which candidates somehow emerge from the mass of possible contenders. The earliest part of this season begins immediately after the previous election, when potential candidates begin to position themselves for the future. Particular politicians are mentioned in news reports as possible or likely presidential candidates. Indeed, speculation about possible candidates for the next presidential election takes place even as the current campaign is under way. In its coverage of the 1992 Republican convention, *Newsweek* included a highly visible article on possible GOP candidates in 1996. Often, ambitious political figures will try to persuade prominent journalists to identify them in this way, so they can begin to gauge how well they may be received by party leaders and activists.[17]

As the presidential election year draws near, prospective candidates will arrange to be seen and heard in contexts that will assist their campaigns should they decide to run. They will travel extensively to make speeches on national affairs, especially in New Hampshire and other key primary states. They will look for and take advantage of opportunities to appear in the national media. They may write autobiographies (Jimmy Carter wrote *Why Not the Best?* and George Bush, *Looking Forward*) or books on the problems facing the nation (Howard Baker wrote one in anticipation of a 1988 run, and Walter Mondale wrote one before the 1976 campaign).[18] As time marches on, potential candidates will organize exploratory committees, as required by the federal campaign finance law. These groups provide for the recording and disclosure of contributions and spending on behalf of the almost-candidates.

By the late fall of the year preceding the election, the list of actual candidates begins to take shape. Declarations of candidacy occur, as do recusals from the race by those who might have been important candidates but who believe that now is not their time. Those in the race continue to make appearances to test themes and issues they might use in the campaign, build their staffs, raise money, and position themselves for the contests to come. Everyone studies the opposition with an eye toward highlighting differences and finding weak spots in the enemy's armor.

The winnowing stage. The real campaign begins with the dawn of the election year. Intensive coverage of the Iowa caucuses and the New Hampshire primary makes these contests important tests for contenders for the nomination. As soon as the results are in, the field of candidates begins to separate, with two or three leaders out front and everyone else struggling to stay in the race. Hopefuls who perform poorly, or who may at this point be short of funds, begin to drop out.

The breakaway stage. In the middle phase of the race for the nomination, a large number of primaries and caucuses are held in a short space of time. This highly compressed array of events tests which candidates have broad appeal, good organization in several states, a full war chest (and skill at keeping it full), media savvy, and the momentum to put together a winning coalition within the party. The most important primaries and caucuses take place on Junior Tuesday and Super Tuesday.

The consequences of the breakaway stage are substantial: more than one-third of all convention delegates are selected during a relatively brief period in early March. The field of contenders for the nomination, which once may have been as large as seven or eight, has now been reduced to a single front-runner who is defending that status from the one or two remaining challengers. By this time in 1988 George Bush dominated the Republican race, and only Senate minority leader Bob Dole and televangelist Pat Robertson remained to offer token opposition. Momentum becomes the key; the front-runner is working to make the nomination seem inevitable.

The mop-up stage. In this phase of the process, the front-runner accumulates enough delegates to secure the nomination. The candidate may not win every primary or caucus but over time will be able to declare title as the standard-bearer of the party. A number of important contests take place during the mop-up stage, such as primaries in New York, Ohio, and California, but these do not alter the ultimate outcome of the process. The primaries and caucuses are over in early June. Strategy and issues for the fall campaign now occupy the attention of the eventual nominee.

The convention stage. In the final phase of the nominating process, the presumed nominee attempts to put a personal stamp on the party by accomplishing three important tasks. First, the nominee must select a vice presidential running mate. A variety of considerations may go into that decision, from ideological and geographical balance with the presidential candidate to age, experience, and ethnic or religious affiliation. But the essential goal is to find someone who the nominee believes will best complement his or her own qualities as a candidate for president. John Kennedy chose Lyndon Johnson because of Johnson's base in the South; George Bush chose Dan Quayle to strengthen Bush's ties to the Republican right.

Before the reform era ushered in a process in which the nomination is all but decided before the convention, contenders concentrated on winning their party's endorsement almost to the last minute. Vice presidential candidates were selected in haste after the nomination was won, with exhausted nominees considering their own political interests and the best way to heal whatever wounds in the party had been caused by the fight for victory. In the age of reform the nominee has more time to consider and even interview potential running mates. Media speculation on vice presidential candidates is a common feature of news coverage; indeed, this free media may aid the campaign.

Jimmy Carter invented a vice presidential selection process in 1976 that all his Democratic successors have imitated in one form or another. Carter invited potential seconds on the ticket to his home for interviews, giving him and them time to discuss issues and qualifications. This process also gave Carter's staff a chance to check up on his potential choices. The Carter campaign considered this check important because in 1972 they had seen what happened when George McGovern selected Sen. Thomas Eagleton of Missouri as his second with little prior investigation. When the press discovered that Eagleton had once undergone psychiatric treatment and electroshock therapy, he was forced out of the race and McGovern was embarrassed by the revelation. Walter Mondale used the Carter process in 1984, with his interviewees even being questioned outside his home by reporters. (One wag compared Mondale's well-publicized selection system to the Publishers' Clearinghouse sweepstakes.) Michael Dukakis also interviewed candidates in 1988, while Bill Clinton created a search committee to help him find a running mate in 1992.

Republicans have tended to take a more secretive approach. Although they have had the time to discuss vice presidential contenders with their staffs and meet with their potential choices, GOP nominees have not used a public process akin to that pioneered by Carter and Mondale. Indeed, in 1988 George Bush kept his choice of Dan Quayle a secret from even his most senior aides until shortly before he announced his decision.

The second task facing the nominee is to oversee the writing of the party's platform. Although that document is drafted by a committee of the convention, and not by the standard-bearer's representatives, it has always borne the nominee's stamp. As each convention approaches, the media devote considerable time to the nuances of language in the platform to assess how closely that language follows the nominee's own positions. In general, the platform usually adheres to the leader's views or is ambiguous enough not to contradict pledges made during the primaries.

Finally, the nominee must oversee the preparations for a good show at the convention and plan for the fall general-election campaign. The convention is a sustained period of free media for the candidate and the party and represents the best opportunity the nominee will have to introduce himself to the nation. An important element of this preparation is the writing of the nominee's acceptance speech, which will outline the themes and issues for the fall campaign. As with vice presidential selection, what was once done after an exhaustive convention fight (often in the wee hours of the morning) is now polished well ahead of time and delivered on prime-time television. George Bush used this opportunity in 1988 to reintroduce himself to voters as a man dedicated to pursuing missions, as an opponent of tax increases ("read my lips"), and as an advocate of voluntarism ("a thousand points of light").

The Ins: Forward the Incumbent

The party of an incumbent president seeking reelection is not spared the selection process. But there is a crucial difference between this situation and the identification of a new nominee: the incumbent usually dominates the process, and progress toward renomination is far simpler and more predictable than the opposition's elaborate five-stage affair. Indeed, in the reform era only one internal challenger (Ronald Reagan in 1976) has been able to threaten seriously the renomination of an incumbent president.

Occasionally, presidents face token opposition from disaffected elements in their own party. Richard Nixon was challenged in 1972 by liberal

Republican representative Paul McCloskey of California and conservative John Ashbrook of Ohio, but the president hardly noticed. Sometimes, the challenge is stronger. In 1980 an unpopular Jimmy Carter faced the prospect of a challenge for the nomination by Sen. Edward Kennedy of Massachusetts, who enjoyed support from the liberal wing of the Democratic party and was favored over the president in early polls of Democrats. But Carter was able to employ his standing as president, the political organization he had developed to first win office in 1976, and the loyalty of party members to their incumbent to stop Kennedy's challenge. Carter won in Iowa and New Hampshire (the latter so close to Massachusetts as to be interpreted by the media as a serious blow for Kennedy) and most other early delegate contests. In the momentum-driven nomination environment of the reform era, Kennedy was unable to stop Carter.

Stronger still was Ronald Reagan's challenge to Gerald Ford in 1976. But even Reagan, darling of the party's conservative wing and a two-term governor of California, was unable to defeat the man who only months before assuming the presidency had been the House minority leader. Although Ford had never before campaigned for president (and so had no personal organization or coalition), he won because he was the incumbent, was known to party leaders in Congress and in the states, and enjoyed support from rank-and-file party members for bearing well the burden cast upon him by the collapse of Nixon's presidency in 1974. Reagan came close to denying Ford the GOP nomination, but in the end he was unable to do so.

Thus the lengthy and complex nomination system of the reform era clearly favors the president, who is poised to organize a national campaign, can raise lots of money, has access to the media, can use the powers of the office to win attention and supporters, and has a claim on the loyalty of partisans and the public at large.

The Wild Card:
An Independent or Third-Party Challenger

In each presidential election, voters in many states are surprised to find that their ballots contain more choices than the two offered by the major parties. The Socialist Workers party, the Right to Life party, the Libertarians, the Citizens party, and other groups not only nominate presidential candidates but manage to win a place for them on the official list from which voters choose the chief executive. Although these alternatives usually do not constitute a threat to the monopoly over American politics enjoyed by the Democrats and Republicans, every so often an independent or third-party challenger becomes a potentially important element in the election.

Historically, the most important third parties have been those like the Progressive (Bull Moose) party in 1912, the State Rights party (Dixiecrats) in 1948, and the American Independent party (George Wallace's group) in 1968 that represent disaffected elements in one of the two dominant parties.

These breakaway groups have the advantage of support from established politicians with experience in major-party politics, such as former president Theodore Roosevelt (1912), Dixiecrat Strom Thurmond of South Carolina (1948), and Gov. George Wallace of Alabama (1968). In 1948 and 1968 third-party candidates also took advantage of a single galvanizing issue (hostility to civil rights) and a strong regional base in the South to threaten the Democratic party from which they had bolted.

A new development in the reform era has been the arrival of independent candidates whose stated reason for running is to break the monopoly of the Democrats and Republicans and end "politics as usual." In 1980 and 1992 independent candidates sought the presidency by promising an alternative to the dominant parties. John Anderson, a member of Congress from Illinois, entered the 1980 Republican nomination process but declared himself an independent when Ronald Reagan seized front-runner status that spring. Anderson conducted what he called a national unity campaign to confront issues that his major-party rivals were ducking and to break the deadlock of two-party government. Similarly, in 1992 Ross Perot announced as an independent presidential candidate, promising to run if he could be placed on the ballot in all fifty states and to spend as much as $100 million of his own money to win the presidency back "for the people" from the professional politicians.

Both of these candidacies were to some extent made possible by the age of reform. The reformed nominating system has separated presidential nomination from the rest of each party's activities, so presidential candidates cannot make much of a claim to leading a united national party. Moreover, since the 1960s there has been a sharp rise in the number of voters not affiliating with either party, making appeals to go outside the normal two-party realm more attractive than they might have been in the past. Even those citizens who express a party preference do not necessarily vote that party's ticket from president down to sheriff. Southern Democrats, "Reagan Democrats," and other voters have often supported presidential candidates of the other party; it is always possible that they will support an independent candidate.

Serious independent and third-party candidates are essentially self-nominated. Strom Thurmond led southern delegates out of the 1948 Democratic convention; his nomination as leader of the State Rights party was no surprise. When George Wallace created the American Independent party in 1968, no serious observer saw it as anything but Wallace's personal fiefdom. Anderson and Perot proceeded without even the illusion of a party base: their candidacies were built on the argument that the solution to America's problems involved transcending parties.

The Process at Work in 1992

Although many different elements shape a presidential election, the 1992 race was heavily influenced by breathtaking changes in international affairs, especially the Persian Gulf war of 1991, that occurred during the administration of George Bush. These events affected how the president conducted himself in the White House, who ran against him, and what issues were important in the nomination races.

The Exhibition Season

The exhibition season of 1992 illustrated the power of conventional wisdom in American politics. Widespread belief in the inevitability of George Bush's reelection kept top Democrats out of the race, leaving the nomination race to "second tier" candidates. Among the Republicans, certainty about Bush meant that only nontraditional candidates would challenge him.

The Democrats. In the important period when potential Democratic presidential candidates were contemplating a run for the White House, George Bush seemed invincible. The Persian Gulf crisis, which dominated the middle months of his term, gave him an enormous boost. Shortly after the war ended in the spring of 1991, Bush scored nearly a 90 percent job-approval rating in opinion polls, and his reelection seemed certain. He had the good fortune to be in office when the Berlin Wall was dismantled and the Soviet Union collapsed. He could claim at least some credit for assisting in the reunification of Germany and the other changes underway in Eastern Europe. He had marshaled an unprecedented international coalition against Iraq, and his efforts as war leader seemed overwhelmingly successful.[19]

Clearly, Bush's popularity influenced the decisions of many potential candidates not to run. For example, Tennessee senator Al Gore, a presidential candidate in 1988, still harbored presidential ambitions and was expected to run in 1992. But Gore had joined the chorus of support in Congress for the Gulf war and had observed George Bush's triumph there. When an attempted coup in August 1991 against President Mikhail Gorbachev threatened to derail reform in the Soviet Union and Bush once again had an opportunity to display his diplomatic skill, Gore announced publicly that he would not be a candidate for president. Although he attributed his recusal to the need to spend time with his family, a wide range of political observers concluded that Gore had been done in by Bush's role in the "new world order."

The Democratic candidates who emerged in the fall and winter of 1991-1992 were not from the front ranks of the party's national leadership. Sen. Bill Bradley of New Jersey, politically wounded by a close reelection fight in 1990, was not in the race. Nor were prominent Democrats such as Senate majority leader George Mitchell, House majority leader Dick Gephardt, New York governor Mario Cuomo, or Sen. Sam Nunn of Georgia. Instead, those declaring themselves in the race were from the party's second tier: Gov. Bill Clinton of Arkansas, Gov. Douglas Wilder of Virginia, senators Tom Harkin of Iowa and Bob Kerrey of Nebraska, former senator Paul Tsongas of Massachusetts, and former California governor Jerry Brown. Each proclaimed himself an outsider who was offering to change the direction of national policy. At this point in the race, the White House regarded Kerrey as the strongest contender because of his record as a decorated war hero, his youthful good looks, his success as an entrepreneur, and his intellectual style.

As 1991 drew to a close, national attention shifted away from foreign affairs to the weakened state of the American economy. The candidates attacked the president for his seeming inattention to domestic concerns and offered solutions ranging from Tsongas's probusiness economic plan to Kerrey's call for national health insurance. In October the president's job-approval rating, which had been declining slowly since its March high, took a dip to near 50 percent. It continued to fall as the economy remained stagnant. By early 1992 many Democrats hoped the president's declining political fortunes would entice a prominent national figure such as Governor Cuomo to enter the race. (Indeed, Bill Clinton believed that Cuomo would run in 1992 and saw the New York governor as his major rival for the nomination.) None did, however, and the announced candidates engaged in the usual round of exhibition-season activities.

Prominent among these activities was fund raising. Governor Clinton was the clear winner in this enterprise, amassing $3.3 million (not including federal matching funds) by the end of 1991. Much of this money came from contributors in Arkansas. He was followed by Senator Harkin of Iowa, whose press secretary acknowledged Clinton's lead with the comment, "I think we all recognize that Governor Clinton has been ordained the front-runner. He had a great December [for fund raising]." [20] Figure 2-2 gives the results of the Democratic money primary in 1991.

In addition to fund raising, active campaigning was under way. The candidates were jockeying for position, each attempting to portray himself as centrist enough for general-election voters but liberal enough for Democratic primary participants. Only two of the group stood out: Brown, who adopted the label of outsider with all the fervor of a convert (as the son of a governor, a former governor himself, and the recent California Democratic party chair, he was more of an insider than most of his opponents), and Harkin, who unrepentantly called himself a traditional New Deal Democrat.

At a debate in January 1992, Democratic prospects seemed dim. The candidates met in a forum moderated by NBC news anchor Tom Brokaw, who conducted the event much like a daytime talk show. The six challengers, all largely unknown to the nation, squabbled among themselves and attacked George Bush. They impressed few observers. Brown, who had raised little money, chanted a mantra-like message about change and recited his toll-free number for making campaign pledges. He forswore any contribution of more than $100, which made all of his money eligible for federal matching funds (the government matches donations only up to $250) but limited his ability to buy expensive television time. Kerrey, Harkin, Clinton, and Tsongas competed for opportunities to criticize the president. Wilder revealed himself to be generally unprepared and uninformed on most issues.

Figure 2.2 Democratic "Money Primary" Through December 1991

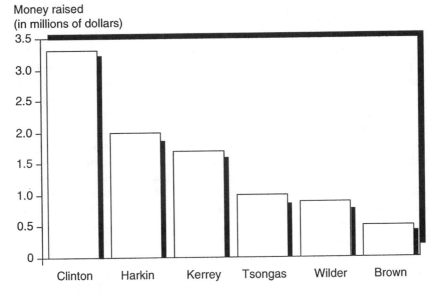

Money raised
(in millions of dollars)

Source: Washington Post, Jan. 3, 1992 A4.

When the debate was over, the spectacle alarmed several prominent Democrats and made the field of contenders the butt of several jokes. Asked who he thought had won the event, President Bush indicated himself.

Soon after this shaky start, however, things began to improve. Governor Wilder, apparently surprised by the amount of time and energy required for a campaign, dropped out of the race. As the first real contests in Iowa and New Hampshire drew near, the five remaining contenders accelerated the pace of their efforts.

The Republicans. In the aftermath of the Gulf war, no one expected President Bush to have any serious opposition to renomination. Although Bush had never gotten along well with the conservatives in his party, who had been Ronald Reagan's base, his war victory and persistent opposition to abortion seemed to protect him from trouble on his right flank. The only opponents willing to take on the president were a white supremacist from Louisiana and a conservative television commentator.

David Duke had existed for several years on the fringes of American politics, as imperial wizard of the Ku Klux Klan, a member of the American Nazi party, and an activist for white supremacy. In the 1980s he changed his approach, running first for state office in Louisiana as a Democrat and then winning a state senate seat as a Republican. He avoided talking about his involvement with the Klan and the Nazi party, professing himself a born-again Christian who was interested in defending working-class voters against "welfare cheats" and unfair affirmative-action programs. Duke gained national media attention in 1991, when he won enough support among white voters to earn a spot in a runoff race for the Louisiana governorship against former state chief executive Edwin Edwards. The national Republican party repudiated Duke, and prominent party members endorsed his Democratic opponent, but Duke wore their scorn as a badge of honor. He proclaimed that he would take on the president in 1992, and several analysts thought he might attract substantial support from white middle-class voters who were unhappy with the state of the economy and Bush's inattention to it.

The other challenger, Patrick Buchanan, was an equally unlikely presidential candidate. He had spent most of his career in politics, as a campaign aide and presidential speechwriter. In the Nixon White House, he was famous as the author of Vice President Spiro Agnew's harsh attacks on the media. As director of communications in the Reagan administration, Buchanan was the man conservatives looked to to maintain the president's ideological purity. During the Bush years, he achieved national celebrity as a panelist on various political talk shows on cable and public television. He could be counted on to advance his conservative positions in often strident language.

Buchanan's differences with Bush centered on two closely related issues. First, with the fall of communism, Buchanan had reverted to an old-fashioned form of conservative isolationism in his foreign policy views. He attacked George Bush's internationalist foreign policy and intervention in the Persian Gulf crisis, attributing the president's involvement to pressure from Jewish interest groups. Second, he maintained that Bush paid little attention to domestic affairs and thus was allowing the American economy to decline. Buchanan hit the president especially hard for breaking his "no new taxes" pledge and signing a tax bill in 1990. He hinted throughout the fall of 1991 that he might run against Bush in the Republican primaries, if only to force the president to the right and to make him shift his attention to domestic matters.

The Winnowing Stage

As the early contests of the nominating process got under way, the big questions were whether one Democrat would emerge from the field of contenders and whether George Bush would really have to fight for renomination. To the surprise of nearly everyone, these issues were somewhat eclipsed by the sudden emergence of a wild card in the race.

The Democrats. In early 1992 many Democratic party leaders feared that no front-runner would emerge and that the quest for the nomination would not be resolved until the convention in July. They worried that the absence of a first-tier Democrat in the race would cause the various hopefuls to divide the party, thus making it nearly impossible to unseat the incumbent, whose party probably would be united. Party chair Ron Brown and others wanted the nomination to be decided sooner rather than later, but they feared that the political bases of several candidates made that outcome unlikely: Harkin would win Iowa, Tsongas's home state of Massachusetts was next door to New Hampshire, Clinton was a southerner, and Brown a westerner. Conceivably, the convention could resemble the old-style deadlocked nomination contests from which a weak compromise nominee might emerge.

At first, it seemed that Ron Brown's worst fears might come true. The Iowa caucuses ended predictably. Favorite-son Tom Harkin won 76.4 percent of the delegates, followed by 12 percent who were uncommitted to any candidate. Paul Tsongas came in third (4.1 percent), with Bill Clinton behind him (2.8 percent).[21] But polls indicated that Clinton was leading in the upcoming New Hampshire primary.

Clinton's lead in the Granite State suggested that as a southern governor who could win votes in the Northeast, he might emerge early as the front-runner and dominate the spring. Clinton had prepared for the first primary with money and organization, employing a strategy designed to build momentum early and knock out his opponents on Super Tuesday.

But all hopes were dashed when Clinton became embroiled in scandal over two episodes in his past. First, widely published stories alleged that the Arkansas governor had had an extramarital affair while in office. Clinton's handling of allegations of infidelity was quite different from Gary Hart's. He appeared on "Sixty Minutes" along with his wife and in general terms acknowledged past marital problems. (He was not specific but admitted to having "caused pain" in his marriage in the past.) Hillary Clinton demonstrated resolve and trust in her husband. By attacking the problem, Clinton ensured that the issue soon died.

Clinton's performance on the infidelity issue contrasted with the way he handled charges that he had avoided the Vietnam-era draft. He tried to dodge the issue with a series of explanations that never quite provided a complete story. Consequently, the issue continued to come up until the end of the campaign in November. During one of the October presidential debates, the candidate confessed that he had handled the whole matter poorly.

In any event, scandal broke Clinton's stride in New Hampshire, and he found himself fighting hard to hold on to his lead. The chief threat came from Paul Tsongas, whom many observers previously had written off as an unlikely nominee. As a former senator and cancer survivor, Tsongas was regarded as a risky choice who would not be able to attract broad voter support. In response, the probusiness Tsongas maintained that he would be more likely to woo Republicans in November than would Clinton.

Tsongas surprised the skeptics, and Bill Clinton, by winning the bellwether New Hampshire primary on February 18. He received 33.2 percent of the votes to Clinton's 24.7 percent, with the other contenders finishing well behind. But as a sign that some party members still were not satisfied with the field, Mario Cuomo won 4 percent as an undeclared write-in candidate.[22] Tsongas took advantage of his regional proximity to New Hampshire and the allure of his economic program in the economically depressed state. Ever searching for the front-runner, journalists turned their attention from the wounded Clinton to the emerging Tsongas.

Tsongas followed his first New England victory with another in the Maine caucuses on February 23, in large part because Clinton had headed south to prepare for Super Tuesday. Two days later Kerrey, a Nebraskan, won the primary in neighboring South Dakota. His victory, along with Jerry Brown's strong second-place finish in Maine, suggested that the nomination contest might indeed drag on for as long as Ron Brown and others had feared. In the winnowing stage, each candidate had demonstrated strength in his native region. As yet, the demand for a coordinated strategy of money and momentum had not decided the race.

The Republicans. The major question in the Republican contest was whether Pat Buchanan would win enough votes to embarrass the president. He did not, although it seemed for a time that he might. In a way, Buchanan even performed an important service for George Bush.

As the New Hampshire primary approached, Buchanan worked hard to stir up resentment against the president. Republican voters in the conservative state were especially open to Buchanan's appeal. New Hampshire had been hit hard by the recession and seemed fertile ground for the commentator's challenge. Nevertheless, the White House struck back with an intense effort to hold on to a strong lead, even bringing in former president Reagan to endorse Bush at a political dinner on February 9.

Buchanan urged New Hampshire voters to "send a message" to the White House about Bush's backing down on the "no new taxes" pledge he had made in 1988. At one point, the challenger's staff and some journalists predicted that Buchanan might receive as much as 40 percent of the vote. As a result, this number became a kind of threshold for determining the strength of the send-a-message campaign.

But Buchanan was unable to reach 40 percent. Instead, he received 37.4 percent to the president's 53 percent. This result gave him enough momentum to stay in the race but prevented him from embarrassing Bush. He had not performed in the expectations game as predicted. Buchanan continued to be a factor in the race, however, because his showing had demonstrated Republican discontent with the president.

In any event, Buchanan did Bush a service in New Hampshire by offering a viable, mainstream alternative to David Duke. Although Duke did not contest the New Hampshire primary, Buchanan's candidacy gave Republican voters who wanted to send a message a choice other than the former Nazi. Many party leaders had feared that Duke would win substantial support simply by being the only alternative to the president and thus would gain legitimacy as a Republican. The last thing that the White House or Republican leaders wanted was for Duke to claim respectability in a party already struggling against charges of insensitivity to minority Americans. Although

Buchanan was not yet out of the race, in retrospect it is clear that Duke was winnowed out by the New Hampshire results.

Ross Perot emerges. On February 20, two days after the New Hampshire primary, the presidential race was thrown into turmoil by the sudden entry of businessman Ross Perot. Perot was a billionaire who had secured a high public profile by attempting to take control of General Motors, sending mercenary soldiers to rescue some of his employees trapped in Teheran during the Iranian revolution in 1979, and making several well-publicized efforts to win the release of American prisoners of war during and after the Vietnam War.

Perot had been highly critical of both parties for perpetuating a political deadlock that, he maintained, prevented effective action to deal with the federal deficit and other pressing national problems. On CNN's "Larry King Live," he expressed a willingness to run for president if the American people could "register me [for a place on the ballot] in fifty states," pledging to spend up to $100 million dollars of his own money in a "world class campaign." [23]

The public reaction to Perot's announcement was impressive. With Bush vulnerable and the Democratic field weak, many disenchanted voters were looking for a "white knight" whom they could support with enthusiasm. Petition drives sprang up in several states, coordinated and financed by the Perot headquarters in Dallas. (The Perot campaign tried hard to make the state drives appear spontaneous and autonomous.) Although he continued to demur on whether he was actually in the race, Perot kept up his round of television and radio appearances to promote his apparent candidacy. His process of self-nomination was under way.

The Breakaway Stage

Despite the ambiguities of the winnowing stage in 1992, the middle, or breakaway, phase of the nominating process in the two major parties proceeded as expected: the Democrats found a front-runner and the president halted his challenger. But the presence of Ross Perot in the campaign continued to provide an element of uncertainty.

The Democrats. After losing the New Hampshire primary to Paul Tsongas, Bill Clinton preempted his opponent's victory speech with a televised pronouncement that he was "the comeback kid." [24] He denied that his twenty-point drop in the polls from first to second place meant the end of his candidacy, and he proclaimed his determination to stay in the race. Clinton's effective use of spin control, coupled with the media emphasis on Pat Buchanan's showing in the Republican primary, meant that Tsongas was unable to take full advantage of his New Hampshire victory.

Clinton's perseverance was rewarded in the delegate-rich period from Junior Tuesday to Super Tuesday in early March. On March 3 the Junior Tuesday contests showed that Clinton and Tsongas were the leaders of the pack, with Jerry Brown able to exploit an environmentalist message in order to stay in the race. Clinton won the Georgia primary with an impressive 57.2 percent of the vote, establishing him as a force to be reckoned with in the upcoming, southern-dominated Super Tuesday. Tsongas won in Maryland and Utah, while Brown narrowly beat Clinton in Colorado. By the end of the day, the winnowing process had resumed: Bob Kerrey's poor showing led him to withdraw formally on March 5; he was followed a few days later by Tom Harkin. Each of these candidates lacked the money to campaign effectively and so could not draw the votes needed to raise more money. The downward spiral of fund raising and vote getting ended each man's hopes.

The Junior Tuesday contests were crucial for Clinton because they demonstrated that he could endure attacks on his personal life and military record and still win votes in the South, where such issues traditionally have been important. The intensity of so many events clustered together also increased the personal attacks and negative tone of the campaign. Tsongas accused Clinton of being a "pander bear" who was willing to promise anything to any group to win votes, while the Arkansas governor compared the former senator's economic philosophy to the "soulless" and "coldblooded" policies of Ronald Reagan.[25]

The question as Super Tuesday approached was whether the southerner in the race could deliver a knock-out punch to establish himself as the undisputed front-runner and claimant to the title of nominee. The answer Clinton received on March 10 was definite. His strong showing was reported as a "sweep" and a "rout," with the normally phlegmatic *Congressional Quarterly Weekly Report* commenting that "the architects of Super Tuesday finally got what they wanted this year when a moderate Southerner swept Dixie's Democratic primaries." [26] Clinton won primaries in Florida (50.8 percent), Louisiana (69.5 percent), Mississippi (73.1 percent), Oklahoma (70.5 percent), Tennessee (67.3 percent), and Texas (65.6 percent), as well as caucuses in Hawaii (51.5 percent) and Missouri (45.1 percent). In contrast, Tsongas won only in the northeastern states of Massachusetts (66.4 percent), Rhode Island (52.9 percent), and Delaware (30.2 percent).[27] The delegate count told the story. Of the 2,415 delegates needed to win nomination, Clinton already could claim the support of 728. The next greatest number was uncommitted, followed by 343 delegates for Tsongas. The media were now describing Clinton as the clear front-runner, portraying Tsongas as a regional candidate and Brown as a fringe candidate.

One week later, on March 17, Clinton effectively clinched the nomination with primary victories in Illinois and Michigan. His success in these contests showed that he could win votes in the industrial Midwest, an important element in any Democratic presidential coalition. Tsongas faltered, finishing second in Illinois and third behind Brown in Michigan. Because he had spent nearly all of his money on Super Tuesday, Tsongas had little left to devote to the industrial Midwest, where he might have done much better.

On March 19 he suspended his campaign, virtually ensuring that the Arkansas governor would be the party's nominee.

Clinton's breakaway victory can be attributed to his ability to work effectively within the nominating environment. He raised money early and used it to build an organization, put out his message, and take advantage of his southern roots. In contrast, Tsongas raised little money in advance and began too late to put together a campaign in the South. He could not halt the momentum Clinton had built up.

The Republicans. For George Bush, the breakaway stage of the renomination campaign proceeded as he had hoped. Some observers believed that Pat Buchanan might be able to upset the president in one or more southern states, where he could appeal to conservatives on social issues, race, and the economy. Indeed, the Buchanan campaign launched a determined attack against Bush on several fronts, criticizing him for signing the 1991 Civil Rights Act (a "quota bill"), for the government's supporting a film that supposedly celebrated homosexuality, and for breaking his pledge not to raise taxes. But all was for nought; the challenger never could exceed his New Hampshire peak of 37.4 percent.

As the important contests of Junior Tuesday and Super Tuesday proceeded, Buchanan came to be seen as less and less a threat to the president. Eventually, some cynics began calling him the "thirtysomething" candidate, because he could never do much better than 30 percent of the vote. After the Illinois-Michigan follow-up to Super Tuesday, Buchanan virtually conceded that his campaign against Bush had failed. On March 20 he told reporters that only "celestial intervention" could stop the president from winning the nomination.[28] Buchanan promised to continue campaigning but said that he would focus his efforts only on North Carolina (May 5) and California (June 2). Assured of the nomination, Bush announced that he was scaling back his campaign.

Ross Perot at large. While his opponents secured their grips on their parties' nominations, the independent candidate, marching to his own drummer, engaged in activities reminiscent of the exhibition season. On March 18 Perot delivered a speech to the National Press Club, attacking both Democrats and Republicans as part of the same Washington establishment. "In plain Texas talk," he proclaimed, "it's time to take out the trash and clean out the barn." Two days later Perot's supporters opened offices in Dallas to coordinate his campaign efforts, especially the petition drives that were necessary to put him on state election ballots. A Perot spokesman claimed that his toll-free number for voters to call to offer assistance and support had received two thousand calls an hour in its first few days of operation.[29]

The Mop-Up Stage

Even as Bill Clinton was securing his nomination and George Bush was putting the Buchanan challenge behind him, each had to look over his shoul-

Table 2-1 1992 Democratic Party First-Round Caucus Winners

Caucus States	Turnout	Brown	Clinton	Harkin	Kerrey	Tsongas	Others	Uncommitted
Iowa (Feb. 10)	30,000*	1.6	2.8	76.4	2.5	4.1	0.6	12.0
Maine (Feb. 23)	13,500*	30.3	14.8	5.2	3.0	29.0	1.7	16.1
Idaho (March 3)	3,090	4.5	11.4	29.7	8.0	28.4	0.8	17.2
Minnesota (March 3)	50-60,000*	8.2	10.3	26.7	7.6	19.2	3.9	24.3
Utah (March 3)	31,638	28.4	18.3	4.0	10.9	33.4	2.7	2.3
Washington (March 3)	60,000*	18.6	12.6	8.2	3.4	32.3	1.5	23.2
American Samoa (March 3)	n.a.	—	4.3	—	8.7	—	—	87.0
North Dakota (March 5-19)	5,000*	7.5	46.0	6.8	1.2 [a]	10.3	2.4	25.9
Arizona (March 7)	36,326	27.5	29.2	7.6	—	34.4	—	1.3 [d]
Wyoming (March 7)	1,500*	23.0	28.5	14.2	—	11.7	0.4	22.3
Democrats Abroad (March 7-9)	4,000*	12.2	26.6	6.9	—	36.8	17.5	—
Nevada (March 8)	6-7,000*	34.4	26.6	—[b]	—	19.6	—	19.4 [d]
Delaware (March 10)	2,500*	19.5	20.8	—	—	30.2	—	29.6
Hawaii (March 10)	3,014	13.6	51.5	12.7	0.4	14.3	—	7.5
Missouri (March 10)	20-25,000*	5.7	45.1	—	—	10.2 [c]	—	39.0
Texas (March 10)				——— Not available ———				
Virgin Islands (March 28)	343	4.1	39.7	—	—	—	—	56.3
Vermont (March 31)	6,000*	46.7	16.8	—	—	9.3	2.2	25.0
Alaska (April 2)	1,100*	33.1	30.9	—	—	1.3	—	34.7
Virginia (April 11, 13)	n.a.	11.6	52.1	—	—	—	—	36.3
Guam (May 3)	1,000*	20.0	49.0	—	—	—	—	31.0

Source: Congressional Quarterly Weekly Report, July 4, 1992, 70.

Note: By and large, caucus results were compiled by the state parties and reflect either the share won of delegates to the next stage of the caucus process or a tally of the presidential preferences of caucus participants. No results were available from the March 10 precinct caucuses in Texas. In most cases, the turnout figures are estimates. An asterisk indicates estimated turnout. A dash (—) indicates that the candidate was not listed on the caucus ballot or that his votes were not tabulated separately.

[a] Kerrey withdrew from the race March 5.

[b] Harkin withdrew from the race March 9.

[c] Tsongas suspended his campaign March 19.

[d] Vote for uncommitted and others was combined in tally.

der. The shadow of Ross Perot was looming: Perot appeared to be the only viable alternative to either of the major candidates. This made the mop-up stage of the campaign both normal and unusual. What was normal was that there were no surprises in either major party; what was different was the fear that an independent challenger just might defeat the major-party nominees.

The Democrats. With Paul Tsongas out of the race, the only obstacles standing between Clinton and the nomination were Jerry Brown's unorthodox challenge and the possibility that Clinton's own character and record would make him unacceptable to voters.

Jerry Brown's antiestablishment campaign never really threatened to undo Clinton's hold on the nomination, but it had enough life to continue to lend an air of suspense to the rest of the primary season. Brown was running a bare-bones campaign: he slept in the homes of supporters, not in hotels; he bought radio time, not television; and he exploited free media by appearing incessantly on talk shows. As the former California governor found out, however, his ability to draw votes away from Clinton was a function of his status as the only alternative left in the race after Tsongas's withdrawal.

The high point of Brown's challenge came just days after Tsongas suspended his campaign. On March 24 Brown scored a victory in the Connecticut primary (37.2 percent to Clinton's 35.6 percent). He attacked Clinton as the representative of a bipartisan, money-corrupted "incumbent party" and criticized the Arkansan's "smugness" in playing golf at an all-white country club. Accused by some party leaders of being a "spoiler" intent on bringing down Clinton, Brown told reporters, "What is this, the Politburo? There is only one candidate picked by the power structure? I'm not the spoiler. Slick Willie [Clinton] is the spoiler. If he gets the nomination, he's going to ruin the whole Democratic Party." [30]

One week later Brown won the Vermont caucuses. But his campaign would never be as forceful again. In New York's April 7 primary, he took on Clinton as aggressively as he could but came in third, trailing even behind the noncandidate Tsongas. More than a third of Brown's voters in Connecticut had told pollsters that they would have voted for Tsongas had he still been in the race. [31]

Clinton won nearly all the remaining events, including the California primary on June 2. In Brown's home state, the front-runner (47.5 percent) beat the challenger (40.2 percent). Clinton had survived the media's revelations about his personal life and military record as well as attacks from members of his own party. Having shown himself to be the "comeback kid," he looked forward to the convention and the tasks that lay ahead.

Meanwhile, however, Perot's candidacy gained momentum. With polls in May showing Perot ahead in some states, and second nationally behind Bush, the Clinton campaign worried that all their efforts ultimately might be fruitless. [32] As the primary season ended, no one was quite sure what Clinton's success in capturing the nomination would mean. Tables 2-1 and 2-2 present the results of the 1992 Democratic caucuses and primaries.

Table 2-2   1992 Democratic Primary Results

State	Turnout	Brown	Clinton	Harkin	Kerrey	Tsongas	Other	Uncom-mitted
N.H. (2-18)	167,819	8.1%	24.7%	10.2%	11.1%	33.2%	12.7%	—
S.D. (2-25)	59,503	3.9	19.1	25.2	40.2	9.6	2.0	—
Colo. (3-3)	239,643	28.8	26.9	2.4	12.3	25.6	1.6	2.2%
Ga. (3-3)	454,631	8.1	57.2	2.1	4.8	24.0	—	3.8
Md. (3-3)	567,243	8.2	33.5	5.8	4.8 [a]	40.6	0.8	6.4
S.C. (3-7)	116,414	6.0	62.9	6.6 [b]	0.5	18.3	2.6	3.1
Fla. (3-10)	1,123,857	12.4	50.8	1.2	1.1	34.5	—	—
La. (3-10)	384,397	6.6	69.5	1.0	0.8	11.1	11.0	—
Mass. (3-10)	792,885	14.6	10.9	0.5	0.7	66.4	5.4	1.5
Miss. (3-10)	191,357	9.6	73.1	1.3	0.9	8.1	0.8	6.2
Okla. (3-10)	416,129	16.7	70.5	3.4	3.2	—	6.2	—
R.I. (3-10)	50,709	18.8	21.2	0.6	0.9	52.9	4.1	1.4
Tenn. (3-10)	318,482	8.0	67.3	0.7	0.5	19.4	0.1	3.9
Texas (3-10)	1,482,975	8.0	65.6	1.3	1.4	19.2	4.5	—
Ill. (3-17)	1,504,130	14.6	51.6	2.0	0.7	25.8	0.7	4.5
Mich. (3-17)	585,972	25.8	50.7	1.1	0.5	16.6 [c]	0.5	4.8
Conn. (3-24)	173,119	37.2	35.6	1.1	0.7	19.5	2.7	3.1
Kan. (4-7)	160,251	13.0	51.3	0.6	1.4	15.2	4.7	13.8
Minn. (4-7) *	204,170	30.6	31.1	2.0	0.6	21.3	8.8 [d]	5.6
N.Y. (4-7)	1,007,726	26.2	40.9	1.1	1.1	28.6	2.0	—
Wis. (4-7)	772,596	34.5	37.2	0.7	0.4	21.8	3.4	2.0
Pa. (4-28)	1,265,495	25.7	56.5	1.7	1.6	12.8	1.7	—
D.C. (5-5)	61,904	7.2	73.8	—	—	10.4	—	8.5
Ind. (5-5)	476,849	21.5	63.3	—	3.0	12.2	—	—
N.C. (5-5)	691,875	10.4	64.1	0.9	0.9	8.3	—	15.4
Neb. (5-12)	150,587	21.0	45.5	2.8	—	7.1	7.1	16.4

continued

The Republicans. The mop-up stage of the Republican nomination process was relatively uneventful. George Bush ran out the string of primaries and caucuses, with Pat Buchanan far behind and David Duke even farther behind. Table 2-3 gives the Republican party primary results. (Democrats require a tally of first-round caucus results; Republicans do not. In only a few states was there a public tally of the presidential preferences of the GOP caucus voters.) As with the Clinton campaign, however, the real unknown that began to concern the Republicans was whether Bush could prevail in a three-way race.

Ross Perot peaks. By mid-April the Perot campaign was in full gear. A CBS News/*New York Times* poll in late April showed that the independent Texan enjoyed the support of 23 percent of respondents, compared with Clinton's 28 percent and Bush's 38 percent.[33] Only a month before, Perot had been seven points lower and Bush six points higher. Perot was clearly

Table 2-2 *Continued*

State	Turnout	Brown	Clinton	Harkin	Kerrey	Tsongas	Other	Uncom-mitted
W.Va. (5-12)	306,866	11.9	74.2	0.9	1.0	6.9	5.0	—
Ore. (5-19)	354,332	31.2	45.1	—	—	10.5	13.2	—
Wash. (5-19) *	147,981	23.1	42.0	1.3	1.0	12.8	19.8 d	—
Ark. (5-26)	502,617	11.0	68.0	—	—	—	2.9	18.0
Idaho (5-26) *	55,124	16.7	49.0	—	—	—	5.2	29.1
Ky. (5-26)	370,578	8.3	56.1	1.9	0.9	4.9	—	28.0
Ala. (6-2)	450,899	6.8	68.2	—	—	—	4.8	20.2
Calif. (6-2)	2,863,609	40.2	47.5	—	1.2	7.4	3.8	—
Mont. (6-2)	117,471	18.5	46.8	—	—	10.7	—	24.0
N. J. (6-2)	392,626	20.3	62.1	—	—	11.5	6.1	—
N. M. (6-2)	181,443	16.9	52.9	1.8	—	6.2	2.7	19.4
Ohio (6-2)	1,042,335	18.9	61.2	2.4	2.2	10.6	4.5	—
N.D. (6-9) *	32,786	—	14.5 e	—	—	—	85.5 d	—
Total	20,239,385	20.1%	51.8%	1.4%	1.6%	18.1%	3.4%	3.7%

Source: Alice V. McGillivray, *Presidential Primaries and Caucuses, 1992: A Handbook of Election Statistics* (Washington, D.C.: Congressional Quarterly, 1992), 4-5; and *Congressional Quarterly Weekly Report,* July 4, 1992, 69.

Note: Results are based on official returns. An asterisk indicates nonbinding "beauty contest" primaries. A dash (—) indicates that the candidate or the uncommitted line was not listed on the ballot. Percentages may not add to 100 because of rounding.

[a] Kerrey withdrew from the race March 5.

[b] Harkin withdrew from the race March 9.

[c] Tsongas suspended his campaign March 19.

[d] Perot write-in votes totaled 2.1 percent of the Democratic primary vote in Minnesota, 19.1 percent in Washington, and 29 percent in North Dakota (which was the winning total).

[e] Clinton's vote in North Dakota came on write-ins.

gaining on the major-party candidates. The price of success was that while once he had been treated with a considerable deference by journalists Perot now found his statements subjected to increasing scrutiny. In a speech to the American Society of Newspaper Editors in April, he was pressed to outline his positions on a variety of issues. The candidate angrily responded, "Do we have to be so rude and adversarial? Can't we just talk?" [34]

Reporters also investigated his life and career in greater detail. In April and early May a flurry of stories swirled around the question of why Perot, a graduate of the U.S. Naval Academy, had resigned from the navy. Perot maintained that he had done so because of a dispute with his commanding officer on the USS *Sigourney,* who had wanted him to use a sailors' recreation fund for the skipper's personal benefit. Several journalists followed the story and could find no corroboration for the candidate's claims.

Table 2-3   1992 Republican Primary Results

State	Turnout	Buchanan	Bush	Duke	Others	Uncommitted
N.H. (2-18)	174,165	37.4%	53.0%	—	9.7%	—
S.D. (2-25)	44,671	—	69.3	—	—	30.7%
Colo. (3-3)	195,690	30.0	67.5	—	2.5	—
Ga. (3-3)	453,990	35.7	64.3	—	—	—
Md. (3-3)	240,021	29.9	70.1	—	—	—
S.C. (3-7)	148,840	25.7	66.9	7.1%	0.3	—
Fla. (3-10)	893,463	31.9	68.1	—	—	—
La. (3-10)	135,109	27.0	62.0	8.8	2.1	—
Mass. (3-10)	269,701	27.7	65.6	2.1	0.9	3.8
Miss. (3-10)	154,708	16.7	72.3	10.6	0.4	—
Okla. (3-10)	217,721	26.6	69.6	2.6	1.2	—
R.I. (3-10)	15,636	31.8	63.0	2.1	0.3	2.8
Tenn. (3-10)	245,653	22.2	72.5	3.1	—	2.0
Texas (3-10)	797,146	23.9	69.8	2.5	0.3	3.5
Ill. (3-17)	831,140	22.5	76.4	—	1.2	—
Mich. (3-17)	449,133	25.0	67.2	2.4	0.1	5.3
Conn. (3-24)	99,473	21.9	66.7	2.3	—	9.1
Kan. (4-7)	213,196	14.8	62.0	1.8	4.8	16.6
Minn. (4-7)	132,756	24.2	63.9	—	8.8 [b]	3.1
N.Y.		No presidential preference vote held				
Wis. (4-7)	482,248	16.3	75.6	2.7 [a]	3.7	1.8
Pa. (4-28)	1,008,777	23.2	76.8	—	—	—
D.C. (5-5)	5,235	18.5	81.5	—	—	—
Ind. (5-5)	467,615	19.9	80.1	—	—	—
N.C. (5-5)	283,571	19.5	70.7	—	—	9.8
Neb. (5-12)	192,098	13.5	81.4	1.5	3.7	—
W. Va. (5-12)	124,157	14.6	80.5	—	4.9	—
Ore. (5-19)	304,159	19.0	67.1	2.2	11.8	—
Wash. (5-19)	129,655	10.2	67.0	1.2	21.6 [b]	—
Ark. (5-26)	52,141	12.6	87.4	—	—	—
Idaho (5-26)	115,502	13.1	63.5	—	—	23.4
Ky. (5-26)	101,119	—	74.5	—	—	25.5
Ala. (6-2)	165,121	7.6	74.3	—	—	18.1
Calif. (6-2)	2,156,464	26.4	73.6	—	0.0	—
Mont. (6-2)	90,975	11.8	71.6	—	—	16.6
N.J. (6-2)	310,270	15.0	77.5	—	7.5 [b]	—
N.M. (6-2)	86,967	9.1	63.8	—	—	27.1
Ohio (6-2)	860,453	16.7	83.3	—	—	—
N.D. (6-9)	47,808	—	83.4	—	16.6 [b]	—
Total	12,696,547	22.8%	72.5%	0.9%	1.5%	2.3%

Source: Alice V. McGillivray, *Presidential Primaries and Caucuses, 1992* (Washington, D.C.: Congressional Quarterly, 1992, 2-3); *Congressional Quarterly Weekly Report,* Aug. 8, 1992, 63.

Note: Results are based on official returns. A dash (—) indicates that the candidate or the uncommitted line was not listed on the ballot. Percentages may not add to 100 because of rounding.

[a] Duke withdrew from the race April 22.

[b] Write-in votes for Ross Perot totaled 2.7 percent of the Republican primary vote in Minnesota, 19.6 percent in Washington, 7.5 percent in New Jersey, and 8.1 percent in North Dakota.

Perot also became the target of attacks by his opponents. For example, Clinton challenged Perot's pose as a businessman unsullied by politics. He charged that Perot was as "political as anybody else has been" and accused the Texan of making lavish campaign contributions in order to influence legislation that was favorable to his own interests.[35] George Bush suggested that Perot was unprepared for the rough-and-tumble of a presidential campaign.

Not only was Perot being treated as a candidate, despite his official claim only to be "considering" a run for the White House, but he also acted more like a candidate. He continued to appear on television interview shows, his preferred method of public communication, but he was also making more public appearances and speeches. In April he resigned from two private clubs that excluded minority members. He began assembling a staff that included veterans of previous major-party campaigns, with former Carter aide Hamilton Jordan and Reagan aide Ed Rollins as co-chairs of the campaign.

On May 11 Perot qualified for his first state ballot: Texas. By the end of the month he was on the November ballot in nine states. Eventually he would qualify in all fifty states. Although not technically a candidate, Perot clearly was a significant contender.

The Convention Stage

The convention phase of the nominating process opened on what appeared to be a transformed political landscape. Early June was an anxious time for Bush and Clinton, as they contemplated Perot's challenge. But later in the summer the Democratic and Republican conventions were held in what by then seemed to be the circumstances of a "normal" election. The atmospheric change between June and July was stimulated by an event of singular importance: Ross Perot's sudden withdrawal from the race.

Ross Perot departs. Just as commentators and scholars were speculating on how the independent candidate might make history, he withdrew from the race. Perot had been riding high in the polls; he had drawn even with his opponents nationally and was leading them in the West and the South. Pundits were spinning scenarios in which Perot might draw enough support to deny anyone a majority of votes in the electoral college, thus turning the election over to the House of Representatives. No one was quite sure what would happen if the House had to choose the next president.

As for Perot himself, until he withdrew he was a candidate in every way except declaring himself one. He was building a national campaign organization, making frequent appearances and speeches, and spending millions of dollars to win a place on state ballots and spread his message. But he was dogged by opponents' attacks and continued media scrutiny of his statements and background. His style of business management, past contributions to political campaigns, involvement with the Nixon White House, and various investments all came under investigation. Perot claimed that Republican "dirty tricks" underlay many of the revelations in the news, but he offered no real response to his critics. Nevertheless, his campaign maintained credibility with the voters.

Suddenly, however, Perot's enthusiasm for the race seemed to wither. He angrily resisted advancing specific positions on most issues, despite increasing pressure to do so. He would not name a running mate, although he would need one to be a candidate.[36] And he showed that he had not mastered the protocols of national politics. On July 11 Perot addressed the National Association for the Advancement of Colored People (NAACP), the country's leading civil rights group. In his remarks, he characterized his audience as "you people" and "your people," suggesting insensitivity in matters of race relations. The critical reaction to that speech shocked Perot.

The euphoria of the Perot campaign began to evaporate. In mid-July reports began circulating of dissension between the candidate and his advisers. On July 15 Rollins resigned as co-chair, and some reports speculated that Jordan would leave as well. The next day Perot withdrew from the race as suddenly as he had entered it. He told supporters and reporters in Dallas that he had concluded he could have no more effect on the election than to throw it into the House of Representatives, a development he described as "disruptive." After a testimonial to the people who had worked for him, he left the campaign.

The Democrats. With the primary season over, Bill Clinton faced the task of preparing for the Democratic convention with what must have been great trepidation. Polls in June showed him in a three-way tie with Bush and Perot, and some analysts were suggesting that the independent from Texas might push Clinton into third place. But the Arkansas governor pressed on with his preconvention duties.

First, he picked Tennessee senator Al Gore as his running mate. Gore's selection was the outcome of a quiet but intensive search managed by a committee under the direction of former deputy secretary of state Warren Christopher. It surprised many party leaders because Gore was so like Clinton in his age (fortyish), region (the South), religion and ethnicity (WASP), and place on the political spectrum (moderate liberal). Some saw the ticket as narrow, but Gore complemented Clinton in several ways. He was a Vietnam veteran, a member of the Washington establishment, and a specialist in defense and environmental matters. More than anything else, picking Gore was intended to highlight Clinton's theme of change: the entire Democratic ticket would be of a different generation from that of George Bush and Ross Perot. Moreover, Gore could help reinforce Clinton's base in the South, a region that the Democrats had lost in several presidential elections and in which Perot was expected to be strong.

After the selection of a running mate, there was the platform and convention. As expected, the party's manifesto generally reflected the themes and positions of its nominee. It was more centrist than many past Democratic platforms, stressing the need to return to "basic American values" and proclaiming "We honor business as a noble endeavor." [37]

Between the issuing of the platform and the convening of the delegates in July, Ross Perot had announced his withdrawal. This surprise development left his backers looking for someone to support at the very moment that Clinton was in the spotlight. Clinton's pollster detected a surge of support for the governor: a tracking poll just before the convention put the race at 58 percent for Clinton and 38 percent for Bush.[38] Clearly, this confluence of events affected the mood of the convention in New York City. The assembled delegates and those who addressed them were enthusiastic about Clinton and about their party's chances for winning in November. Even Jerry Brown, who had resisted endorsing Clinton, returned to the fold. The only real dissension at the convention was over Clinton's refusal to allow Pennsylvania governor Robert Casey to address the delegates. Casey had unsuccessfully challenged the platform's prochoice language on abortion. He wanted to urge the convention to turn away from what he considered to be a mistaken and losing position. The nominee refused, giving the Pennsylvania governor media attention and the Republicans ammunition to attack Clinton for his handling of disagreement within his own party.

In the end, however, Clinton and Gore were nominated without incident. The Democrats, always a diverse and shaky coalition, seemed to be more united than they had been in years. They eagerly looked forward to the fall campaign.

The Republicans. For George Bush, the preconvention story was somewhat similar. He, too, had to be concerned about the future, having fallen from his post-Gulf war high in the polls into a three-way race with a small-state governor and a computer entrepreneur.

Throughout June and July journalists and pundits speculated that the president might replace Dan Quayle as his running mate. The vice president's qualifications had been questioned ever since Bush chose him in 1988, and he continued to be a lightning rod for criticism. Quayle was dismissed as intellectually weak (he recently had misspelled *potato* in a campaign appearance at an elementary school), too willing to protect business at all costs (his White House Council on Competitiveness earned the ire of environmentalists and others critical of deregulation), and too conservative. In May the vice president delivered a speech attacking the "Hollywood media elite" as dangerous to American values, citing the television series "Murphy Brown" as evidence that the entertainment industry was opposed to the family. But Quayle managed to survive all these attacks because of his unwavering loyalty to the president. On July 24 Quayle announced that the matter of his place on the ticket was "closed." The president, who had named his personal speedboat *Fidelity*, was not about to dump his faithful vice president.

With the Quayle question out of the way, only the platform and convention remained. The Republican manifesto was more conservative than it had been in 1988, with firm opposition to abortion prominent in the document. Because of Buchanan's challenge, Bush felt the need to strengthen his ties to the right; the platform was a convenient way to do so. The GOP attempted to highlight its differences from the Democrats, however, by allowing prochoice speakers such as Massachusetts governor William Weld to address the delegates. Although the party's official positions clearly were conservative, the implicit (and sometimes explicit) message of the convention was that Republicans were more tolerant of dissent than their opponents.

With Perot out of the race in July, the August convention in Houston focused its attention on Bill (and often Hillary) Clinton. The major theme of the gathering was Republican devotion to "traditional family values," an undefined term meant to suggest excessive Democratic tolerance of homosexuality, feminism, abortion, and unwanted social change. Speakers such as Pat Buchanan, Marilyn Quayle, and Barbara Bush (along with the Bushes' children and grandchildren) emphasized the Republican commitment to family values and charged that the Democrats disdained the American mainstream.

His renomination confirmed, Bush turned his attention to the fall campaign. But because of the sagging economy he now was far behind Clinton in the polls. Nor was it clear that the issue of family values would woo voters back from the Democratic message of economic and political change.

Conclusion

Why did the 1992 nomination races turn out as they did? The answers are different for each party. The Republicans did the predictable thing: they renominated their incumbent president. What is interesting is that Bush's victory within the party did not give him the boost in the polls that usually accrues to candidates in their moments of triumph. Why not? The answer lies in Bush's approach to the campaign: basically, he campaigned only when necessary. He became active in New Hampshire when it seemed Buchanan might embarrass him but was rather lethargic for most of the time between March and Labor Day. Instead of aggressively seeking his renomination and reelection, he gave his attention and energy to foreign problems and other issues. Even so, he seemed generally ineffective when it came to the central problem on voters' minds: the state of the economy.

As for the Democrats, their contest ended with two southerners ready to take on the president. Why was Bill Clinton nominated? We suggest three reasons.

First, Clinton was the strongest candidate in a weak field of contenders. Because of the Gulf war and the 1991 Moscow coup, many prominent Democrats stayed out of the race. Clinton himself fully expected Mario Cuomo to run and was surprised when the New York governor's decision to stay in Albany opened the way for his own victory.[39] Understanding the environment of presidential nominations, Clinton began early to raise money, build an organization, hire competent staff, and develop a strategy for winning. His strategic planning included preparing for contests down the road, not just for the next primary. Lacking sufficient resources, his opponents were unable to do the same.

Second, Clinton's regional base helped him at a crucial time. He used good spin control to turn New Hampshire from defeat into momentum, thus positioning himself to take full advantage of the events to come on Junior and Super Tuesdays. When the delegate hunt went south, Paul Tsongas foundered from lack of money, while Bill Clinton's early planning began to pay off. He emerged from the breakaway stage as a clear front-runner with lots of momentum.

Finally, Clinton managed scandal well enough to stay in the race. He was unable to eliminate these problems completely, especially the issue of his draft status, but he handled them well enough to keep them from derailing his progress toward the nomination.

In the end, George Bush and Bill Clinton won their party standards because they worked effectively within the system of presidential nominations. Nominees are selected in an environment that is relatively stable, even as the specific details and issues change with each election. The age of reform has brought the nation long and tortuous presidential campaigns. Already, the next race is under way for the Republican nomination. Hopefuls such as Housing and Urban Development secretary Jack Kemp, Vice President Quayle, former secretary of state James Baker, and Texas senator Phil Gramm are weighing their prospects. All those who think they may want to run for president have already begun planning for the next election.

Notes

1. Rhodes Cook, "The Nominating Process," in *The Elections of 1988*, ed. Michael Nelson (Washington, D.C.: CQ Press, 1989), 26.
2. Stephen Wayne, *The Road to the White House 1992* (New York: St. Martin's, 1992), 88.
3. The process of reform has been described by several authors. For a good summary, see James Ceaser, *Reforming the Reforms* (Cambridge, Mass.: Ballinger, 1992). On selection in the prereform era, see James Ceaser, *Presidential Selection* (Princeton: Princeton University Press, 1979), 231-236.
4. See Wayne, *Road to the White House*, 92-97. See also Nelson Polsby and Aaron Wildavsky, *Presidential Elections*, 8th ed. (New York: Free Press, 1991), 110-122.
5. Wayne, *Road to the White House*, 99.
6. See Polsby and Wildavsky, *Presidential Elections*, 126-127. See also Herbert B. Asher, *Presidential Elections and American Politics*, 4th ed. (Chicago: Dorsey, 1988), 232, 352-353.
7. Wayne, *Road to the White House*, 99.
8. See Polsby and Wildavsky, *Presidential Elections*, 111.
9. Larry M. Bartels, *Presidential Primaries and the Dynamics of Public Choice* (Princeton: Princeton University Press, 1988), esp. 21-27.
10. On the media's role in politics, see Doris A. Graber, *Mass Media and American Politics*, 2d ed. (Washington, D.C.: CQ Press, 1984).
11. Bartels, *Presidential Primaries*, 35.
12. Not only is spin control an art practiced by candidates and their staffs, but the

journalists on whom they practice it are conscious participants in the act.

13. Wayne, *Road to the White House*, 116.

14. Ibid., 116.

15. Ryan J. Barilleaux, *The Post-Modern Presidency* (New York: Praeger, 1988), 70.

16. Quoted in Bartels, *Presidential Primaries*, 25.

17. Eleanor Clift, "Eyes on the Prize," *Newsweek*, Aug. 31, 1992, 30-31. A discussion of the "mentioning" process and some historical examples are presented by Stephen Hess in *The Presidential Campaign* (Washington, D.C.: Brookings Institution, 1988), 38-39.

18. Jimmy Carter, *Why Not the Best?* (Nashville: Broadman, 1975); George Bush with Victor Gold, *Looking Forward* (New York: Doubleday, 1987); Howard Baker, *No Margin for Error: America in the Eighties* (New York: Times Books, 1980); Walter F. Mondale, *The Accountability of Power: Toward a Responsible Presidency* (New York: McKay, 1975).

19. For a discussion of Bush's role in German unification and the fall of communism, see Ryan J. Barilleaux, "George Bush, Germany, and the New World Order," in *Shepherd of Democracy?* ed. Carl C. Hodge and Cathal J. Nolan (Westport, Conn.: Greenwood, 1992).

20. *Washington Post*, Jan. 3, 1992, A4.

21. *Facts on File*, Feb. 13, 1992, 93-94; *Congressional Quarterly Weekly Report*, July 4, 1992, 70.

22. *Facts on File*, Feb. 20, 1992, 108-110; Alice V. McGillivray, *Presidential Primaries and Caucuses, 1992: A Handbook of Election Statistics* (Washington, D.C.: Congressional Quarterly, 1992), 4-5.

23. *Congressional Quarterly Weekly Report*, March 14, 1992, 641.

24. *Facts on File*, Feb. 20, 1992, 110.

25. *Facts on File*, March 5, 1992, 149-150.

26. *Congressional Quarterly Weekly Report*, March 14, 1992, 641.

27. *Facts on File*, March 12, 1992, 164-166; *Congressional Quarterly Weekly Report*, July 4, 1992, 70; McGillivray, *Presidential Primaries and Caucuses*, 4-5.

28. *Facts on File*, March 26, 1992, 208.

29. Ibid.

30. Ibid., 207.

31. Ibid.

32. "New Rules for Old Political Game," *National Journal Convention Preview*, June 16, 1992, 1, 35.

33. *Cincinnati Enquirer*, April 26, 1992, A10.

34. *Facts on File*, April 16, 1992, 268.

35. *Facts on File*, April 30, 1992, 307.

36. Although retired admiral James Stockdale eventually became Perot's running mate, the billionaire candidate said when he selected Stockdale that the admiral was an "interim" candidate to satisfy state ballot laws.

37. *Facts on File*, July 9, 1992, 497-498.

38. "Manhattan Project '92," *Newsweek*, special election issue, November-December, 1992, 56.

39. "Six Men and a Donkey," *Newsweek*, special election issue, November-December, 1992, 30.

3

The Election: A "New Democrat" and a New Kind of Presidential Campaign

Paul J. Quirk and Jon K. Dalager

Winners and losers abound in presidential elections. The most obvious winner in 1992 was Bill Clinton, the Democratic nominee for president. Paul J. Quirk and Jon K. Dalager describe the general election campaign that preceded Clinton's victory, along with the defeats of George Bush, the Republican incumbent, and independent candidate Ross Perot. In the course of doing so, Quirk and Dalager analyze a variety of long-term and short-term explanations of why Clinton won.

The voters also can be winners and losers in elections, depending on the quality of the campaign. Are the major issues facing the country discussed in a reasonable and specific way by the candidates? Are the voters able to learn about these positions and about the aspects of the candidates' records and character that bear on their competence to be president? In most recent presidential election campaigns, Quirk and Dalager argue, the answer to these questions has been "no." In 1992, however, the quality of the campaign was somewhat improved. Polls indicated that on election day the voters felt more like winners.

A year in advance the presidential election of 1992 seemed likely to be a dull and predictable affair. President George Bush held such a commanding lead in opinion polls that his reelection, and a fourth consecutive Republican victory, appeared all but inevitable. The only suspense was whether any of the leading Democrats would bother to seek their party's nomination.

In the actual event, the 1992 election was one of the most surprising and significant presidential elections of the twentieth century. For one thing, the Democrats won. The victory of Gov. Bill Clinton and Sen. Al Gore over Bush and Vice President Dan Quayle upset the common view that the Republican party had a "lock" on the presidency. Indeed, although there were no guarantees that Clinton and Gore would succeed in office and win reelection in 1996, much postelection commentary speculated that the Democratic party might dominate presidential politics for a long time to come. Second, despite the formidable barriers built into the U.S. two-party system, an independent candidate, Ross Perot, played an unusually important role in the campaign. For a short time he led in the polls. In the end, he won no electoral votes, but his presence may have changed the dynamics of the campaign.

Third, after a series of elections in which the public had become increasingly distressed about the quality of campaign debate, the 1992 campaign was widely seen as greatly improved. Compared with other recent presidential campaigns, it offered more discussion of issues and more informative and penetrating news coverage. The voters ended up more pleased with both the candidates and the process than they had been in years, and they turned out at the polls in large numbers.

This chapter reviews the events of the campaign in an effort to answer two central questions: First, why did the Democrats win? Was their victory foreordained by the weak performance of the economy? Did the campaign make a difference? Did Perot? And second, how much better was the campaign than previous campaigns? Specifically, does the record of the 1992 election suggest that the mechanisms of discussion and debate in presidential campaigns, after years of increasingly serious criticism, have decisively improved?

The Candidates, Organizations, and Strategies

In the spring of 1991 Democrats with presidential aspirations had to be skeptical about their chances of winning the 1992 election. In the aftermath of the U.S.-led victory in the Persian Gulf war, President George Bush enjoyed an approval rating of 89 percent, a Gallup poll record.[1] He also had the inherent advantages of incumbency. And recent history had favored the Republicans, who had won five of the past six presidential elections.

But as the election year approached, the situation changed. East and West Germany were reunited, and the Soviet Union abandoned communism and eventually dissolved. The end of the Cold War suddenly rendered irrelevant one of the major issues, anticommunism, that had benefited the Republicans for forty years. On the home front, the economy, beginning to falter after the boom times of the 1980s, slid into recession. The gross domestic product (GDP) fell slightly during the first half of 1991, followed by minimal growth during the rest of the year. Unemployment remained stuck at an uncomfortable 6.8 percent.[2] By the time Bill Clinton had nailed down the Democratic nomination in the spring of 1992, he clearly had a usable issue in the economy.

In many ways, the terms of the emerging contest were familiar. Bush and Clinton could each count on the support of a core group of party loyalists amounting to about 30 percent of the electorate. The real competition was for the remaining, swing voters—independents, potential switchers, and first-time voters. The Democrats wanted to recapture the so-called Reagan Democrats, mostly white working-class people with conservative views on cultural issues such as abortion and school prayer. The Republicans hoped to incorporate these voters permanently into their coalition. Both parties also aspired to do well with suburban voters. Although they had supported Reagan in 1980 and 1984, many suburbanites did not approve of the Republicans' conservative positions on the cultural issues. A large number of new voters were expected in 1992, in part because many eligible voters had not turned out in 1984 and in 1988.

The strength of the Perot candidacy complicated both parties' strategies. Typically, independent or third-party candidates have a hard time meeting the requirements to be listed on the ballot in all fifty states. Because they also have trouble raising adequate funds to campaign and are dismissed as incapable of winning, their support usually wanes as the election approaches. In 1980 Republican representative John Anderson of Illinois, who ran as an independent, reached a peak of 15 percent support in the polls but faded to a modest 6.6 percent in the actual vote. Perot's candidacy was different. At his peak of 39 percent in early June, he led the race.[3] His army of paid staff and volunteers got him on the ballot in every state. And he promised to spend up to $100 million of his own money, almost double the amount that is directly available to each major-party candidate.

For much of 1992 Perot's influence on the election was impossible to predict. If he could win some states—as third-party candidate George Wallace had done in 1968, with five states and forty-six electoral votes—he could possibly deprive both major-party candidates of an electoral-vote majority and throw the election into the House of Representatives. Failing that, if he drew his support mainly from voters who otherwise would support one of the major-party candidates, he could tip the balance toward the other. Because Perot was from Bush's home state of Texas, it was especially possible that he could steal enough of the favorite-son vote from Bush to give the state's thirty-two electoral votes to Clinton. Even if he pulled voters from both candidates about equally—as he ultimately did—Perot could change the other candidates' strategies and the dynamics of the competition between them. In fact, Perot's presence affected the competition between Bush and Clinton in several ways, mostly to the latter's benefit. It also affected the quality of the debate. Ironically, even though Perot largely avoided taking specific positions, he helped to deepen the discussion of certain issues.

The Bush Campaign

As he approached the campaign to win reelection, Bush as a candidate had both considerable strengths and glaring weaknesses. In one respect—experience—his qualifications for the presidency were almost unparalleled. The son of a U.S. senator, Bush had been a war hero, successful businessman in the Texas oil industry, member of Congress, ambassador to the United Nations, chair of the Republican National Committee, emissary to China,

director of the Central Intelligence Agency, and vice president. Most important, of course, he had been president.

Bush's first-term record, however, did not provide him with a strong
basis for a reelection campaign. His imposing résumé was a mixed blessing in
a year in which the voters were impatient with incumbents and suspicious of
Washington. Because of world events and his own predilections, Bush had
devoted most of his attention to foreign policy, where he had enjoyed considerable success. The Berlin Wall was torn down in November 1989, leading
to the reunification of Germany; U.S. troops invaded Panama and arrested
dictator Manuel Noriega in January 1990; the Soviet Union formally dissolved in December 1991; and U.S.-led forces defeated Iraq in the Gulf war
in February 1991. For most of the first three years of his term, these successes helped sustain Bush at high levels of popularity, but eventually the
bloom faded. Saddam Hussein remained in power in Iraq, suppressing domestic opposition and violating the terms of the cease-fire. Critics charged
that before the war Bush had helped to build up the Iraqi military and failed
to warn Saddam convincingly about the American intention to resist an invasion of Kuwait and that at the end of the war he had missed the chance to
remove Saddam from power. Although Bush claimed credit for "ending the
Cold War," most people believed that Soviet communism had died mainly of
natural causes.

In domestic and economic policy, Bush had engaged in a running battle
with the Democratic Congress, producing a state of inaction that was widely
decried as "gridlock." In truth, Bush signed major legislation on clean air,
civil rights, and the disabled. But he fought unproductive, frequently bitter
battles with Congress over abortion, crime, child care, school prayer, family
leave, and capital-gains taxation, among other subjects. And he made frequent use of the veto power. The enormous costs of the savings and loan
crisis were revealed on Bush's watch, and in part because of them, he did not
reduce the federal budget deficit. In the view of many economists, Bush's
refusal to take the lead on deficit reduction during his first two budget cycles
was the central policy failure of his presidency.

Three other features of Bush's domestic performance, however, were
more directly harmful to his campaign. First, he responded only belatedly
and unpersuasively to intense public concerns about health care. As the
election approached, Bush offered a limited proposal for broadening insurance coverage that had no prospect of being passed by Congress. Second, to
reach an agreement with the Democrats on a fiscal 1991 budget, he accepted
a substantial tax increase, openly reneging on his 1988 campaign pledge not
to raise taxes. Bush's reversal angered the public and was widely ridiculed.
"Reread my lips" was one parody of his new stance.

Third, and most important, Bush suffered the misfortune of a prolonged
economic slump. The outstanding feature of the slump, which began in mid-
1990, was its duration. The recession phase was brief and mild, and unemployment never rose above 7.8 percent. But instead of undergoing a typical,

strong recovery, the economy remained sluggish throughout 1991 and the first half of 1992. As a result, the performance of the economy during Bush's term was exceptionally poor. His administration oversaw the slowest rate of growth in GDP since the Nixon-Ford years (1973-1977), and the slowest rate of growth in nonfarm jobs since Eisenhower's second term (1957-1961).[4] More businesses failed during the Bush administration than during any other presidency since World War II.

Despite the public's growing distress, Bush opposed the demands of many Democrats for fiscal measures to stimulate the economy. In doing so, he followed the advice of most economists, who argued that the economy could not afford a further increase in the budget deficit. But however justified Bush's refusal to act may have been economically, it was a disaster politically, creating the impression that he was unconcerned about the economy. Because of the duration of the slump and his lack of action, Bush was far more vulnerable to criticism on the economy than the 2 percent annual growth rate during the first half of the election year ordinarily would suggest. A Gallup poll found in May 1992 that 76 percent of the public disapproved of Bush's handling of the economy.[5]

In a sharp break from the pattern of three skillful Republican campaigns, Bush's 1992 campaign was hampered by organizational weaknesses. For the most part, the architects of Bush's 1988 victory were no longer with the campaign: Lee Atwater, the chief strategist in 1988, was dead; and Roger Ailes, who directed the advertising campaign, had left politics. James Baker, who chaired the 1988 campaign, had become secretary of state and stayed out of the reelection campaign until August 23, 1992, when he came to the White House and assumed control in a desperate attempt to rescue the campaign.

Until Baker's return, the 1992 campaign was run by White House chief of staff Samuel Skinner; Robert Teeter, who served as campaign chair; consultant Charles Black, as senior political adviser; political strategist Mary Matalin, the political director and deputy campaign manager; and Republican activist Fred Malek, who was named the general manager. This team suffered from internal bickering and had a difficult time choosing a consistent focus for the campaign. A separate advertising team, called the November Group, also experienced internal conflicts and had difficulty producing usable advertisements.

The Bush campaign cast about for a strategy that could make up for a weak record. In the spring and early summer it sought mainly to appease the Republican right. Pat Buchanan's strong showing in the early Republican primaries had raised fears that Bush had alienated the conservative wing of the party. Bush's strategists believed that regaining solid support from the right would give the president most of the votes he would need to win a three-candidate race. Calling his reversal on taxes a mistake, Bush promised that he would not make the same mistake again. Vice President Quayle stressed cultural conservatism under the new rubric of "family values," even

attacking a popular television program, "Murphy Brown," for allegedly ignoring those values. As the campaign developed, however, the public showed
little interest in the family-values issue.

The Bush campaign also sought to repeat the Republicans' extraordinary 1988 success in "defining" the opponent for the electorate. Campaign
officials portrayed Perot as a fringe candidate and accused him of using
private investigators to intimidate opponents. In the same language that had
worked against Democrat Michael Dukakis in 1988, they called Clinton a
tax-and-spend liberal. But it was hard to make the charges stick. Perot
launched a counterattack against "Republican dirty tricks." And Clinton was
an implausible left-winger. He was the governor of a conservative southern
state; he had campaigned as a moderate in the primaries; and he had headed
an organization, the Democratic Leadership Council, that sought to move
the party in a conservative direction.

Bush was an inconsistent, seemingly ambivalent performer in his own
campaign. He was at times forceful and indefatigable; at other times he was
listless and unfocused. It was often apparent that he simply did not like to
campaign. He avoided mentioning his opponents by name. Uncomfortable
with the new media formats of the 1992 campaign, he criticized Clinton
and Perot for appearing on "weird talk shows," although he too later appeared on "Larry King Live" and MTV. Most important, Bush started
late—assuring impatient Republicans that he would get into "campaign
mode" after the national convention. Yet he hit his stride as a candidate
only in late October.

Bush's candidacy had other problems. Quayle was widely dismissed as
an intellectual lightweight. Already a frequent butt of comedians' humor,
Quayle exacerbated the situation during the campaign when he prompted a
schoolboy in a spelling bee to add an *e* to the word *potato*. The spectre of the
Iran-contra scandal also haunted the president. Bush had repeatedly denied
that he had participated in Reagan-administration decisions to exchange arms
for hostages with Iran and to use the proceeds illicitly to fund the Nicaraguan
contras. But a series of documents and statements by witnesses revealed
during the campaign linked him directly to discussions of the transactions.
Finally, Bush labored under popularity ratings that fell steadily as the election approached. In a poll conducted in July 1992, his job approval rating fell
to 32 percent, with 59 percent of the respondents disapproving of his performance as president.[6]

The Clinton Campaign

Except for one major flaw, Bill Clinton was virtually the ideal Democratic candidate for president. That flaw, however, almost derailed his candidacy entirely.

Clinton had been relatively unknown to the American public before his
campaign for the Democratic nomination. But at the age of forty-five he had

a distinguished record of public service and played a prominent role in the national Democratic party. In 1978 he had been elected governor of Arkansas—at thirty-two, the youngest governor in the nation. Although defeated in 1980, he was elected again in 1982 and in three succeeding elections—generally by comfortable margins. Although Arkansas remained one of the nation's poorest states, his governorship was marked by significant accomplishments in education, welfare reform, and economic growth. Recognized as one of the leading governors, he was elected chair of the National Governors' Association in 1987.

More than most Democrats, Clinton was well positioned ideologically to pursue the presidency. He favored the death penalty, supported abortion with restrictions, and sought alternatives to welfare. Appropriating a Republican epithet, Clinton pronounced that he was not a tax-and-spend Democrat. He was therefore relatively immune to the ritual Republican charge of extreme liberalism.

Clinton assembled a highly competent campaign organization. To ensure that it would have adequate experience, he relied largely on professional consultants and the national party organization. His chief strategist was James Carville, the consultant who had masterminded Democrat Harris Wofford's surprise victory in the 1991 Pennsylvania Senate election. Although campaign chair Mickey Kantor was a personal friend, other campaign officials were drawn from a broad and experienced talent pool. Paul Begala served as a senior strategist, George Stephanopoulos was the communications director, Stan Greenberg ran the polling operation, and Frank Greer was a media adviser. Impressively, the Clinton campaign avoided serious mistakes and was mostly free of internal conflict.

Because of a combination of intelligence and the availability of effective themes, the Clinton team managed to devise a strategy and stick with it throughout the campaign. To gain the support of the moderates and independents who had flocked to the Republicans in the 1980s, the campaign proclaimed that Clinton was a "new kind of Democrat." To appeal to the voters' dissatisfaction with the direction of the country, it adopted the theme of change and emphasized the two issues that were uppermost in voters' minds: the economy and health care. The simplicity of the strategy was captured in a sign (often quoted incompletely) that was posted in Clinton's Little Rock headquarters: "Change vs. more of the same. The economy, stupid. Don't forget health care." [7] Accordingly, Clinton repeatedly attacked Republican "trickle-down economics" and pointed to the lack of job growth during Bush's term.

Promising to do better, Clinton offered a relatively specific economic program—with plans to tax the wealthy, increase public investment in job training and infrastructure, and reform the educational system. He also proposed an ambitious program for universal access to health care. If the economy had rebounded vigorously during the summer, the Clinton campaign might have had an awkward time improvising new themes. But no rebound occurred, and surveys indicated that the economy was the issue that most concerned the voters.

The Clinton campaign took an important lesson from the Democrats' vulnerability to negative campaigning in 1988. Although Dukakis had tried to avoid responding to Bush's attacks in order not to draw attention to them, the tactic was clearly unsuccessful. In 1992 the Clinton campaign made it a policy to respond immediately to every attack. When Bush aired a television advertisement alleging that Clinton would raise taxes on the middle class, Clinton answered the next day with an advertisement of his own. The Clinton response showed segments of the Bush ad and quoted newspaper reports criticizing it as deceptive.

Apart from attacking Bush's record on the economy, the Clinton campaign mostly refrained from negative campaigning. It ignored the issue of Quayle's competence and did not take up Bush's role in the Iraqi military build-up before the Gulf war. Through most of the campaign, the Clinton team declined to exploit Bush's increasing vulnerability in the Iran-contra scandal, allowing embarrassing news stories of Bush's involvement to pass by almost unnoticed. Rightly or not, Clinton's strategists evidently judged that the public was tired of negative politics and that attacking Bush or Quayle personally would backfire by shifting the focus of the campaign from the economy.

In contrast with Bush, Clinton was a tireless, skilled, and enthusiastic campaigner. Rather than looking for excuses to delay campaigning, he seemed to relish it; he stayed on the hustings for long hours and seldom took a day off. Clinton carefully managed the impression he made on voters. When told that his habit of speaking with a slight smile was seen as smirking, for example, he abandoned the habit. To give the public a better sense of "the real Bill Clinton," he attended town meetings and appeared on talk shows, even playing the saxophone in dark glasses on "The Arsenio Hall Show." Clinton's rapport with audiences, coherence in speech, and thorough command of the issues enabled him to perform well at all kinds of campaign events.

The major weakness of Clinton's candidacy, nearly a fatal one, was the issue of his character. In a stretch of several weeks during the primaries, Clinton endured a succession of allegations that raised questions about his honesty and integrity: rumors of extramarital affairs (which, in general terms, he essentially admitted); claims by Gennifer Flowers, an employee of the Arkansas state government, of an affair with him (which he denied); allegations that he had used marijuana as a student at Oxford (which he lamely half-denied, saying he had puffed but had not inhaled); and stories indicating that he had somewhat underhandedly sought to evade the draft (which he denied in several, incompatible ways). The rapid accumulation of accusations created the impression of Clinton as someone who regularly cut corners. Most important, Clinton appeared to respond to questions on these matters with inaccurate or misleading answers.

Fortunately for Clinton, this period of troubles occurred at just the right time—late enough that he already had a fairly secure lead in the nomination contest and early enough that by the time of the general election the allegations seemed stale. Crucially, despite Republican attempts to make an issue of a trip Clinton made to Moscow and his participation in organizing anti-Vietnam War protests in London during the early 1970s, no significant revelations of scandal occurred during the summer or fall.

The Perot Campaign

One cannot assess the strengths and weaknesses of Ross Perot's candidacy in conventional terms. From one perspective, he was unsuccessful, running third in a three-way race. Yet, from another perspective, he was remarkably successful: He substantially exceeded early predictions by capturing 19 percent of the popular vote, and he established his ability to remain a significant political force after the election. Quite possibly, winning the election was not even Perot's main objective.

Perot had hardly any of the standard qualifications of a presidential candidate. Although he had been involved as a prominent citizen-volunteer in public issues ranging from Texas school reform to POW-MIA investigations, he had neither held nor sought elective office. After college, he served in the navy, worked for IBM, started a data-processing company, and built it into a multi-million dollar business. Except for his hard-line insistence that the budget deficit be rapidly reduced, Perot's ideology and policy views were mostly undefined. He had no particular social or geographic constituency. Most important, he had no party affiliation. As the history of independent and third-party candidates (none of whom has ever won) demonstrates, the lack of a strong base of reliable party voters made victory a long shot, at best, for Perot.

The basis of Perot's support was a combination of the public's widespread frustration with the status quo; the attraction of his engaging, plain-speaking manner; and an acceptance by many voters of his simple prescriptions for the problems of government. Perot spoke bluntly, used folksy metaphors and analogies, and said things that ordinary citizens could understand. He attributed the poor performance of the economy largely to the national debt. He attacked the president and Congress for playing "the blame game" and talked about "getting under the hood" and "hammering out a solution"—even appropriating the Nike slogan, "Just do it!" Presumably, many voters credited Perot's ability to get the job done because of his undeniable success in business.

Perot did not attempt to run a full-scale presidential campaign. In the first phase of his campaign, which lasted from February until he withdrew from the race in July, he tried to get his message out primarily by making appearances on national television programs, such as "20/20," "Dateline NBC," and "Larry King Live." After reentering the race in October, Perot again frequented the national television programs, but he also ran an extensive television advertising campaign, which he paid for with his own money.

Perot ignored many of the usual considerations of campaign strategy. He put much of his advertising money into half-hour "infomercials," which featured him discussing the problems of the American economy. Political candidates had long abandoned such advertisements because the audiences were small and limited mostly to the already convinced. Although Perot's long advertisements drew large audiences, they probably still failed to reach most of the voters. Perot declined to participate in the daily campaign grind of touring the country to attract local interest and media coverage. He had no regional strategy. Even though he had concentrations of supporters in Texas, California, and a few other western states, he refused to focus his efforts there. Nor did Perot consistently attack the front-runner. For the most part, he attacked Bush even when Clinton was in the lead.

A plausible interpretation of Perot's campaign is that, being realistic, he did not expect to win the election. He preferred Clinton to Bush and did not want to be responsible for a Bush victory. Mostly, he wanted to make a statement, draw attention to the deficit, and establish himself as a force in American politics. His campaign was well designed for those purposes.

The Dynamics of the Campaign

The terms of the competition in 1992 were shaped by two distinctive features of the campaign. One was the interaction between the candidates in a three-way race. Perot's presence was felt in a variety of ways. He bickered with Bush. Some of his campaign themes, especially the need for change, resembled Clinton's. As he entered, abandoned, and reentered the race, he changed calculations about the breadth of support necessary to win. Finally, Perot's feisty, colorful performance overshadowed both Bush and Clinton during their most critical confrontation, the October debates.

The other notable feature of the 1992 campaign was that the media and even the public applied lessons from the 1988 election. The media had been stung by criticism of what was widely seen as superficial campaign coverage. As a result of what one television executive called "endless postmortem conferences at all the networks," they resolved to do better in 1992—covering issues, resisting manipulation, and checking facts.[8] The television networks and many newspapers provided lengthy treatments of major issues. They instituted regular features, with names like "Reality Check" and "Fact or Fiction?" to assess the accuracy of commercials and other statements from the campaigns.

Very likely, the public too had learned something from the 1988 campaign. The Democrats' complaints about Republican campaign tactics and critical discussions in the media heightened the public's resistance to negative, emotional messages and created a demand for serious discussion of the issues.

The Preconvention Campaign

Although Bush and Clinton had both wrapped up their nomination contests by April, Perot's candidacy prevented them from savoring their victories. Even though only 12 percent of the public said in an April poll that they knew "quite a bit" about Perot, he had the support of 25-30 percent in most polls. By June his appearances on talk shows and news programs had brought him into a virtual tie with Bush. Remarkably, an early June CNN/*USA Today* poll actually showed the independent candidate leading the presidential race, with 39 percent supporting Perot, 31 percent Bush, and 25 percent Clinton.[9]

In late spring the Bush campaign turned its attention to fighting off Perot, generating news stories that criticized Perot's history of using private investigators. Perot responded with charges of Republican "dirty tricks." But he also began encountering troubles in his own campaign. At a speech to the annual convention of the NAACP on July 11, Perot offended many in the audience by referring to African Americans as "you people." Perot volunteers complained to the press that they were being pushed aside by professional consultants from Dallas. In mid-July Perot broke off relations with his advertising director, Hal Riney, and his campaign co-chair, Ed Rollins, resigned, saying that his advice was being ignored.

The main beneficiary of the dispute between Bush and Perot and of Perot's other troubles was Clinton, who set about the task of restoring his public image. Serenely declining to comment on the Bush-Perot conflict, Clinton made several serious speeches on the economy. To overcome weaknesses that had been discovered in focus-group research, he made a point of directly challenging some liberal interest groups. He provoked a fight with Jesse Jackson at a Jackson-sponsored event by criticizing the allegedly inflammatory remarks of a black rap singer, Sister Souljah. Clinton and his wife, Hillary, worked to show a warm family relationship as their daughter, Chelsea, began traveling with the campaign. Clinton also sought to unite his party before the convention. He obtained the endorsements of all his rivals for the nomination except Jerry Brown, patched up a quarrelsome relationship with New York governor Mario Cuomo (who agreed to place Clinton's name in nomination), and even brought Jackson on board.

With Bush and Perot savaging each other and Clinton discussing issues and improving his image, the race tightened. A CBS News/*New York Times* poll shortly before the Democratic convention showed Bush leading narrowly at 33 percent; Clinton was a close second at 30 percent; Perot had slipped to third place, at 25 percent. Underlying this shift, Clinton in one month had reduced the frequency of "unfavorable" opinions of him from 40 percent to 31 percent and increased his "favorable" ratings from 16 percent to 20 percent. Bush's ratings had not changed significantly, but Perot's had deteriorated, with only 19 percent favorable.[10]

The Party Conventions

Because Bush and Clinton were already assured of receiving their respective party nominations, the purpose of each party's national convention was to showcase its candidates and begin to set forth its messages. In fact, the conventions were highly revealing of the respective campaigns.

The Democratic convention was an extraordinary feat of political management and a resounding success for the Clinton campaign. In choosing another moderate southerner, Sen. Al Gore of Tennessee, as his running mate, Clinton dispensed with the traditional ideological and geographical ticket balancing. Yet, in many ways, Gore was the perfect complement to Clinton: he was a Washington insider; he had served in Vietnam; he was strong on environmental issues; he was an expert in defense; and he, his wife, Tipper, and their four children were undeniably a solid family. Together, Clinton and Gore represented the coming of age of the baby-boom generation. Gore's reputation as a highly competent, exceptionally knowledgeable senator provided a favorable contrast with his Republican counterpart, Dan Quayle. The choice of Gore demonstrated Clinton's intention to make a serious challenge to the Republicans' control of the South. More important, it generated a surge of enthusiasm for the ticket.

With the help of national party chair Ron Brown, the New York City convention was perfectly choreographed. The party platform was less liberal and less indulgent of Democratic constituency groups than in recent years. The speakers at the convention hammered away in support of Clinton's themes of change and the economy, adding healthy doses of Bush bashing. An unexpected development on July 16, the last day of the convention, added measurably to the building momentum: Perot withdrew from the presidential race. Observing that the Democratic party had "revitalized itself," Perot said he had concluded that he would not win in November but would only cause the election to be decided by the House. By evening, Clinton had quickly rewritten his acceptance speech to make a warm appeal to Perot's supporters to join him in seeking change. (Bush, although lacking an implicit endorsement from Perot and a comparable television audience, made a similar appeal from a vacation campsite in Wyoming.)

The main purpose of Clinton's speech was to proclaim a new philosophy of government for the Democratic party, one firmly grounded in the concerns of the middle class. Accusing the Bush administration of paying lip service to America's problems, Clinton declared that during his presidency the middle class would be "forgotten no more." Speaking in general terms, with few specific proposals, he stressed that the new philosophy was "not conservative or liberal, Democratic or Republican." Rather, it envisioned a "new covenant" in which the people would take greater responsibility for their own well-being, but the government would support their efforts by ensuring that they had the incentives and opportunities necessary to succeed.[11]

Even though the Clinton camp expected to receive a boost in the polls after the convention, the extent of the increase was surprising. On the day after the convention, almost every poll showed Clinton leading the race with the support of more than 50 percent of the public. The CBS News/*New York Times* poll showed Clinton ahead with 55 percent to Bush's 31 percent. Former Perot supporters were going to Clinton over Bush by 45 percent to 25 percent.[12] In the space of a few days, Clinton had raised his share of public support by an extraordinary 25 percentage points.

In a stroke of public-relations genius, Clinton, Gore, and their wives jumped on a bus to campaign from New York to St. Louis. At every stop they were met by large, enthusiastic crowds and local media, and each day the network news showed attractive images of Clinton and Gore tossing a football, talking to ordinary citizens, or sharing a joke with their wives.

The Republican convention in August, in stark contrast, was poorly managed and failed to convey an effective message. In the weeks after the Democratic convention, Republicans were understandably anxious about their party's rapidly deteriorating prospects and showed signs of serious dissension. Bush rejected advice, offered mostly in unattributed remarks to reporters, to drop Quayle from the ticket, to fire his economic team as a sign that he would now address the economy, and even to step aside and let another candidate carry the Republican banner.[13] But he did bring Secretary of State James Baker to the White House as chief of staff to take over the campaign.

Whether through inadvertence or miscalculation, the tone of the convention in Houston was aggressively and divisively conservative on cultural issues. On a number of points the party platform was to the right of President Bush. It opposed counseling on birth control, called for a constitutional amendment to ban abortion in all circumstances, and proposed a fence along the U.S.-Mexican border to keep out illegal aliens.[14] More important, in remarks not cleared with the Bush campaign, Pat Buchanan attacked Hillary Clinton as a radical feminist and accused her of likening marriage to slavery; television evangelist Pat Robertson denounced gay rights and complained that the Democratic platform did not mention God; and Marilyn Quayle held herself up as a model for women because she had sacrificed a legal career for the sake of her family. Television commentary highlighted the strident conservatism of the convention.

The Republicans may have believed that the party's only hope for the election was to provoke what some called a "culture war." But to profit from such a war, the party would have to be on the winning side. In fact, public and media response to the Republican convention's emphasis on "family values" was massively negative, with many people repelled by the divisive message or concerned that their own lives or families were under attack.

In view of Bush's downward slide in the polls, some commentators suggested that he had to "hit a home run" with his acceptance speech. But in the confusion of the campaign reorganization and the changing strategic situation, Bush's speech was hastily drafted in a Houston hotel room and was strictly ordinary. Bush touted his record in foreign policy, recalling his leadership in the Gulf war and taking credit for ending the Cold War. He blamed Congress for the country's economic troubles. He apologized for raising taxes under pressure from the Democrats; drew a contrast between himself and Clinton, who he claimed had raised taxes 128 times in Arkansas and enjoyed doing it; and promised to cut taxes and spending in his second term. Unlike many other speakers at the convention, Bush discussed family values only in a brief and noncontroversial passage.[15]

According to the polls, the convention gave Bush only a small, temporary surge in public support. Clinton's lead dropped from about 19 percentage points a week before the convention to about 10 percentage points the day after.[16] Within a week it had returned to the preconvention level. In 1988, by contrast, the Republican convention enabled Bush to overcome a Dukakis lead and propelled him to a 5-point lead of his own.[17]

The Fall Campaign

By the end of summer the presidential race had assumed a definite shape. For the rest of the campaign Clinton stuck with the strategy that had helped produce his significant lead. Bush, whose previous efforts had come up short, cast about for a new strategy.

The Bush campaign used several approaches to try to get back into contention. For one thing, Bush began making overt political use of his power to dispense federal funds. After Hurricane Andrew devastated parts of Florida and Louisiana in late August, Bush came up with a generous package of federal disaster assistance and promised to rebuild Homestead Air Force Base. Within a few weeks, usually during campaign appearances, Bush made several announcements: the government would sell U.S.-made F-16 planes to Taiwan; he would provide $1 billion for increased agricultural subsidies; and he would give $755 million for crop damage to farmers in Texas and Florida. Several of these and similar decisions reversed longstanding policies of the administration.

In addition, the Bush campaign redesigned its message. It dropped the failed issue of family values. It continued to portray Clinton as a tax-and-spend liberal—even though the press had criticized its main evidence for that charge, the purported 128 tax increases, as misleading. Most important, the campaign began a sustained attack on Clinton's character, hoping to convince voters that they could not trust him as president. Despite Bush's full-time involvement in the campaign, however, some observers remarked about a lack of vitality in his efforts.

The ad war. The previous election had featured controversial, yet highly effective television commercials; in 1992, in part because of the increased readiness of candidates and the media to respond, the advertising was less dramatic and consequential than in 1988. The Bush and Clinton campaigns each began with positive ads recounting its candidate's record as president or governor. Each turned toward negative ads in the fall.

One effective Bush ad sped up footage of Clinton signing legislation to a comical pace, accompanied by "hillbilly" music, as a narrator discussed Clinton's record of raising taxes in Arkansas. The most controversial Bush ad showed several middle-class people and claimed to report the tax increases each would face if Clinton were elected. Clinton officials called the claims blatant falsehoods, but the Bush team defended the figures, explaining that it had simply assumed that Clinton would raise taxes on the middle class to pay for all the programs he had proposed. Some of the most effective Bush ads, broadcast in October, showed ordinary people discussing Clinton's character and trustworthiness.

The Clinton team followed an initial round of positive advertising with ads that took aim at Bush. One ad showed the president saying that the economy was healthy, then displayed economic indicators demonstrating that it was weak. Another reminded the audience of some of Bush's 1988 campaign promises—not to raise taxes, to be "the education president," and to be "the environmental president"—and presented facts suggesting his failure to keep those promises.

Perot's reentry. In late September, Perot began to say that he was having second thoughts about his withdrawal from the campaign. He complained that neither Bush nor Clinton was paying adequate attention to the budget deficit. Considering that Perot had kept his staff and volunteers working to place his name on the ballot in every state, however, it is possible that he never intended to stay out. After a highly peculiar meeting with his state coordinators and representatives of the Bush and the Clinton campaigns, Perot said he would reenter the race if his volunteers wanted him to do so. He then set up a spurious poll—with a toll-free number that counted every call as a vote in favor—to measure his support and announced on October 1 that he was again a candidate.

At the time the significance of Perot's decision to reenter the race was hard to assess. Few commentators believed that he would win any electoral votes. And polls consistently had shown that he was pulling his support almost equally from Bush and from Clinton. Nevertheless, the Bush campaign—looking for almost anything that would change the dynamic of the race—greeted Perot's return as a source of hope.

The televised debates. Aside from the dramatics concerning Perot, public and media attention in September and October focused largely on televised presidential debates—whether they would occur, how they would be conducted, and who would win.

In theory, a mechanism for organizing the debates had been established before the campaign began. A Commission on Presidential Debates had been created by the two parties to work out a plan for the 1992 debates. Headed jointly by a former national committee chair from each party, the commission in early September proposed a series of three debates between the presidential candidates, and one between the vice presidential candidates, to take place between September 22 and October 15. Taking account of criticisms of past debates, it proposed a format in which a single moderator would ask the questions, with time for follow-up questions and direct exchanges between the candidates.

Clinton immediately accepted the commission proposal, but the Bush campaign rejected it, calling the proposed format unacceptable. One reason for Bush's position, according to Republican insiders, was that his strategists believed that the announcement of the debates would "freeze" the race: voters who might otherwise be persuaded to shift to Bush would wait for the debates to consider doing so. Bush's strategists also may have considered that Clinton, the challenger, would benefit from appearing on the same platform with the president and that he was exceptionally articulate and likely to do well in a demanding format. Whatever the reasons, the Bush campaign's decision proved costly. Worse for the president than having the campaign frozen, the debate on the debates dominated the news for two weeks. When the first scheduled debate was canceled, Clinton appeared at the planned site and accused Bush of refusing to discuss the issues. At campaign rallies Bush was mocked as "Chicken George."

In a bold move to turn the tables and create some possibility of catching Clinton, Bush on September 29 suddenly challenged Clinton to four weekly debates with a mix of formats. He also invited Perot to participate. After several days of meetings, the two campaigns agreed on three presidential debates and one vice presidential debate, with varying formats, all squeezed into the nine-day period from October 11 to October 19. Perot agreed to participate.

In the first debate, with the traditional format of a moderator and a panel of three reporters, Bush performed competently but failed to launch the aggressive attack on Clinton that his advisers had planned. In contrast, Clinton focused on economic issues and the need for change, and he effectively chastised Bush for raising questions about his patriotism. Perot boosted his candidacy with charm and humor, although he shied away from any specific discussion of his proposals.

The vice presidential debate probably had little effect on the campaign. Both Quayle and Gore gave generally strong performances, although Gore was criticized for appearing programmed and Quayle was faulted for some "unpresidential" lapses of decorum. Perot's running mate, Admiral James Stockdale, who had been hurriedly pressed into service when Perot reentered the race, was obviously unprepared. Indeed, he surrendered much of his time for lack of something to say.

The second presidential debate, with a single moderator soliciting questions from an audience of undecided voters, was a field day for Clinton. Bush again failed to make his points about Clinton's character—this time because members of the audience insisted that they wanted to hear only discussions about issues. The president looked out of touch when he failed to understand a misspoken question about how the "national debt" had affected him personally. And he was twice caught on camera checking his watch, as if eager for the debate to end. Clinton displayed the skills and experience at answering voters' questions he had gained from numerous appearances on talk shows. In a highly effective performance, he occasionally left his chair and walked over to speak directly with a questioner.

The last debate, which combined the single-moderator and panel-of-reporters formats, was widely seen as Bush's last chance to build momentum. He finally made the most of it, jumping at every opportunity to attack Clinton's character. The effect was diminished, however, when Perot turned the character issue against Bush. He blamed Bush for the Iraqi military build-up, and, suggesting a cover-up of the administration's failure to deter the invasion of Kuwait, demanded that Bush release the instructions that had been given to the American ambassador to Iraq. To a lesser extent, Perot also criticized Clinton, arguing that Clinton's experience as the governor of a small state was irrelevant to the presidency. Again, Clinton was forceful and articulate, returning blow for blow.

Sorting out the effects of the debates on the election is complex. The various opinion polls taken after each debate showed that Clinton either won or was the co-winner with Perot in all three encounters. Because Clinton was already ahead in the election, he was the only candidate who clearly did what he needed to do—hold his own against Bush and demonstrate presidential stature. But Perot did the most to raise his standing. Coming into the debates with strong negative ratings and barely more than single-digit support, he gave appealing performances and increased his credibility with many voters.

Bush was not judged the winner of any debate. Nevertheless, he performed well enough, especially in the last debate, to gain some momentum. He probably convinced some Republican-leaning holdouts that he was indeed a plausible choice. Thus it was Bush, not Clinton, who along with Perot made gains in the preference polls. In a CBS News/*New York Times* poll before the first debate, Clinton had a 13-point lead, with 47 percent of the respondents to Bush's 34 percent and Perot's 10 percent. After the final debate the same poll found Clinton leading Bush by only 5 percentage points, 42 percent to 37 percent. Perot's support had risen to 17 percent.[18]

Apart from their effect on the candidates, the debates were a success with the public. The voters were able to see the candidates in action, form impressions of their character and abilities, and hear them discuss a range of issues—the economy, health care, gun control, education, fuel-efficiency standards, term limits, lobbyists, civil rights, the budget deficit, and free trade, among others. They saw each candidate challenged on at least one topic he would rather not have discussed—Bush on his pre-Gulf war policy toward Iraq, Clinton on paying for his programs, and Perot on his use of private investigators. On average, the debates were seen in thirty-nine million homes, and eighty-eight million people watched the final debate.[19]

The final weeks. With the debates over, each campaign settled on a strategy for the last two weeks. Bush continued his attack on Clinton's character and his record on taxes, asking the voters to consider carefully whom they would trust in a crisis. But because he did not have strong evidence to support his charges, Bush had to resort to marginally effective complaints about Clinton's anti-Vietnam War protests and his vague or inconsistent positions on certain issues. Clinton, having found no need to alter the strategy that had been devised in the spring, continued to run on the economy and the need for change. Perot argued that he alone would overcome gridlock and reduce the deficit.

In early October, Perot began running a series of television advertisements that set aside conventional methods. Instead of using the thirty- and sixty-second spots that are the staple of contemporary campaigns, he bought several half-hour blocks of prime network television time. In the first of these "infomercials," Perot, displaying hand-held charts, sat at a table and discussed the economy, the federal deficit, and the economic condition of the United States compared with the conditions of Germany and Japan. The advertisement was seen by 16.5 million people, beating the competition in its time slot. In his later advertisements, Perot described some policy proposals; he was interviewed about his background; his friends and family talked about him; and he criticized the records and experience of his opponents. Even though Perot's unconventionally long advertisements were seen by millions of people, they probably missed a majority of the voters.

On October 25 Perot made a remarkable announcement: the real reason he had withdrawn from the presidential race in July was that he had learned that the Republicans were planning to embarrass his daughter and disrupt her August wedding. He also alleged that the Republicans had tried to sabotage his computer, attempting to interfere with his stock trading and prevent him from buying advertising time. The Republicans denied these farfetched charges, and Perot refused to provide any evidence. The episode prompted news stories that reviewed a number of bizarre claims of conspiracies and attempts to assassinate him made by Perot in the past. But the controversy did not affect his standing in the polls.

As election day drew near, the Clinton team became increasingly confident of victory and began campaigning seriously in traditionally Republican states such as Louisiana, Florida, and Georgia. Clinton was trying to make inroads into the Republican South and, evidently, to achieve an electoral vote landslide. That ambition was curtailed during the final days of the campaign, however, when evidence that the race was tightening forced Clinton to concentrate largely on pivotal states, especially in the Midwest.

By most accounts, Bush did his most effective campaigning in the two weeks after the debates. He spoke forcefully at campaign rallies and drew large, enthusiastic crowds. But although Bush followed the campaign strategy of attacking Clinton and Gore, he appeared sometimes to lose control of his rhetoric. He referred to Clinton and Gore as "bozos." Attacking Gore as an environmental extremist, he called him "Ozone Man." (He even combined the names and called Gore "that bozo Ozone Man.") And he said that his dog Millie knew more about foreign policy than either of the Democrats. Bush's lapses into playground invective drew cheers from rally audiences, but campaign aides worried about how they would sound on the evening news.

Some national polls indicated that the race was tightening at the end. In polls taken two weeks before the election Clinton's lead over Bush ranged from 3 to 19 percentage points, with an average lead of 10.7 percentage points.[20] In the week before the election Clinton's lead in four major polls varied from 1 to 10 percentage points, with an average of 4.25.[21] The poll with the 1-percentage-point margin, conducted by the Gallup organization for CNN/*USA Today,* caused considerable excitement, but questions were raised about its methods of identifying likely voters.

In any case, the tightening stopped in the last three or four days. Bush's gain may largely have run its course; the wavering Republicans who were disposed to come back to their party may have all returned by that point. But, in addition, Bush suffered a major embarrassment with a new revelation of his involvement in the Iran-contra scandal. As noted earlier, on several occasions during the campaign documents or testimony emerging from Independent Counsel Lawrence Walsh's investigation had impugned Bush's repeated denial that he had approved of or even known about the arms-for-hostages deal with Iran. The Democrats, sticking rigidly to their strategy of avoiding personal attacks, did not exploit the revelations. But on October 31, four days before the election, Walsh released an indictment of Reagan's secretary of defense, Caspar Weinberger, that included copies of Weinberger's personal notes of meetings during the episode.[22] One note stated that Bush had been present at a crucial meeting that he had long denied attending and that he had supported the arms-for-hostages deal. Clinton and Gore seized on the scandal to turn around Bush's attacks on the character issue, arguing that it was Bush, not Clinton, who could not be trusted. The last three days of the campaign were dominated by Bush's unpersuasive, and sometimes testy, efforts to dismiss the new evidence. The final polls showed Clinton's lead widening again—with a range of 4 to 9 percentage points, and an average of 7.1 percentage points.[23]

On the day before the election Perot saturated the national television market with a final wave of spot advertisements. Bush campaigned in five states. And in a thirty-hour marathon tour, Clinton campaigned in nine states, including a rally in Colorado at 3:00 a.m. on election day.

The Result

The voters, by a decisive margin, chose Bill Clinton to be the forty-second president of the United States. Clinton received 43.0 percent of the popular vote to Bush's 37.4 percent and Perot's 18.9 percent. (See Table 3-1.) He carried thirty-two states and the District of Columbia for a total of 370

Table 3-1 Presidential Election Results by State

State	Clinton Popular	%	Bush Popular	%	Perot Popular	%
East						
Connecticut	682,318	42.2	578,313	35.8	348,771	21.6
Delaware	126,054	43.5	102,313	35.3	59,213	20.4
D.C.	192,619	84.6	20,698	9.1	9,681	4.3
Maine	263,420	38.8	206,504	30.4	206,820	30.4
Maryland	988,571	49.8	707,094	35.6	281,414	14.2
Massachusetts	1,318,639	47.5	805,039	29.0	630,731	22.7
New Hampshire	209,040	38.9	202,484	37.6	121,337	22.6
New Jersey	1,436,206	43.0	1,356,865	40.6	521,829	15.6
New York	3,444,450	49.7	2,346,649	33.9	1,090,721	15.7
Pennsylvania	2,239,164	45.1	1,791,841	36.1	902,667	18.2
Rhode Island	213,299	47.0	131,601	29.0	105,045	23.2
Vermont	133,592	46.1	88,122	30.4	65,991	22.8
West Virginia	331,001	48.4	241,974	35.4	108,829	15.9
Midwest						
Illinois	2,453,350	48.6	1,734,096	34.3	840,515	16.6
Indiana	848,420	36.8	989,375	42.9	455,934	19.8
Iowa	586,353	43.3	504,891	37.3	253,468	18.7
Kansas	390,434	33.7	449,951	38.9	312,358	27.0
Michigan	1,871,182	43.8	1,554,940	36.4	824,813	19.3
Minnesota	1,020,997	43.5	747,841	31.9	562,506	24.0
Missouri	1,053,873	44.1	811,159	33.9	518,741	21.7
Nebraska	216,864	29.4	343,678	46.6	174,104	23.6
North Dakota	99,168	32.2	136,244	44.2	71,084	23.1
Ohio	1,984,919	40.2	1,894,248	38.3	1,036,403	21.0
South Dakota	124,888	37.1	136,718	40.7	73,295	21.8
Wisconsin	1,041,066	41.1	930,855	36.8	544,479	21.5
South						
Alabama	690,080	40.9	804,283	47.6	183,109	10.8
Arkansas	505,823	53.2	337,324	35.5	99,132	10.4
Florida	2,071,651	39.0	2,171,781	40.9	1,052,481	19.8
Georgia	1,008,966	43.5	995,252	42.9	309,657	13.3
Kentucky	665,104	44.6	617,178	41.3	203,944	13.7
Louisiana	815,971	45.6	733,386	41.0	211,478	11.8
Mississippi	400,258	40.8	487,793	49.7	85,626	8.7
North Carolina	1,114,042	42.7	1,134,661	43.4	357,864	13.7
Oklahoma	473,066	34.0	592,929	42.6	319,878	23.0
South Carolina	479,514	39.9	577,507	48.0	138,872	11.5
Tennessee	933,521	47.1	841,300	42.4	199,968	10.1
Texas	2,281,815	37.1	2,496,071	40.6	1,354,781	22.0
Virginia	1,038,650	40.6	1,150,517	45.0	348,639	13.6

continued

Table 3-1 *Continued*

State	Clinton Popular	%	Bush Popular	%	Perot Popular	%
West						
Alaska	78,294	30.3	102,000	39.5	73,481	28.4
Arizona	543,050	36.5	572,086	38.5	353,741	23.8
California	5,121,325	46.0	3,630,575	32.6	2,296,006	20.6
Colorado	629,681	40.1	562,850	35.9	366,010	23.3
Hawaii	179,310	48.1	136,822	36.7	53,003	14.2
Idaho	137,013	28.4	202,645	42.0	130,395	27.0
Montana	154,507	37.6	144,207	35.1	107,225	26.1
Nevada	189,148	37.4	175,828	34.7	132,580	26.2
New Mexico	261,617	45.9	212,824	37.3	91,895	16.1
Oregon	621,314	42.5	475,757	32.5	354,091	24.2
Utah	183,429	24.7	322,632	43.4	203,400	27.3
Washington	993,037	43.4	731,234	32.0	541,780	23.7
Wyoming	68,160	34.0	79,347	39.6	51,263	25.6
Total	44,908,233	43.0	39,102,282	37.4	19,741,048	18.9

Source: Adapted from "Official 1992 Presidential Election Results," *Congressional Quarterly Weekly Report,* Jan. 23, 1993, 190.

Note: Vote percentages may not add to 100 because of votes for minor-party candidates.

electoral votes, 100 more than he needed to win. Bush won eighteen states and 168 electoral votes. Despite Perot's impressive showing in the popular vote, he did not come close to winning any state.

Clinton's winning margin was significantly narrower than Ronald Reagan's in the landslide elections of 1980 and 1984. But his victory over Bush, among voters who voted for either major-party candidate, was roughly comparable to Bush's victory over Dukakis in 1988. In 1988 Bush won 53.9 percent of the two-party vote; in 1992 Clinton won 53.5 percent.

Although Clinton did not win in a landslide, he assembled an unusually broad coalition. Most important, he defeated Bush soundly in the crucial contest for swing voters. According to the exit poll by Voter Research and Surveys, Clinton won support from 38 percent of the voters who identified themselves as "independent/other," while Bush won 32 percent; not surprisingly, Perot did well with these voters. (See Table 3-2.) Clinton was even stronger with self-identified moderates, outpolling Bush by 47 percent to 31 percent. The most striking element of Clinton's coalition was his massive support among first-time voters, who preferred Clinton to Bush by 46 percent to 32 percent.

Like all recent Democratic presidential candidates, Clinton gained his strongest support from several traditionally Democratic groups: liberals, racial minorities, women, people with lower incomes, people with less education, Jews, and union members. But he ran relatively well among every

Table 3-2   Voting Choice by Demographic and Political Groups in the
1992 Presidential Election (in percentages)

	Clinton	Bush	Perot
All (100%)	43%	38%	19%
Men (47)	41	38	21
Women (53)	45	37	17
Whites (87)	39	40	20
Blacks (8)	83	10	7
Hispanics (2)	61	25	14
Did not complete high school (7)	54	28	18
High school graduate (25)	43	36	21
Some college (29)	41	37	21
College graduate (23)	39	41	20
Postgraduate (16)	50	36	14
Age 18-24 (11)	46	33	21
25-29 (10)	41	36	23
30-39 (24)	40	38	22
40-49 (22)	43	38	20
50-59 (13)	41	40	19
60+ (20)	50	38	12
Family income			
Less than $15,000 (14)	58	23	19
$15,000-$30,000 (24)	45	35	20
$30,000-$50,000 (30)	41	38	21
$50,000-$75,000 (20)	40	41	18
More than $75,000 (12)	36	48	16
Protestants (42)	36	45	18
Catholics (27)	44	35	20
Jewish (4)	80	11	9
Family financial situation compared with 1988:			
Better (24)	24	61	14
Worse (34)	61	14	25
Same (41)	41	42	17
Democrats (38)	77	10	13
Republicans (35)	10	73	17
Independents/others (27)	38	32	30
Liberals (21)	68	14	18
Moderates (49)	47	31	21
Conservatives (30)	18	64	18
1988 vote			
Bush (53)	21	59	20
Dukakis (27)	83	5	12
Did not vote (15)	48	26	26
First-time voters (11)	46	32	22

Source: Voter Research and Surveys exit polls.
Note: Percentages may not add to 100 because of rounding.

Figure 3-1 Electoral Votes by State, 1992

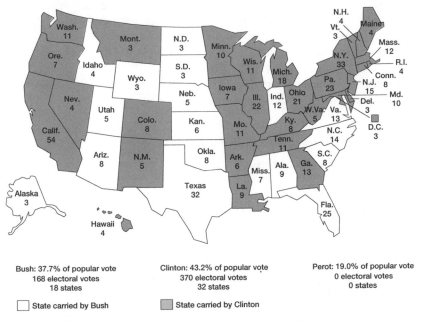

Bush: 37.7% of popular vote
168 electoral votes
18 states

Clinton: 43.2% of popular vote
370 electoral votes
32 states

Perot: 19.0% of popular vote
0 electoral votes
0 states

☐ State carried by Bush

▨ State carried by Clinton

Source : Congressional Quarterly Weekly Report, Nov. 7, 1992, 3549.

identifiable group of voters. He won a plurality among both men and women, although a narrower one among men. He won among blacks and Hispanics and virtually tied with Bush among whites. Clinton won in every age group and in every income group except the two highest—those with family incomes of $50,000 or more. Looking only at votes that went to either Clinton or Bush, we find that even the groups that are most inclined to vote Republican gave Clinton considerable support. Clinton received 44 percent of the two-party vote among Protestants, 43 percent among people in the highest income category, and 22 percent among self-identified conservatives.

Clinton also won electoral votes in all regions of the country. (See Figure 3-1.) He carried every state in the largely Democratic East, even normally Republican New Hampshire and New Jersey. He defeated Bush decisively in the Midwest, carrying all the large states in the region—Michigan, Ohio, and Illinois, with 61 electoral votes—and holding Bush to five small states with 29 electoral votes.[24] Although Bush won most of the South, the moderate, all-southern Democratic ticket made inroads there, winning not only the candidates' home states, Arkansas and Tennessee, but also Georgia, Louisiana, and Kentucky. Clinton also broke into Republican territory in the West. He won by 13.4 percentage points in California, a normally competitive state that was in severe economic distress. He carried competitive Oregon and Washington by generous margins and traditionally Republican Montana, Nevada, Colorado, and New Mexico more narrowly. In elections from 1968 to 1988, Republican presidential candidates had enjoyed a seemingly secure base in the twenty-six states of the Southeast and the Rocky Mountains, which had 223 electoral votes in 1992. Except for Jimmy Carter's victory in his home state of Georgia in 1980, Republicans had won every one of these states in 1980, 1984, and 1988. In 1992 Clinton won eight of these states, with 63 electoral votes.

Explaining the Outcome

Why did the Democrats win? What were the crucial elements of their success? At one level the answer is easy: On the issues and qualities of the candidates that the voters considered most important, they judged Clinton superior to Bush. In the exit poll, 42 percent of the voters said the issue of jobs and the economy was important to their decision, making it by far the most important issue of the election. (See Table 3-3.) These voters supported Clinton over Bush by more than a 2-1 margin, 52 percent to 25 percent. Twenty percent of the voters identified health care as important. They preferred Clinton by an even larger margin, 67 percent to 20 percent. The issues that favored Bush—taxes, foreign policy, and family values— were important to smaller numbers of voters, 14 percent, 8 percent, and 15 percent, respectively. Significantly, a large number of voters, 21 percent, said that the budget deficit was important, but this judgment did not drive them strongly to either candidate. They supported Clinton over Bush by only a modest margin.

The most important candidate qualities also worked to Clinton's advantage. Thirty-six percent of the voters mentioned the ability to bring about change and 24 percent mentioned having the best plan for the country as important to their decision; by wide margins, the voters who cited these considerations favored Clinton. The qualities that helped Bush—having the right experience and having good judgment in a crisis—were important to smaller numbers of voters, 19 percent and 16 percent respectively.[25]

There are two grounds for suspecting that in 1992 the campaign was crucial to the election outcome. One is the contrast between the predictions of most forecasting models, such as the one developed by Michael Lewis-Beck and Tom W. Rice, and the actual result.[26] These models base predictions on past relationships between election outcomes and various relevant conditions, such as presidential popularity and the performance of the economy during the election year. In 1992 most such models predicted a Bush victory. The other is that the Bush campaign was widely criticized for mismanagement, the lack of a strategy, and a lackluster performance by the candidate—all charges with some foundation. In contrast, the Clinton campaign was much admired by pundits and politicians for its intelligence and effectiveness. Taken together, these observations suggest that Bush was in a

Table 3-3   Reasons for Candidate Preference in the 1992 Presidential Election (in percentages)

	Percent voting for		
	Clinton	Bush	Perot
Which issues mattered most in deciding how you voted?			
Health care (20%)	67%	20%	14%
Budget deficit (21)	36	27	37
Abortion (12)	36	55	9
Education (13)	60	25	16
Economy/jobs (42)	52	25	24
Environment (5)	72	14	13
Taxes (14)	26	57	18
Foreign policy (8)	8	87	5
Family values (15)	22	67	12
Is the condition of the economy:			
Excellent (1)	53	35	12
Good (18)	8	82	10
Not so good (47)	43	37	20
Poor (32)	64	12	24
Which candidate qualities mattered most in deciding how you voted?			
Has the right experience (19)	7	84	9
Will bring about needed change (36)	67	5	28
Is my party's candidate (5)	56	42	2
Cares about people like me (13)	64	11	25
Is honest and trustworthy (14)	14	63	23
Has the best plan for the country (24)	58	17	25
Would have good judgment in a crisis (16)	8	88	4
His choice of vice president (8)	85	13	2
Has strong convictions (14)	27	45	28
Was your vote mainly:			
For your candidate (69)	44	38	18
Against his opponents (27)	40	40	20
Would you rather have government:			
Provide more services but cost more in taxes (36)	65	21	14
Cost less in taxes but provide fewer services (55)	28	50	23
In the House election, did you vote for:			
The Democrat (54)	74	11	15
The Republican (46)	10	72	18
Independent (0)	0	0	0
Which should be the highest priority for the next president?			
Cutting taxes (14)	41	44	15
Reducing the budget deficit (54)	35	43	23
Expanding domestic programs (22)	63	25	12

Source: Voter Research and Surveys exit polls.
Note: Percentages may not add to 100 because of rounding.

strong position to win the election but managed to lose it by running a campaign that was markedly inferior to his opponent's.

Such reasoning, however, is questionable. Although models such as Lewis-Beck and Rice's are undoubtedly useful forecasting tools for most presidential elections, their reliance on very recent economic performance as a major predictor failed to capture Bush's difficulties with the economy. Bush's problem was not, for example, the marginally below-average growth rate of the gross national product (GNP) in the first half of the election year—the variable used by Lewis-Beck and Rice. It was that growth was still sluggish after more than two years of stagnation and that because of his attempts to assure the public and his opposition to fiscal stimulation, Bush was seen as out of touch and unconcerned about the economy. As a result, the Clinton campaign could easily identify its major issue—"the economy, stupid." In the exit poll, 79 percent of the voters described the economy as "not so good" or "poor," and those voters chose Clinton by a substantial margin.

Moreover, the differences in the effectiveness of the two campaigns were mostly a matter of their respective circumstances. The weaknesses of the Bush campaign reflected the serious problems it faced: the poor economy, Bush's lack of domestic accomplishments, the sudden irrelevance of anticommunism that accompanied the end of the Cold War, the competence and political centrism of the opposing candidate, and the public's desire for change. Admittedly, the Bush campaign shifted from one ineffective issue, family values, to another that was almost as ineffective, character and trust. But if a more effective campaign appeal had been available, in all likelihood the Bush team would have discovered it. Similarly, Bush was a lackluster candidate at times. But if his prospects for reelection had been better, he probably would have had more energy.

The converse is true of the Clinton campaign: Its strengths reflected a wealth of strategic opportunities. Any Democratic campaign organization in 1992 would have discovered the issues of change, the economy, and health care. The potential efficacy of each of these issues was abundantly evident in the history of presidential elections, recent opinion polls, or both. The main novelty in Clinton's strategy was arguably his refusal, through most of the campaign, to exploit Bush's problems with the Iran-contra scandal and the Iraqi military build-up before the Gulf war. But the wisdom of that strategy was questionable, and it was abandoned, apparently with good results, in the last days.

If the campaign was probably not the source of Clinton's victory, Perot's involvement was not either. Perot drew his support equally from potential supporters of both Bush and Clinton. When Perot voters were asked in the exit poll whom they would have voted for had Perot's name not been on the ballot, they divided almost evenly between Bush and Clinton.[27]

Perot may have affected the outcome of the election by changing the dynamics of the campaign. But if he did it is not clear whom he benefited.

There are several ways that Perot may have helped Clinton. At an early stage, he gave some voters a halfway house—a candidate to support temporarily, without becoming committed to Bush—when Clinton's image problems were most severe. Through most of the campaign, Perot reinforced Clinton's attack on Bush's record and his call for change. And in the televised debates, Perot's presence distracted attention from the confrontation between Bush and Clinton, diminishing Bush's opportunity to narrow the gap between them.

Another view of Perot's effect is possible. According to the polls, it was Clinton who defeated Bush in the debates. If Perot had not been involved, the debating skills of the two front-runners would have been put to a harder test—with longer statements, more follow-up questions, and more direct exchange between the two. In these circumstances, Clinton might have won even more decisively. Even if not, the public and the media would have paid more attention to his victory. Ultimately, assessing Perot's effect on the dynamics of the campaign is entirely speculative.

There is no doubt that the campaign was important in 1992. As we have noted, the candidates' standing fluctuated with major events in the campaign. (See Figure 3-2.) Moreover, if Clinton had made serious mistakes in his choice of positions (for example, advocating cuts in Social Security or a middle-class tax increase), if he had failed to demonstrate competence in the televised debates, or if the Republicans had turned up genuine evidence of significant improprieties on his part, he might have lost the election.

But, more than anything, the 1992 campaign represented the unfolding of the fundamental political strengths and weaknesses that the two major-party candidates had going into it. A presidential campaign depends above all on the appeals the candidates are in a position to make—in short, their ammunition. In 1992 the Democrats had more ammunition.

Evaluating the Campaign

Recent presidential election campaigns, especially the campaign of 1988, have played to almost uniformly bad reviews. In the view of most commentators, the candidates relied on simplistic, emotional, and negative appeals and neglected the issues facing the country. Voters were irritated by the campaigns, wished there were other candidates, and stayed home in large numbers on election day.[28] As many observers have noted, the 1992 presidential campaign showed marked improvement over its predecessors in many respects. But, as very few have pointed out, there were still serious deficiencies in the campaign.

To play a constructive role in the larger process of democratic government, a presidential campaign must enable voters to act on their genuine preferences, those they would have if they were fully informed.[29] Furthermore, it must elicit positions and commitments from the candidates that permit the winner to serve those genuine preferences after the election. To

Figure 3-2 Support for Presidential Candidates, March - October, 1992

Percentage of support

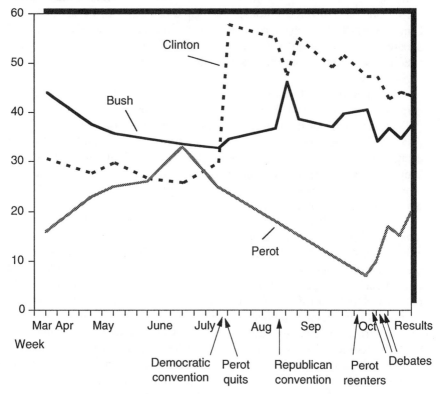

Source: CBS News/*New York Times* poll.

accomplish these things, a presidential campaign must have several features. The candidates must take reasonably specific positions on a variety of issues. They must also discuss their records of past performance and capabilities as leaders. Crucially, all of this discussion must be firmly connected to reality. The candidates must not overlook major issues or problems facing the country. And, for the most part, they must not mislead or distract the voters with irrelevancies, unsupportable claims, or impossible promises. The voters' job is hard enough without having to filter out an enormous amount of disinformation.

The improvement in the 1992 election was apparent in three aspects of the campaign. First, there was extensive discussion of issues. The candidates took positions, often in detail, on numerous matters of public policy. They discussed the issues not only in obscure position papers but on talk shows, in best-selling books, and during the televised debates. The news media, for their part, covered the issues more thoroughly than in previous elections. Second, the candidates largely avoided using the most blatantly deceptive or manipulative methods of persuasion. There was no equivalent of the racially inflammatory "Willie Horton" ad that was run in Bush's behalf in 1988 or of the Dukakis campaign's unsubstantiated allegations about Bush's relationship with Panamanian dictator Manuel Noriega. Presumably because the 1992 advertising was being monitored closely by the media and the opposing candidates, it was more responsible, less controversial, and probably less consequential for the election.

Finally, the voters, perhaps feeling that they had been treated with respect by the candidates, were satisfied with the campaign. In a postelection poll, 77 percent said they had "learned enough about the candidates and issues to make an informed choice"—up from 59 percent in 1988.[30] On the whole, they also were pleased with what they learned about the candidates. In a *Los Angeles Times* exit poll, about 60 percent of the voters said they had chosen their candidate because they liked him and his policies, not merely to avoid the others or register a protest.[31] And, reversing the downward trend of recent years, a larger share of the voters turned out at the polls than in any election since 1968. The rate of participation of the voting age population increased from 50.1 percent in 1988 to 55.2 percent in 1992.[32]

It is significant that these changes in the quality of the campaign were accomplished merely through learning and interaction between all the participants in the presidential election process; they did not require new laws, regulations, or institutional devices to bring them about. Of their own accord, the news media responded constructively to criticism of their past coverage. In their constant search for ways to attract an audience, the entertainment media employed talk-show formats to provide new opportunities for discussion with the candidates. The candidates learned to reply aggressively to misleading attacks. The public probably became more resistant to persuasion through such attacks. And all three campaign teams adjusted their strategies and rhetoric to the opportunities and constraints that arose from all these other changes. In the context of recent history, these unplanned favorable developments come as a pleasant surprise: They prove that there is no law of ceaseless deterioration in presidential campaign debate.

Yet, in certain respects, the 1992 campaign still had serious deficiencies and, indeed, was not perceptibly superior to the campaigns of the 1980s. For one thing, the candidates avoided several of the most pressing issues facing the country. Despite the concerted effort by Perot to prompt a debate on the budget deficit, neither Bush nor Clinton joined in. The candidates were oblivious to the momentous issue of American support for the transition to democratic capitalism in the former Soviet Union. They did not discuss the American role in guaranteeing human rights in troubled countries such as Somalia and Bosnia-Herzegovina. Just weeks after Los Angeles had one of the worst race riots in American history, they did not discuss the persisting problems of race or the cities in American society.

Moreover, on some issues that the candidates did address, the discussion was so superficial and loosely tied to reality that it was useless or worse for informing the voters. Clinton and Bush traded wildly contradictory assertions about the tax consequences of Clinton's economic program: Clinton said he would raise taxes on families with annual incomes above $200,000 per year; Bush said that Clinton's programs would require significant new taxes even for ordinary working people. Discrepancies of this magnitude on a relatively straightforward budget projection indicate that at least one candidate was going far beyond any supportable claim.

As in all presidential campaigns, assessing the president's performance in managing the economy was reduced to measuring the short-term results. Clinton implied that the economy's poor performance during Bush's term was the result of the president's incompetence or lack of concern. In fact, Bush's decisions on dealing with the recession and slow recovery from 1990 to 1992—including his long resistance to stimulative measures—were consistently in line with mainstream economic opinion.[33] Yet Bush did not even bother to point this out; undoubtedly, he thought that in the circumstances of the campaign such a defense would easily be made to look ridiculous. Bush tried to make an issue of Clinton's character. He did so mostly on the basis of episodes that were so old and remote from any matter of conduct in office that they were monumentally irrelevant to a serious discussion of the point.

Of course, presidential campaign debate in the era of modern mass communication has probably never been any deeper or more closely tied to reality than it was in 1992. Indeed, there are severe limitations to the quality of the debate that is possible; a democratic polity of 250 million people will never resemble the agora of ancient Athens.

Nevertheless, in the view of many observers, the superficiality and unrealism of presidential campaign debate has in recent years been causing havoc with the performance of American government. The effects of such debate apparently are being magnified by changes in American society and political institutions that are making government more open and sensitive to public opinion. In any case, presidential campaigns have been crucially involved in the politics of the budget deficit, by many accounts the central policy failure of contemporary American government. Campaigns also have probably played a major role in government's failure to deal effectively with the drug problem and with the plight of the underclass. As Anthony King and Giles Austin argue, these failures reflect the pressure of simplistic or stereotyped mass opinion on presidents and other policymakers.[34] Such pressures are brought to bear primarily in election campaigns. As a result of the 1992 campaign, it will be difficult for the Clinton administration to respond effectively to the threat of instability or counterrevolution in the former Soviet Union; to impose the genuine sacrifice that will be needed to reduce the budget deficit; or to refrain from stimulating the economy in a period of slow growth, even if there are serious risks in doing so.

It is thus important for the nation to seek means to improve significantly the depth and realism of presidential campaign debate. Clearly, there is no feasible way to enhance dramatically the critical powers of 200 million eligible voters. The key to improvement is to increase the prominence in campaign debate of independent experts on the substantive issues of the campaign. Such experts—journalists, academics, business leaders, and others—must play a larger role as commentators, or better yet as participants, in the ongoing campaign debate. It does not serve democracy for the critical national discussion of who should be president to be reserved entirely to the candidates.

Notes

1. "Bush Job Performance—Trend," *Gallup Poll Monthly*, February 1992, 15.
2. Economic figures are reported in U.S. Department of Commerce, *Survey of Current Business* 72 (September 1992): C2.
3. *Polling Report* 8 (June 22, 1992): 4.
4. "How the Economy Has Fared Under 9 Presidents," *New York Times*, Nov. 4, 1992, B11.
5. *Polling Report* 8 (May 25, 1992): 2.
6. "Bush Job Performance," *Gallup Poll Monthly*, July 1992, 7.
7. Michael Kelly, "Democrat Fights Perceptions of Bush Gain," *New York Times*, Oct. 31, 1992, 1.
8. Alan L. Otten, "TV News Drops Kid-Glove Coverage of Election, Trading Staged Sound Bites for Hard Analysis," *Wall Street Journal*, Oct. 12, 1992, A12.
9. *Polling Report* 8 (June 22, 1992): 4.
10. Robin Toner, "Democrats Display a New Optimism, Reflected in Poll," *New York Times*, July 13, 1992, A1.
11. For a partial transcript of Clinton's remarks, see *New York Times*, July 17, 1992, A12.
12. R. W. Apple, Jr., "Poll Gives Clinton a Post-Perot, Post-Convention Boost," *New York Times*, July 18, 1992, 1.
13. Andrew Rosenthal, "Bush Campaign Issues Stinging Attack," *New York Times*, Aug. 3, 1992, A10.
14. Excerpts of the Republican platform are reprinted in *New York Times*, Aug. 18, 1992, A8.
15. For a transcript of Bush's remarks, see *New York Times*, Aug. 21, 1992, A10.
16. *Polling Report: Campaign '92 Update*, Aug. 31, 1992, 1.
17. *Polling Report: Campaign '92 Update*, Sept. 5, 1988, 1.
18. *Polling Report: Campaign '92 Update*, Oct. 19, 1992, 1; and Oct. 28, 1992, 1.
19. "Final Debate Tops Ratings," *New York Times*, Oct. 21, 1992, A13.
20. *Polling Report: Campaign '92 Update*, Oct. 28, 1992, 1.
21. "Recent Polls," *New York Times*, Oct. 31, 1992, 6.
22. Some Republicans charged that the timing of the indictment was politically motivated. But Walsh had promised the judge handling the case that he would produce an indictment by the end of October.
23. "Presidential Preference: Final Nationwide Polls," *Polling Report* 8 (Nov. 16, 1992): 3.
24. The five states were Indiana, Kansas, Nebraska, North Dakota, and South Dakota.
25. Of course, the voters' responses to questions about what considerations were important partly reflect their candidate choice, as opposed to explaining it: A voter who liked Clinton, for whatever reason, was more likely to identify his themes as the important issues.

26. Michael S. Lewis-Beck and Tom W. Rice, *Forecasting Elections* (Washington, D.C.: CQ Press, 1992), 133-141. On the performance of forecasting models in 1992, see Richard Morin, "Surviving the Ups and Downs of Election '92," *Washington Post National Weekly Edition*, Nov. 9-15, 1992, 37; and Elizabeth Kolbert, "As for All That Lore About Sure-Thing Election Prophecies, Forget About It," *New York Times*, Nov. 5, 1992, B1. For an example of a forecasting model that called the 1992 election correctly, see Alan I. Abramowitz, "An Improved Model for Predicting Presidential Election Outcomes," *PS: Political Science and Politics* 21 (Fall 1988): 843-847.

27. Voter Research and Surveys, General Election, Nov. 3, 1992.

28. See Paul J. Quirk, "The Election," in *The Elections of 1988*, ed. Michael Nelson (Washington, D.C.: CQ Press, 1989), 63-92; for an excellent, full-length assessment of the 1988 campaign, see Bruce Buchanan, *Electing the President* (Austin: University of Texas Press, 1991).

29. For thoughtful treatments of democratic government as a deliberative process, see Jane Mansbridge, *Beyond Adversary Democracy* (New York: Basic Books, 1980); James Fishkin, *Democracy and Deliberation: New Directions for Democratic Reform* (New Haven: Yale University Press, 1991); and Joseph Bessette, *The Mild Voice of Reason* (Chicago: University of Chicago Press, forthcoming).

30. William Schneider, "When Issues, Not Personalities, Rule," *National Journal*, Dec. 5, 1992, 2814. The poll was conducted by the Times Mirror Center for the People and the Press.

31. Ronald Brownstein, "Economic Concerns Fueled Clinton's Drive to Victory," *Los Angeles Times*, Nov. 4, 1992, A1.

32. Adam Clymer, "Turnout on Election Day '92 Was the Largest in 24 Years," *New York Times*, Dec. 17, 1992, A13.

33. See Paul J. Quirk and Bruce Nesmith, "Explaining Deadlock: Domestic Policy in the Bush Presidency," in *New Perspectives in American Politics*, ed. Lawrence C. Dodd and Calvin Jillson (Washington, D.C.: CQ Press, forthcoming).

34. Anthony King and Giles Austin, "Good Government and the Politics of High Exposure," in *The Bush Presidency: First Appraisals*, ed. Colin Campbell and Bert A. Rockman (Chatham, N.J.: Chatham House, 1991), 249-286.

4

The Media Reformation:
Giving the Agenda Back to the People

Philip Meyer

*The role of the media in the electoral process, always controver-
sial, was widely discussed during and after the elections of 1992.
For once, however, the discussion had less to do with shopworn
issues such as "Are the media biased?" and "Are the media too
powerful?" than with more empirical and analytic questions concerning the new ways in which the candidates were using the media
to reach out to the voters and the correspondingly new ways that the
media were covering the candidates. Responding to innovations such
as 800 numbers as a form of fund raising, appearances on entertainment programs ("The Arsenio Hall Show") and networks (MTV),
and town-meeting style presidential debates, most commentary was
devoted to the candidates' side of the relationship.*

*Philip Meyer gives due attention to the candidates' innovative
use of the media in 1992. But he is more concerned with the media's
own innovations. He describes several such experiments, with special
attention to newspapers. Papers in Charlotte, North Carolina, and
Wichita, Kansas, for example, inaugurated new programs of interactive, community-based election coverage that Meyer believes may
spread throughout the industry.*

Sometimes the candidates were bold, and sometimes they were merely
desperate. Either way, they were motivated to find new ways to get
around the traditional news media. And they succeeded. Jerry Brown repeated his 800 number at every opportunity; Bill Clinton had videocassettes
of himself distributed door to door to undecided voters in New Hampshire;
candidates and their staffers interacted with voters through online computer
services, including Prodigy, CompuServe, and other electronic bulletin
boards; Ross Perot used direct-access video to reach the 3.7 million viewers
with satellite dishes; and all the major candidates, even George Bush, appeared on talk shows that once had been considered too frivolous a forum for
presidential aspirants.

The candidates who found new ways to bypass the mainstream news
media and reach the people directly were not the only innovators of 1992.
Some of the smarter managers of the conventional media were already on the

way to making long-term institutional reforms. They had seen the bypass coming, and they opened the year with new mechanisms in place to preserve and strengthen their role as intermediaries between the electorate and the elected. This tension between the new and the old media may prove to be a lasting characteristic of election campaigns in the United States.

Much of the audience was caught by surprise. But when campaign adviser Mandy Grunwald persuaded Bill Clinton to don sunglasses and play the saxophone on "The Arsenio Hall Show," she was working on a problem that is as old as democracy. The future president's rendition of "Heartbreak Hotel" on June 3, 1992, reached out to one of many narrow segments of voters, this one young and politically uninvolved. Donning a flowered tie and strapping on a tenor sax may be a new approach, but it speaks to the same old problem: the peaceable aggregation of a diversity of interests. The "men of factious tempers" [1] that Madison warned us about present a paradoxical problem: the need to consolidate the polity's divergent interests without destroying the divergences. Historians of the twenty-first century may well decide that the 1992 campaign marked the time that the diversity in channels of political communication began to approach the diversity of political interests in American society. As a result, the hegemony of the traditional, mainstream mass media was forever altered.

The Framers of the Constitution did their best to accommodate pluralism by providing for a layered government with many routes of access to power. The exact mechanisms were wisely left to the political marketplace to invent. Like many good inventions, Grunwald's came in a moment of desperation. Clinton was third in the polls, the attention of the mainstream media was turning away from him to Ross Perot, and Grunwald needed to open a new channel to the voters. Her strategy worked, and a new and possibly long-lasting linkage between popular culture and political information was forged.

Even political parties began as a response to the political marketplace. Until recently, it was uneconomical for each candidate or even each interest group to construct an individual platform and sell it to the voters. And so this extraconstitutional form of political organization quickly came to dominate the process and remained dominant for almost two centuries, mediating between the candidates and the voters, consolidating interests, simplifying messages, and competing to form winning coalitions.

Conventional wisdom traces the decline of parties to the so-called political reforms of the late 1960s and the 1970s, which were designed to make candidate selection less elitist and place it more directly under the control of the voters.[2] But even there the hidden hand of the market was at work. New communications technology has made it possible for the work of coalition formation to be performed by individual candidates and their technologically competent managers.

To some analysts it has seemed that the media, regrettably, are taking over the former functions of the parties—"regrettably" because the media lack both a long enough planning horizon and a long-term interest in the outcome.[3] Yet the events of 1992 demonstrated that the same technological changes that made it possible for the media to displace the parties in some functions are also contributing to the fragmentation of the media and placing control of the mediation process in the hands of candidates and managers who are skilled enough to seize the opportunities that the new technologies present.

The managers employed by baby-boomer candidates Bill Clinton and Al Gore had just those skills, as did Ross Perot. Just as the Protestant Reformation displaced the priesthood and allowed the laity to talk directly to God, politicians in the communications reformation learned to go around the media and speak directly to the people. Larry King was among the first in the new wave of passive mediators. Like the Protestant clergy of the sixteenth century, he brought a purifying simplicity to contrast with the ornate rituals of the traditional process. King and his media peers were extremely effective. In a preelection survey of North Carolina voters, John Bare found that exposure to nonconventional media, primarily talk shows, accounted for a far greater increase in public knowledge about the candidates' positions on policy issues than did either print media or conventional TV news.[4]

The Old Media Fight Back

The sixteenth-century Catholic church survived the Reformation by instituting reforms of its own. Signs of a similar process among the mainstream media began to appear in the 1980s and received their first large-scale trial in the 1992 presidential campaign. Newspapers were especially penitent, having sensed that their relative importance was slipping; they blamed their own ineptness and lack of focus. In February 1991 the *Washington Post* reporter and columnist David Broder gave a ringing challenge-cum-confession to his colleagues in an address at the University of California, Riverside. Readers see, he said,

> that politics has become—and has been treated by the press [as]—largely a sport for a relative handful of political insiders. . . . It is no longer meaningful to a great many of our fellow citizens . . . because there is no real connection between their concerns in their daily lives and what they hear talked about and see reported by the press in most political campaigns.[5]

Broder's judgment had a strong factual basis. In recent elections, the mainstream press has tended to overgeneralize the athletic event model. Coverage concentrated on the score of the contest as registered in public opinion polls, on the personal characteristics of the players, and on the tactics of their managers. Campaign reporters had fallen into the trap, as beat reporters often do, of resembling the insiders more than their own readers and projecting their interests and those of the insiders onto their audience.

Broder, like most journalists and many political scientists, accepts the policy government model of American politics, which holds that candidates should be chosen according to their preferred issue positions.[6] This consensus among media professionals helps to explain their widespread mea culpas after hearing Broder's complaint. But one is compelled to wonder whether the outcomes of recent presidential elections also had something to do with the collective media guilt. The journalists who cover presidential elections are, on the whole, more liberal than the average citizen,[7] and three elections in a row had gone to conservative candidates: Ronald Reagan in 1980 and 1984 and George Bush in 1988. At some level of consciousness, the media guilt may have been built on the feeling that the voters had been making some bad choices that could have been avoided if they had been better informed. The traditional ethic of journalism is to give light and let the people find their own way. In 1992 the resolve to provide more light—even in the absence of a conscious bias for the Democratic presidential nominee—was very strong.

There was also a more systemic reason for the intuitive appreciation felt by mainstream media managers for Broder's thesis: economic anxiety. The same technological innovations that had opened up new channels of political communication were making their own positions less secure.

Richard Maisel documented the trend toward media fragmentation as far back as 1973. Information markets were becoming increasingly specialized. Attendance at off-Broadway plays was growing faster than attendance on Broadway. Monthly magazines were growing faster than those produced weekly, and quarterly journals were doing even better. Suburban dailies and neighborhood weeklies were growing faster than big-city dailies. Across a broad spectrum of communication vehicles, the more specialized the medium, the greater its growth. And it was all because of the interaction of market forces and technology.[8]

In their efforts to appeal to increasingly diverse audiences in growing metropolitan areas, newspapers expanded their content to include material for a mosaic of specialized audiences. Where once thirty-two pages was thought to be the maximum efficient size of a newspaper, big-city papers became bulky packages of specialized sections appealing to special interests, such as food, business, entertainment, life styles, and health, as well as to some advertiser-related topics, such as real estate and automobiles. The newest trend is to target sections of the paper for subsets of the audience, such as neighborhoods, or, as in the case of the *Miami Herald*, a foreign language group.[9] Despite such adaptive behaviors, however, newspapers have been losing their hold on their communities. In 1967 reading the newspaper was a daily habit for 73 percent of adults. Beginning about 1970 the proportion of daily readers fell slowly but steadily, hitting bottom at 51 percent in 1988. Since then the number has stabilized in the 51 to 54 percent range, not quite yet breaking below a majority.[10] (See Figure 4-1.)

Because most communities now have only one newspaper, the industry was able to protect and even improve its short-term profitability while losing

Figure 4-1 Daily Readers of Newspapers, 1967-1992

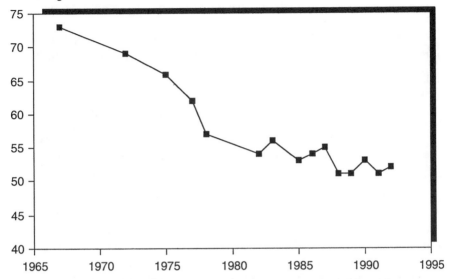

Percentage

Source: For 1972-1992: Sidney Verba and Norman Nie, The General Social Survey (University of Chicago, National Opinion Research Center). For 1967: data collected by the National Opinion Research Center.

its customers. It did this by raising prices, more to advertisers than to readers; by reducing services, mostly to readers; by cutting the space available for news; by reducing staff; and by closing out-of-town bureaus. Collecting more from the customers while doing less for them is, of course, in a competitive marketplace, a start down the road to liquidation. This realization gave many publishers pause, and by the late 1980s some of the more enlightened among them began looking for new solutions.

One of the well-known correlates of newspaper readership is sense of community.[11] As cities decayed at the central core while housing and retail business shifted to the suburbs, community feelings declined as well in most metropolitan areas. The prosperity of suburban media that Maisel noted suggests that the community sense did not vanish but changed in scale and locus. Some publishers began to suspect that for a large umbrella newspaper to survive, it would need to preserve, or even restore, the large-scale sense of community.

In 1989 James K. Batten, chairman and chief executive officer of Knight-Ridder, Inc., the second largest newspaper publishing company (in total circulation), called a meeting of his editorial writers to consider the problem of declining readership. John Gardner, the founder of Common Cause, was a guest speaker. "Newspaper readership is unlikely to turn upward as long as the sense of community continues downward," Gardner said.

"I believe their fate is linked. Newspapers have a stake in the sense of community." [12] In the view of CEO Batten, the decline in voting participation and the decline in readership were more than a coincidence. Strengthening the sense of community could restore both.

In Wichita, W. Davis Merritt, editor of the *Eagle*, had already conceptualized the problem. He saw "broken connections" between the people and policy outcomes:

> The political process, with the full acquiescence of journalists and others, has been hijacked and terribly distorted by the politicians and their handlers. For a couple of decades, our political coverage was suckered in by the thrill of the chase—the ballpark aspects of the election process. We let the politicians bypass the issues, and in the process, we and they together fostered the great frustration and cynicism of the people. [13]

In Merritt's vision of the new role for newspapers, journalists would not stop with reporting the facts and wait passively for somebody to act. They would engage the community in a discussion of its problems, like a town meeting on a large scale. This kind of conversation helps the narrowest groupings of interests find common ground and form larger groupings in which it is possible to give up some of one's original goal in exchange for the strength of the larger consensus. This aggregation of interests used to be one of the main functions of political parties. The newspaper's activism in promoting this process was also endorsed by the editor of the *Charlotte Observer*, who said the newspaper should be "the convener of the community" as well as its chronicler. [14]

These editors were not consciously trying to replace the functions of the fading political parties. But the interest-aggregation function was a logical part of the plan to regenerate large-scale community feeling. The *Wichita Eagle* had gone first with a concentrated effort to increase voter participation and clarify issues in the 1990 Kansas gubernatorial election. It repeated that effort in the 1992 elections and added a related effort, called the people project, that was a frank and self-conscious attempt to foster interest aggregation. Editor Merritt announced the people project in a column on June 21, 1992, with a confession. "We disparaged and dropped out of the political system," he said. "We . . . abandoned the broad concept of community."

The mechanism provided by the *Eagle* for restoring the sense of community was a joint project of the *Eagle*, a local TV station, KSNW, and a talk-format radio station, KNSS. The public was invited to interact with the media by telephone, by fax, in person, in letters to the editor, and by participating on the talk shows. The newspaper placed three related problems on the agenda: crime, education, and unresponsive government. It printed two full pages of the names and addresses of interest groups, agencies, and voluntary associations whose activities related to these problems. The same reporter who wrote about the problems to get the discussion going later wrote about the proposed solutions that emerged from all that discussion.

As an old medium, the newspaper business is tradition-bound, and these new concepts involved new behaviors and unfamiliar theoretical justifications. They were in direct conflict with the tradition of journalistic passivity. To journalists steeped in this tradition, the new activist stance smacked of boosterism, making the newspaper too much like the Chamber of Commerce. Newspaper publishers already were under attack by traditionalists for being too greedy and profit oriented to fulfill their public service obligations.[15] To some, the new activism, and its genesis in owners' concerns for fading profitability, confirmed this fear. And there was a history of pressure for social activism coming from the business side.

As far back as 1964 a high executive from the Newspaper Advertising Bureau, a trade association, had advanced the activist concept and been slapped down. Leo Bogart was an anomaly among newspaper executives. A sociologist by training, he maintained his academic credentials by publishing regularly in scholarly journals and serving actively in professional associations (including terms as president of both the American Association for Public Opinion Research and the World Association for Public Opinion Research). This background gave him a broader historical perspective than other newspaper executives seemed capable of attaining or even tolerating. He sounded an early warning about the coming effects of the decline of central cities on department store revenue and retail prospects generally and advised publishers to get involved in civic rebuilding. On two occasions in the mid-1960s Bogart proposed a conference of publishers and retailers on the problems of the cities. His peers thought he was being too academic. "What we need," he was told the second time he brought the idea up, "is less sociology and more selling." [16]

By 1992 the climate in the newspaper industry was far more favorable to change. To implement the new activism, structural changes were made in newsroom operations. At the *Charlotte Observer*, the election story was dispersed to a broad array of staff specialists, not just to the usual political reporters. For example, the education writer was assigned to compare the education policies of the candidates. The medical specialist worked on the health care issues of the campaign. This structural change is far more radical than it sounds. Newspapers are territorial institutions, with divisions created along subject lines, each presided over by its own desk of editors—the business desk, the metropolitan desk, the sports desk, the national desk, and so on. Editor Oppel assigned Rick Thames of the metro desk to coordinate election coverage and gave him the authority to cross territorial boundaries and assign stories to any department. Thames used his new clout to focus coverage on the substance of policy issues. Coverage of the tactics of the campaign was reduced in relative importance.

One obvious reason that policy issues often get little attention after the earliest days of a campaign is that candidates tend to get their positions on the table early. As the campaign progresses, the substance of these positions does not change and is therefore, by traditional definition, not news. But because campaign strategies and tactics do change, often dramatically, tactical coverage better fits the traditional definition. Both the *Observer* and the *Eagle* consciously broke with this tradition by looping back to policy matters repeatedly even when there was not enough of a new angle to justify such coverage by the old standards.[17]

These newspapers thus replaced the "what's new today" function with a reference function. And they adopted some typographical devices to reflect that change. Among them was the design of a policy grid along the lines of a TV viewing guide and with the same purpose: to enable a reader to navigate quickly to the small subsets of information on, say, a candidate's views on health care or tax policy that he or she most wanted to find without having to read a lot of unwanted material.

To make this process even more systematic, the *Observer* used a January 1992 public opinion poll to identify the policy problems most worrisome to its audience. Then it dealt with these problems week by week. To ensure that the policy grid would be seen, it was always placed on a Sunday section front—a position coveted by editors and advertisers for its high visibility. Readers were guided by pictures of candidates for various offices placed in little boxes with the candidates' explanations of what they would do about the problem of the day.

On the first such effort, on health policy, Sen. Terry Sanford refused to participate. The *Observer* ran his picture anyway, putting white space where his policy position was to have been outlined. After that, the senator never failed to provide his views.

Such an intense focus on policy can be troubling to traditional journalists. "There's a good deal of advocacy journalism involved here, advocacy on the part of the average citizen," observed Rick Thames in the middle of the campaign. "And a lot of [journalists], in the beginning, weren't comfortable with that. They worried about objectivity. But . . . you get beyond being a stenographer, and you say we want to be sure that candidates are listening to voters. So if you're an advocate at all, it's an advocate for the electorate." [18]

The newspaper production process is the product of two hundred years of evolution, and changing the work of the newsroom to affect content in a visible way is no small feat. Content analysis of the *Observer* and other North Carolina newspapers during the peak days of the campaign showed that the effort was effective. In the *Charlotte Observer*, policy issue coverage accounted for 25 percent of all election material in the front section, compared with 21 percent for the *Winston-Salem Journal* (which also had adopted a proissue plan), 14 percent for the *Raleigh News & Observer*, 12 percent for the *Greensboro News & Record*, and 3 percent for the *High Point Enterprise*. In its density of poll coverage, the *Observer* was at the bottom of the same list of newspapers: only 2 percent, compared with a median of 5 percent. (See Table 4-1.)

The *Charlotte Observer* and *Wichita Eagle* may have been the most systematic in their efforts to turn the system of election coverage around, but many of their tactics caught on with other newspapers as well. *USA Today*

Table 4-1 Coverage of Issues and Polls in Selected North Carolina Newspapers

Newspaper	Percentage of paragraphs
Issues	
Charlotte Observer	25%
Winston-Salem Journal	21
Wilmington Star	20
Asheville Citizen-Times	15
Raleigh News & Observer	14
Hendersonville Times-News	14
Sanford Herald	13
Burlington News	12
Greensboro News & Record	12
Shelby Star	10
Henderson Daily Dispatch	9
Concord Tribune	7
High Point Enterprise	3
Polls	
Winston-Salem Journal	10%
Asheville Citizen-Times	7
Shelby Star	7
Henderson Daily Dispatch	7
Burlington News	6
Concord Tribune	6
Wilmington Star	5
High Point Enterprise	5
Raleigh News & Observer	4
Hendersonville Times-News	3
Sanford Herald	3
Greensboro News & Record	3
Charlotte Observer	2

Source: Sue Greer, research in progress, University of North Carolina at Chapel Hill, 1992.

Note: Numbers show the proportion of paragraphs mentioning policy issues or polls in the front section of each newspaper.

had begun in the summer of 1991 to accept recorded telephone messages as letters to the editor, and it applied this technique in the campaign by asking readers to send in questions to be put to the presidential candidates. On eight major issues (selected on the basis of public opinion polling) more than five thousand readers participated. The candidates cooperated, and this "people's press conference" ran weekly from September 7 through November 2, the day before the election.

The new activism was also demonstrated across a variety of media in aggressive attempts to evaluate the truth of charges made in campaign speeches and political advertising. This "ad watch" format, as employed by such papers as the *New York Times*, the *Charlotte Observer*, and *USA Today*, attempted to warn readers of ambiguities, contradictions, and falsehoods in the candidates' messages.

For some editors, the theoretical justification for these reforms was a simplistic vision of elections as policy referenda. Others were motivated by a deeper understanding of the need for interest aggregation. Editors in the latter category could see the parallel with their own marketing efforts. When newspapers first systematically attempted to follow a marketing approach, they commissioned polls to determine their readers' needs and treated the results as a referendum. They quickly discovered that the referendum model was a poor fit to a product that appeals to many divergent and overlapping interests—the newspaper audience is made up not of an easily defined majority but rather of a complex mosaic of highly specialized minority reader interests. (Legend has it that the first editor to discover this was the one who dropped the crossword puzzle because only 8 percent of the readers used it. After the protests were heard and the puzzle restored, analysis revealed that the intensity of the puzzle's following makes it one of the most cost-efficient devices for binding readers to a paper.)

A modern polity is also a mosaic of specialized interests, any one of which might flunk the referendum test. For policy direction to emerge from this diversity, vertical communication between the voters and the policymakers is not enough. There also must be horizontal communication among the voters. That democratic archetype, the New England town meeting, performed just such a function. Representative bodies, with their horse-trading and logrolling devices to attain consensus, also depend on horizontal communication. Even single-issue groups can get a clearer picture of what they stand to gain or lose by attending to the needs of the rest of the community.

Editors with this more complicated agenda see themselves as promoting activities that can restore some of the spirit of the town meeting. If technology is to make democracy more direct, cross-talk among the citizenry is far more important than the technical ability to conduct an instant electronic referendum on any issue. And so some newspapers have continued their quest for innovation since the election. In Charlotte, for example, the *Observer* set up a computer bulletin board to continue the dialogue among varied interests. And the *Wichita Eagle* maintained its people project to promote the exchange of ideas across its community.

Broadcasting: The Rise of the Talk Shows

Paralleling the relative decline in newspaper readership has been the decline in the influence of the major television networks. More and more, viewership is shifting from the networks' broadly targeted offerings to the more specialized content of cable. David Broder's February 1991 message reached the networks, too, but not as swiftly.

In her study of political advertising in the 1980s, Montague Kern showed how political candidates controlled the issue agenda by coordinating their television advertising with staged events on the campaign trail.[19] That the "line of the day" approach continued in 1992 was evidenced when a network producer managed to confront Bill Clinton and ask him about his views on family-leave legislation. "You can't ask about family leave," a Clinton handler shouted. "Today we're talking about welfare." [20]

Leadership in taking back the agenda was offered by CNN with the help of a $3.5 million grant from the John and Mary R. Markle Foundation. The resulting expansion of campaign coverage included polls (with *USA Today*), critiques of political ads, and a grass-roots perspective that included a Larry King town meeting convened in Wichita with the help of the *Eagle*. The aim was to "present issues as voters see them." [21] By scheduling a daily half-hour summary of the campaign at 4:30 p.m., at just the time when decision makers at other media were forming their story budgets, CNN sought to maximize its leadership role.

The more activist media stance eventually diffused to the older networks. In the home stretch of the 1992 campaign, ABC anchor Peter Jennings announced a change of course: "We're aware that a lot of you are turned off by the political process and that many of you put at least some of the blame on us," he told viewers on September 9. The network's new policy: "We'll only devote time to a candidate's daily routine if it is more than routine. There will be less attention to staged appearances and sound bites designed exclusively for television." One of ABC's tactics, introduced that same evening, was to conduct focus groups of undecided voters. It also shifted resources from following the candidates around to doing analytical pieces and feature stories. Jennings vowed to be "less manipulated" by the candidates than in the past.[22]

An innovation at CBS News was a rule to avoid bumper-sticker-length sound bites by letting candidates express their views in twenty- to thirty-second units. NBC's contribution was a conscious effort to report critically on the staged candidate appearances. For example, pictures of President Bush standing statesmanlike with the president of Mexico and the Canadian prime minister while their representatives initialed the North American Free Trade Agreement were accompanied by the following narration: "Was this trip necessary? No, not really. The agreement was reached last summer and it won't be legal until the legislatures in each country accept it. But it gave the president a statesmanlike photo opportunity in a state he must carry: Texas." [23]

Critical coverage is not a new phenomenon. Tough talk by reporters to accompany pretty pictures of candidates has been found in past studies of the networks, and the reason is clear: the candidates supply the photo setting and the reporters try to balance it with realism.[24]

The nontraditional television media were less concerned about being manipulated by the candidates and more interested in providing them with an alternative route to voters who might otherwise be uninvolved. MTV political reporter Tabitha Soren got interviews with all three candidates, although to get an interview with President Bush she agreed not to ask questions about the Iran-contra affair.[25]

Soren came to MTV from an ABC affiliate in Vermont, where she had been a statehouse reporter. She was recruited by a news department that had been opened in 1984 to cover the music scene. The department began to turn serious in 1988 with coverage of policy issues relevant to its young audience, including abortion, drugs, and sexism in the music business. For the 1992 presidential campaign, MTV News inaugurated the "Choose or Lose" campaign to involve its audience with election news coverage, educational specials on how the system works, public service announcements, and polls.[26] Bill Clinton, less than two weeks after his appearance with Arsenio Hall, spent ninety minutes in a special MTV forum answering questions from an audience of eighteen- to twenty-four-year-olds. By the end of the campaign, Ross Perot and President Bush had followed his example.

The most visible television talk show forum, of course, was "Larry King Live," which fell into that role almost by accident. In a February interview with King, Perot said, offhandedly, that he would run for president if volunteers would put him on the ballot in all fifty states. By the end of the campaign, the three major candidates had made more than a dozen appearances on the King show.

Talk show audiences ask different questions from those asked by journalists. Mandy Grunwald, Clinton's innovative media consultant, got her candidate into the talk show business early to give him a boost in the New York primary. He appeared on the Phil Donahue show on April 1 and faced an extended series of aggressive questions from his host concerning marital infidelity and marijuana use. Donahue was in his journalist-as-tough-guy mode, but the members of his own studio audience shouted him down. They wanted to hear about policy issues. "What transpired in Donahue's studio was a sudden shift," wrote Jay Rosen, a journalism professor at New York University. "Rather than Donahue representing the audience's interests to Clinton, it became the audience representing its own interest." [27]

A very few journalists have objected to the talk show development by arguing that the public is not bright enough or aggressive enough to represent itself directly. Jonathan Yardley, writing in the *Washington Post*, called talk show participants "Americans on the margin: people with exaggerated grievances, people who have an excessive liking for the sound of their own voices, people with too much time on their hands.... These aren't the people who ought to be asking the questions." [28]

But more objective evaluations of the kinds of questions asked by journalists and talk show participants revealed a different view. Richard L. Berke of the *New York Times* reviewed hundreds of questions posed to the candidates by audience members and found "a striking difference" with reporters' questions: "Reporters dwell on the process, asking about polls, tactical strategy, and, of course, the story of the day. Questions from the public are far less confrontational, and an overwhelming number of people ask candidates how they would solve problems that would affect the questioner," such as getting jobs, paying for college, or finding health insurance.[29]

The public, not surprisingly, prefers questions from its peers. A Roper survey asked a national sample, "When political candidates appear on radio or television shows, which way do you think you get a better idea of them— when ordinary listeners call in and ask them questions or when regular newspeople ask them questions?" By two to one, ordinary listeners were favored over newspeople.[30]

There is "a new media order," notes Richard Harwood, former ombudsman for the *Washington Post*. And it "could be good for us all if it brings into the loop of American politics some of the millions of outsiders who are now non-participants and if it gets journalists off the stage and back into the audience where they belong." [31]

Political Advertising in Eclipse

A basic aphorism of marketing is that the greater the similarity between competing product brands, the more necessary it is to advertise. It is no accident that one sees so many ads for laundry products on daytime television: all laundry detergent is pretty much the same. In the absence of real distinctions, advertising is needed to "position" a product relative to its competition in the public's mind. In 1992 there were real differences between the candidates, in personality, background, and policy positions. That fact alone may be all that is necessary to explain why political advertising seemed less important than usual in 1992.

Ross Perot's thirty-minute "infomercials" were the exception. While most third-party candidates in the past have faded toward the end of the campaign, Perot gained points under the stimulus of his extended and self-financed advertising campaign. Simple and cheap to produce, his ads gained a respectable audience share. And they helped take him from single digits in the polls at the time of his reentry into the race on October 1 to 19 percent of the popular vote on election day.

The traditional thirty-second spot depends on emotion, not policy explanation. Advertising executive Jerry Della Femina gave the Bush team credit for invoking powerful emotion in ads that ran early and late in the campaign.[32] One spot showed dark clouds rolling across a gray, forbidding landscape that might have come from an Alfred Hitchcock movie, suggesting the unspeakable things that would happen under a Clinton administration. The main strength of Clinton's advertising team was its fast reaction time. Unlike Michael Dukakis in 1988, Clinton responded swiftly to Republican attack ads, getting specific counterattacks produced and on the air within a day or two. Meanwhile, radio was further developed as a "stealth medium for harsh attack ads." [33] Monitoring the competition in hundreds of local markets such as Topeka and Pocatello was difficult for national campaign managers, and they were less likely to answer such ads. News media were also less likely to take notice, and so the candidates' copy writers could get away with more outrageous material.

Polls: Beyond the Referendum Model

In their postcampaign seminars, journalists invariably berate themselves for paying too much attention to polls that merely tell who is ahead. A few reform-minded editors such as Charlotte's Rich Oppel actually made good on their promise to do better in 1992 and reported on fewer polls. One problem with reducing the number of polls, however, is that it increases the salience of those that survive. *USA Today* and CNN tried the opposite strategy: a fresh poll result on the presidential standings every day from September 30 to the election. That greatly reduced the risk of exaggerating the importance of any one day's results. Polling became part of the background, like the scoreboard at a basketball game. A spectator can glance at it or not, depending on whether its information is useful at the moment in providing context to the play on the court.

Nevertheless, the 1992 election was marked by complaints that, on election night at least, exit polls were interfering with the process. In this respect, it was no different from other recent elections.[34] The networks were, however, more restrained in announcing the winner than they had been in the past—so restrained, in fact, that candidate Ross Perot scooped them by announcing Clinton's victory at 10:30 p.m. eastern time, twenty minutes before the networks acknowledged it. "The network anchors stopped being reporters and became actors and civic teachers instead," complained one editorial page writer.[35] An early edition of the *Washington Post* was on the streets announcing the Clinton victory even as Dan Rather was telling his viewers that Clinton "does not have the assurance" of victory.

The networks created this false uncertainty in order to give TV watchers in the West who had not yet voted the illusion of potency. Westerners need this illusion, it is argued, in order to get themselves to the polls to vote for state and local candidates. In fact, the evidence that early calls reduce turnout is slim, and the effect, if any, is slight.[36] Moreover, democratic theory does not demand that state and local elections be decided by people who care so little that they cannot be motivated to vote by interest in those races alone.

Preelection polls also are sometimes criticized for causing bandwagon or underdog effects, undermining "the democratic process of allowing individuals to vote with their own minds."[37] Clearly, the public believes in such effects.[38] The simplest (and least credible) version of the theory is that some people will vote for the front-runner in the polls because they want to side with the majority. Or they will vote for the person trailing in the polls out of sympathy. More complex motivations are possible. A person who saw Clinton leading in the polls might have voted for a Republican senator to keep a Democratic executive in check—or for a Democratic senator to end Washington gridlock. A person seeing his or her first choice trailing in the polls might choose to give up on that candidate and cast a symbolic vote for a third-party candidate. Empirical evidence of any of these effects is quite scarce.

Other effects of preelection polls are more obvious. A low standing in the polls can discourage a candidate's potential contributors, campaign volunteers, and endorsers.[39] A high standing can make a candidate overconfident. The effects are exaggerated if those affected by them are unskilled at interpreting poll data, unaware of the fluidity of campaign standings or unmindful of the proincumbent bias in early polls, which mostly measure name recognition. The problem in such cases is not with the polls but with their misuse.

And polls are misused. Public opinion seems to be such a simple and intuitively comfortable concept that it deceptively appears to need no examination. George Gallup may have been partly to blame. For years, he promoted his poll as an ongoing national referendum on policy issues.[40] The idea of merging electronic technology and polling techniques for national referenda continues to be raised frequently by people who seem credible enough—including Ross Perot, who proposed it as a tool to break government gridlock. Many futurists, like John Naisbitt, are enamored of this old idea.[41]

If referenda are the answer to the problems of democracy, then California, with its many ballot initiatives, ought to be problem free. In fact, many of the state's recent problems can be traced to the ease of getting measures on the ballot, so that each issue is voted up or down independently of all the others, and to the number of issues, which is so great that few can be expected to understand everything they are voting on. The cumulative effect of referenda that mandate expenditures—on widely separated occasions— has been blamed for the state's inability to find the resources to meet new needs.[42] Power belongs not so much to the people who vote on these issues as to those who get them on the ballot and determine the wording of the questions.

The public good is not necessarily the sum of all the particles of individual wants. Most of us want contradictory things: reduced taxes and more government services, personal freedom and social control. Public policy formation requires discussion and horse trading. The best use of public opinion measurement is not to find out what the majority wants on any given issue and then retire as if nothing more needed to be said. Its best use is to give groups and individuals information about each other so that they can "consider their respective and collective wants and possibly modify them" to achieve what Craig Calhoun calls "large-scale societal integration."[43]

Because of the widespread obsession with the problem of how the public can communicate its views to the policymakers, it is easy to forget the importance of communication between subsets of the polity. Well-managed media polls can foster such communication. When the *Miami Herald* followed up on a survey of its black population at the peak of the civil rights movement of the 1960s, it found that the published poll had such an effect. The poll revealed widespread support for the nonviolent tactics of Martin Luther King, Jr., and only token backing for the proviolence activists who were being thrust into the spotlight by the national media at that time.

Discussion of the poll findings affected even those who had not read the newspaper. For example, a sixteen-year-old heard the polls discussed at school. "Our class is integrated . . . quite a few whites . . . I was surprised to see that many people thought the way I thought." And a working mother said, "I was surprised to find that I thought more like even some of what I would call militants, that I thought along certain lines they thought . . . to the extent that they would push, I wouldn't push, but . . . after reading some of the reasoning behind the way they thought about certain things, I agreed." [44]

Such polls of special populations, if carefully managed, can make an obvious contribution to large-scale societal integration. It might be argued that election campaign horse race polls are trivial by comparison and that resources should be directed from that effort to the more interesting special populations. But horse race polls have a redeeming virtue of their own, one that may be underestimated: they help keep the debate interesting. In 1992 Xinshu Zhao and Glen L. Bleske tested this hypothesis in two ways. They looked at poll data and found that people who paid attention to the horse race findings of the polls were more interested in the election—even after the effects of education and voting participation were held constant. The researchers verified the effect in a controlled laboratory experiment.[45]

In multicandidate races, polls are also a reasonable way to track the viability of competing candidates and to help voters consider and modify their wants so that they can try to maximize the utility of voting. A candidate who is the first choice of a few but the second choice of many can gain viability if polls reveal that the first choices are distributed widely across a large field. Something like that may have happened to Paul Tsongas in the 1992 New Hampshire primary. After early polls showed that he stood higher in the rankings than many believed, he climbed to first. Because of the polls, a rational voter whose first choice was, say, Jerry Brown but who would prefer Tsongas if Brown had no chance could make use of the information that Brown was running last and Tsongas was close to the top. Knowing how others feel helps a voter move toward consensus in a constructive, reasonable way. That is no mindless bandwagon effect; it is sophisticated consensus formation.

Even complaining California voters can benefit from early network projections of the national vote. If those projections show the vote to be close, the TV anchors can use the information to motivate California to turn out. (Provided, of course, that the networks can be trusted not to lie. Their election night reticence in 1992 may put them at the same disadvantage as the boy who cried "wolf." When an election really is close, who will believe them?) Even the news that California's vote will not make a difference in the presidential election can add an element of efficacy for a Californian. Knowing that Clinton had won, one might reasonably have cast a vote for Ross Perot, knowing that it would be read as a protest against the mainstream parties but without the danger that it would actually lead to the voluble Texan's election. Tactical voting, decried by some political scientists,[46] can actually be a form of political communication.

In sum, the editors in Charlotte were right to abandon journalistic passivity to the extent that they resolved to follow through on their reporting, including polling on policy issues, and convene citizens' groups and promote action. But their rejection of traditional horse race polling may work against them by depriving the audience of one sure-fire generator of excitement and interest.

Was It an Aberration?

The campaign of 1992 deserves to be recalled as one that the media resolved to cover differently—and for once followed through and did cover differently. That the campaign turned more on issues and less on personalities than usual was documented by Sue Greer in a secondary analysis of two *USA Today* polls, one in early September 1988 and the other in the same period of the 1992 campaign. Both polls contained scalable items asking respondents to assess the candidates on personal or character dimensions and on their policy direction. In 1988 personality explained two and a half times as much variance in voting preference as did policy issues. But in the 1992 campaign the difference was sharply reversed. The policy evaluation of the candidates explained seven times as much variance as did the personality dimension.[47]

Will the reforms persist? Grounds for optimism exist. Journalists tend to imitate one another. Moreover, there are signs that technology-driven structural changes in the way campaigns are conducted are forcing newspaper editors to try policy coverage in order to define their market niche against their real competitors, local TV news. The *Winston-Salem Journal* had a policy density in its coverage almost as great as the *Charlotte Observer's*, and its program was based more on a tactical response to the campaign than on an overarching strategy like the *Observer's*. The pace of the campaign was so fast, with candidates acting and reacting to events and a new fax hitting the editor's desk every few minutes, that Winston-Salem editors decided that print could not compete with broadcast media in event-based coverage. That forced the *Journal* into a theme-based plan of coverage that concentrated on policy issues.[48] This faster pace of communication, spurred by cellular telephones, electronic bulletin boards, portable computers, and fax machines, can put every reporter and every candidate into what Everette Dennis has called a "virtual newsroom," no matter where he or she may physically be.[49] It is a permanent structural change for campaigns and their coverage.

On the other hand, the most important variable of all in explaining strategies for media coverage may be the issue environment of each campaign. The shift toward policy coverage in 1992 may have had more to do with the state of the nation than with any new behavior on the part of the media. The overwhelming power of the economic issue forced both the media and the candidates to focus on it. A sterner test of the new media forms will have to await a campaign that is less dominated by an overriding issue.

Notes

1. James Madison, Federalist No. 10, in *The Federalist Papers by Alexander Hamilton, James Madison, and John Jay,* ed. Gary Wills (New York: Bantam Books, 1982), 47.
2. The 1968 Democratic convention created the Commission on Party Structure and Delegate Selection, also known as the McGovern commission, after its first chair, George McGovern.
3. Gary R. Orren and William G. Mayer, "The Press, Political Parties, and the Public-Private Balance in Elections," in *The Parties Respond: Changes in the American Party System* (Boulder: Westview Press, 1990); Thomas Patterson, "The Press and Its Missed Assignment," in *The Elections of 1988,* ed. Michael Nelson (Washington, D.C.: CQ Press, 1988).
4. John Bare, work in progress, School of Journalism and Mass Communication, University of North Carolina at Chapel Hill, 1992.
5. David Broder, "A New Assignment for the Press," *Press-Enterprise* Lecture Series, no. 26, University of California, Riverside, Feb. 12, 1991.
6. For dissents from the policy government model, see Nelson Polsby and Aaron Wildavsky, *Presidential Elections,* 8th ed. (New York: Free Press, 1991). See also Jean Bethke Elshtain, "Issues and Themes in the 1988 Campaign," in Nelson, *Elections of 1988.*
7. David Weaver and G. Cleveland Wilhoit, "The American Journalist in the 1990s: A Preliminary Report of Key Findings from a 1992 Survey of U.S. Journalists" (Freedom Forum, Arlington, Va., Nov. 17, 1992).
8. Richard Maisel, "The Decline of Mass Media," *Public Opinion Quarterly* 37 (1973): 159-170.
9. *El Nuevo Herald* is a Spanish-language newspaper distributed at no extra cost to *Miami Herald* subscribers who request it.
10. These numbers are from the National Opinion Research Center, University of Chicago. All but the 1967 figures come from the General Social Survey.
11. Keith Stamm, *Newspaper Use and Community Ties: Toward a Dynamic Theory* (Norwood, N.J.: Ablex, 1985).
12. "Newspapers, Community and Leadership: A Symposium on the Editorial Pages" (Miami: Knight-Ridder, November 1989).
13. W. Davis Merritt, "A New Political Contract Must Restore Meaning to Election Campaigns," *Wichita Eagle,* Nov. 13, 1988, 3B. Ideas expressed there were later elaborated in Merritt's speech, quoted here, "Why Telling the News Is Not Enough," on Sept. 16, 1992, to community leaders and Knight-Ridder editors who gathered in Wichita for the Larry King town meeting broadcast.
14. Rich Oppel, The Ralph McGill Lecture, Emory University, Atlanta, Feb. 13, 1992.
15. For example, Bill Kovach, The Fourteenth Annual Frank E. Gannett Lecture, Washington Journalism Center, Washington, D.C., Nov. 20, 1991.
16. Leo Bogart, *Preserving the Press* (New York: Columbia University Press, 1991), 43.
17. In the case of the *Charlotte Observer,* the new approach was promoted and partially funded by the Poynter Institute for Media Studies of St. Petersburg, Fla.

18. Rick Thames, interview with Carol Reese Dykers, Charlotte, N.C., Jan. 28, 1992.
19. Montague Kern, *Thirty-Second Politics: Political Advertising in the Eighties* (New York: Praeger, 1989). See also W. Lance Bennett, *The Governing Crisis: Media, Money, and Marketing in American Elections* (New York: St. Martin's, 1992).
20. James M. Perry, "Caution Rules in Clinton's Campaign, and, So Far, It Hasn't Hurt His Lead," *Wall Street Journal*, Sept. 24, 1992, A18.
21. "The People's Agenda," News release, Turner Broadcasting System, Dec. 23, 1991.
22. Howard Kurtz, "Media Alter Approach to Campaign Coverage: ABC to Play Down Staged Events, Sound Bites," *Washington Post*, Sept. 11, 1992, A10.
23. Alan L. Otten, "TV News Drops Kid-Gloved Coverage of Election, Trading Staged Sound Bites for Hard Analysis," *Wall Street Journal*, Oct. 12, 1992, A12.
24. "Study Finds Differences Among Four Networks in Coverage of 1992 Presidential Campaign," Press release, John F. Kennedy School of Government, Harvard University, Aug. 31, 1992.
25. Leslie Phillips, "Hep Cats," *USA Today*, Nov. 2, 1992, 7A.
26. Dirk Smillie and Martha McKay, "MTV News and 'Choose or Lose,' " in *The Homestretch: New Politics, New Media, New Voters*, by the Research Group of the Freedom Forum Media Studies Center (New York: Freedom Forum Media Studies Center, 1992).
27. Jay Rosen, "Discourse," *Columbia Journalism Review*, November-December 1992, 35.
28. Jonathan Yardley, "Campaign '92: Can We Talk?" *Washington Post*, Oct. 12, 1992, D2.
29. Richard L. Berke, "Why Candidates Like Public's Questions," *New York Times*, Aug. 15, 1992, 7.
30. Press release, *Columbia Journalism Review*, Oct. 28, 1992.
31. Richard Harwood, "The Waning Power of the Press," *Presstime*, Aug. 1992, 25.
32. Jerry Della Femina, "CBS Morning News," Nov. 3, 1992.
33. Kathleen H. Jamieson, "CBS Morning News," Nov. 3, 1992.
34. Paul J. Lavrakas and Jack K. Holley, eds., *Polling and Presidential Election Coverage* (Newbury Park, Calif.: Sage, 1991).
35. Joe Urschel, "Hide 'n' Seek with the News," *USA Today*, Nov. 5, 1992, 18A.
36. The evidence is examined in Lavrakas and Holley, *Polling and Presidential Election Coverage*.
37. Alison Alexander and Jarice Hanson, *Taking Sides* (Guilford, Conn.: Dushkin, 1992), 194.
38. Michael W. Traugott, "Public Attitudes About News Organizations, Campaign Coverage, and Polls," in Lavrakas and Holley, *Polling and Presidential Election Coverage*, 134-150.
39. Richard L. Henshel and William Johnston, "The Emergence of Bandwagon Effects: A Theory," *Sociological Quarterly* (1987): 493-511.
40. George Gallup, *The Sophisticated Poll-Watcher's Guide* (Princeton: Princeton Opinion Press, 1972).
41. John Naisbitt, *Megatrends* (New York: Warner, 1982).
42. Nelson W. Polsby and Aaron Wildavsky, *Presidential Elections: Contemporary Strategies of American Electoral Politics* (New York: Free Press, 1991).
43. For an articulate critique of the role of referenda in democracy, see Craig Calhoun, "Populist Politics, Communications Media, and Large Scale Societal Integration," *Sociological Theory* (1988): 219-241.
44. Philip Meyer, "Aftermath of Martyrdom: Negro Militancy and Martin Luther King," *Public Opinion Quarterly* 33 (1969): 160-173.
45. Xinshu Zhao and Glen L. Bleske, research in progress, University of North Carolina at Chapel Hill, 1992.
46. For example, Michael Traugott, "Marketing the Presidency: Is There a Tyranny of Media Polls?" *Gannett Center Journal*, Fall 1988, 60.

47. Sue Greer, "Evaluating an Alternative Model for Coverage of a Presidential Election: The Case of the *Charlotte Observer*" (Unpublished paper, University of North Carolina at Chapel Hill, 1992).
48. Joe Goodman, telephone interview with the author, Nov. 13, 1992.
49. Everette E. Dennis, "Introduction: The Homestretch," in *The Homestretch: New Politics, New Media, New Voters*.

5

Issues and Themes:
Spiral of Delegitimation or New Social Covenant?

Jean Bethke Elshtain

*Almost all political analysts, including most of the contributors
to this book, have treated the elections of 1992 as being primarily
about economic issues. President Bush's performance on the economy
disappointed the voters, who were not diverted by his attempts to
invoke cultural issues and foreign policy; Governor Clinton's promises for economic reform pleased them; and Perot held both major-
party candidates' feet to the fire, especially on the budget deficit—or
so the argument goes.*

*Jean Bethke Elshtain takes a different view. She regards the
public discontent with the economy in 1992 as just one aspect of a
national "spiral of delegitimation" that has its origins in widespread
cynicism about government and politics, excessive individualism, a
pervasive sense of powerlessness, and other cultural phenomena. She
bemoans the lack of public concern for foreign affairs at a time when
events in the world press hard upon the conscience and self-interest
of the United States. Elshtain concludes by calling upon President
Clinton to take seriously his rhetoric about a "new covenant" that
will bind Americans together with a renewed sense of citizenship
and competence.*

Stalemate. Gridlock. Cynicism. American politics is a miasma, so argue
many experts, journalists, and ordinary citizens. Rather than Abraham
Lincoln's "last best hope on earth," America seems to embody more and
more the worst of what a liberal democratic regime can become. "Nothing
seems to get done." "Politicians just lie to us anyway." "It's all about who
has power. Nobody cares what we think." Growing cynicism about politics
and its possibilities—one important book published in 1991 said it all in the
title, *Why Americans Hate Politics*—promotes a spiral of delegitimation.

How does the spiral of delegitimation get a society in its grip? Over a
period of time, a "culture of mistrust" grows, aided and abetted by scandals
(Watergate and all the little Watergate-type scandals since), a press that
feeds off scandals, and a public that seems insatiable in its appetite for
scandal (even as it berates scandal mongering by the media); by an ever
more litigious society; by declining levels of public trust and a determination

to "get mine" no matter what may happen to the other guy; by unresponsive incumbents who seem more interested in returning to Washington than in serving their constituents; by salacious snooping into the private lives of public figures, which further fuels cynicism about how untrustworthy our leaders are even as we delight in their downfall. This, in part, is the story Suzanne Garment tells in her depressing volume, *Scandal.*[1] That public figures sink lower and lower in our estimation further delegitimates politics and justifies our deepening cynicism about this scandal-ridden land.

E. J. Dionne's *Why Americans Hate Politics* offers yet another story of what has gone awry. According to Dionne, both liberals and conservatives are failing America. He laments in particular a "false polarization" in American politics that is cast in the form of a cultural civil war, the dynamic of which creates what might be called gridlock. Liberal Democrats wish to tame the logic of the market in economic life but allow a nearly untrammeled laissez faire in cultural and sexual life—in the latter realm individual rights are trumps. Thus, for example, one cannot, in the liberal scheme of things, permit any regulation or restriction of abortion on demand but one can and must constrain the unbridled individualism of economic exchange and transfer. Conservative Republicans present a precise mirror image—a story of constraints and controls in the cultural and sexual sphere but a nearly unconstrained economic market. These competing partisan logics not only cancel each other out, but they also gather round them, like so many burrs on a Tennessee coon hound, determined clumps of clienteles that feed happily off the status quo, thus making it tremendously difficult for politicians who might want to break out of ideological deadlock to do so.[2]

A third perceptive analysis of America's recent political travail is *Chain Reaction*, the account by Thomas Byrne Edsall and Mary D. Edsall of (as the subtitle tells it) "the impact of race, rights, and taxes on American politics." [3] The Edsalls, who appear to have been wrong in their particular conclusion that the Republicans had a lock on the White House for the foreseeable future, nonetheless unpack a larger conundrum that will not disappear any time soon. Theirs is a story of how, over the years, long shopping lists of programs targeted specifically at black and underclass Americans lost legitimacy. Those who paid most of the bills—lower middle class inner-city ethnic whites, middle-class suburban whites—not only saw no benefit flowing from such programs to the polity as a whole (as they were presented with evidence of growing welfare dependency, crime, out-of-wedlock births, and the like) but saw instead a pattern of unfair redistribution of forms of assistance to people who were not as committed as they were to following the rules of the game, paying the price for one's actions, and not expecting government to bear one's burdens. This, at least, is a widespread conviction.

In other words, the Edsalls argue, programs that are targeted to particular populations have lost legitimacy—a legitimacy accorded almost automatically to such universal programs as Social Security. Expanding networks of government agencies have become receptive, notes the historian Hugh Davis

Graham, to more "aggressive, results-centered methods. . . . Following the traditional practice of clientele capture, whereby interest groups seek a dominant voice in programs and agencies that enter their turf . . . the minority constituencies—especially African Americans and, in bilingual programs, Hispanics—rapidly dominated the new civil rights bureaucracies." [4] The debate about social policy that the Edsalls call for has yet to occur: the 1992 presidential debates only muddied the waters on this question, despite Clinton's rather anemic calls for a "new covenant." I will return to this theme in the conclusion, for if a robust version of a new social covenant is in fact not in the offing, American politics will continue to be dominated by a series of entanglements, deadlocks, and narrow interest group, clientele-dominated policy entrenchments. The Edsalls concluded:

> At stake is the American experiment itself, endangered by a rising tide of political cynicism and alienation, and by basic uncertainties as to whether or not we are capable of transmitting a sense of inclusion and shared citizenship across an immense and diverse population—whether or not we can uphold our traditional commitment to the possibilities for justice and equality expressed in our founding documents and embedded in our most valued democratic institutions.[5]

It is perhaps worth noting that the growth in American cynicism about government shifts America toward, not away from, a more generalized norm. Most people in other societies are somewhat cynical about government, including those in the democracies of Western Europe. As James Q. Wilson points out, Americans "are less optimistic and less trusting than we once were. And rightly so: if Washington says that we should entrust it to educate our children, to protect our environment, and to regulate our economy, we would be foolish not to be cautious and skeptical." [6] The problem, according to Wilson, is that government has become less effective, not so much as a result of its size per se but because government since the 1960s has taken on more and more issues that it is simply ill-equipped to handle well—abortion and race relations, to name but two of the most volatile. Too many such "wedge issues" were created, not by cynical demagogues, as some pundits like to insinuate, but by well-meaning federal judges and courts who made decisions in the 1960s and 1970s on a whole range of cultural questions without due consideration of how public support for the mandated outcomes might be generated.

Government itself, then, importantly though not exclusively through its judicial arm, "having embarked on policies that inevitably raise the most profound philosophical issues, has necessarily called forth an intense ideological debate over the ends sought and the means deployed." [7] We have effectively guaranteed that government cannot work. In a civic world riven by cultural wars generated from decisions made by judicial fiat, such as *Roe v. Wade*, one cannot simply put things right similarly to the way that government in an earlier era was able, say, to build the world's greatest interstate highway system. As ideologically driven clientele groups grow in importance, the political parties wither on the vine. Politicians become beholden not to a party institution before which they can be called to account but to the contributors to their particular campaign coffers and, most important, to their own entrepreneurial skills at retailing themselves to the voters from one election to the next. The spiral of delegitimation thus is powerfully manifest and will not disappear any time soon.

Those who assert that the cultural questions somehow got put behind us in 1992 because economic matters were first and foremost the issues and themes of the presidential election are pushing an illusory hope. The cultural questions—abortion, family values, drugs, and race relations—were all joined in 1992, often in language that underscored just how much people of all political persuasions still look to government as the remedy for every ill, personal and political. The problem with such reliance is this: democratic politics can reasonably offer hope, but it cannot promise deliverance. Yet deliverance, a dramatic and rapturous sea change to bring in the new and sweep out the old and corrupt, is what loud voices and dominant groups on both the left and the right seek. The very gridlock that the two major parties and Ross Perot's angry, antiparty protesters all decried is generated by their own actions in promising deliverance and in deepening cultural cleavages rather than alleviating them by removing some questions from government's purview, or at least from government's control as the final arbiter.[8] Despite rejoicing from media pundits about a postelection restoration of faith in government, the "return of the Reagan Democrats" to the Democratic fold, and the upsurge in "women's issues," as if all of this betokened a return to some long-lost Democratically dominated sanity, the harsh truth of the matter is that voters are volatile, angry, and deeply disaffected. One comedian captured the mood immediately after the election by doing monologues on "the failed Clinton administration." With this backdrop in mind, I offer a critical interpretive analysis of the issues and themes of the 1992 elections, encouraging readers to debate these and other matters further.

The Economy: What Do People Want?

In the immediate postelection afterglow, President-elect Clinton declared that he would "focus like a laser beam on this economy" and "foreign policy will come into play in part as it affects the economy." [9] Because of a stubborn economic downturn and his broken promise ("read my lips") not to raise taxes, President Bush was vulnerable on the economic issues during the campaign, and candidates Clinton and Perot fully exploited this vulnerability. The economy appears to have been Bush's Achilles' heel—that and his dispirited campaign. But the economy may prove to be President Clinton's *bête noire* as well for this reason: most people do not vote their economic self-interests as narrowly defined.[10] Rather, they vote out of confidence or apprehension about how the economy as a whole is doing: Are things getting worse for the country or getting better? And this assessment takes place against a backdrop of promises made or kept by the president. Bush failed to keep a highly visible promise on taxes, and this failure, combined with the anemic performance of the economy, did him in. Clinton will be able to take advantage of the recovery that was already under way at the time of his election, but he too may become the prisoner of his own promises.

During the campaign, with Bush vulnerable and Perot threatening, Clinton offered up a shopping list of economic remedies and desiderata: a substantially reduced budget deficit, urban renewal, enhanced productivity, job training, investment in infrastructure (especially transportation and construction), family and medical leave, a comprehensive health care program, defense downsizing and conversion to civilian industries, and information technologies. To pay for all these programs, Clinton promised he would generate $300 billion over five years by raising taxes on foreign corporations that do business in the United States, raising the income tax rates on those earning $200,000 or more a year, increasing fines on delinquent taxpayers and on corporate polluters, and cutting defense and other spending.

Before the election both Bush and Perot insisted that Clinton could not generate sufficient revenues to underwrite his ambitious economic programs; after the election the Clinton forces themselves admitted that they might have to increase the deficit "short term" and that spending plans might have to be reduced to the level of available revenues. Otherwise, Clinton would be forced to raise the tax burden on that loosely defined entity, the middle class, to whom he pitched his campaign rhetoric—calling them the beleaguered backbone of the country. Talk during the Clinton transition period revolved around the rhetoric of "no quick fixes," clearly an attempt to set the stage so that public disappointment would not curdle into anti-Clinton "negatives."

Having won the election on economic discontent, the Clinton team was worried about the unrestrained campaign promises and the expectations they may have created for a miracle recovery, a promise the voters may take all the more seriously because it was coupled to another: the promise to end gridlock by having the legislative and executive branches dominated by one party. With gridlock ended (in favor of the Democrats) the electorate is likely to be impatient, especially since "change" is the main thing Clinton promised. "Change" also is the slogan that was trumpeted all over *USA Today* and the sensationalist press the day after the election: "Now, Voters Expect 'Changes,'" "Senate's New Women," "Change Is Afoot," "Landslide: A Clarion Call for Our Country," and the like. All the constituencies that, rightly or wrongly, felt shortchanged or aggrieved during the Bush years are waiting impatiently for their "rightful due."

Five days after the election, Jesse Jackson "led a group of about 150 prominent advocates for minorities, women, and other political groups in celebrating Bill Clinton's victory and in urging that the new administration make good on the candidate's promise on a variety of economic and social issues." [11] Jackson insisted that public pressure would be required to guarantee that the Clinton administration followed through on the entire menu of jobs programs, education, health care, and "civil rights matters." The last phrase, in Jackson's repertoire, means racial quotas in all levels of industry, government, and education, as well as other highly visible—and divisive—programs. This agenda is more a picture of a fractious free-for-all than of a new social covenant.

Is this picture of the situation Clinton faces too bleak? Probably not, given the force of the spiral of delegitimation. It is important to remember that Clinton's popular vote was well under 50 percent and that one big reason for this was the astonishingly successful candidacy of Ross Perot, whose 19 percent of the popular vote was the highest of any independent or third-party candidate since Theodore Roosevelt ran on the Progressive party ticket in 1912. With the largest increase in turnout in forty years (55.2 percent of eligible voters went to the polls in 1992, in contrast to barely 50.1 percent in 1988), Perot benefited heavily. Postelection studies suggest that about 15 percent of Perot's voters would have stayed home had Perot not been on the ballot.[12] Some might argue that such voters, having been drawn into the campaign by Perot's promise to balance the budget and end the deficit, will stay involved and become more content as Clinton moves to fix things. But what was most salient about the Perot campaign was less his specific economic proposals than the widespread anger with the system to which his candidacy was a response. In turn, Perot's success probably will fuel, not abate, the public's anger as the predictable course that presidents follow of satisfying only some of the people some of the time stretches out over the next four years.

Americans seek rough-and-ready fairness. But particular constituencies construe fairness as getting "their" entitlements because those in group X, Y, or Z got theirs. As one Clinton aide put it, "Labor, minorities, environmentalists, blacks, Hispanics, women, retired people, you name it, all see the pot of gold at the end of the rainbow. And somebody is going to be very disappointed." [13] With various Democratic constituencies holding his feet to the fire and with Republicans able to point out, over and over again, that 57 percent of the electorate did *not* vote for Clinton, gridlock on economic policy looms. (Indeed, Clinton's vote percentage—43 percent—is the fourth lowest of anyone ever elected president.) In those areas in which the president can take the lead and Congress can take action, Clinton will find himself entangled immediately in the most divisive and troubling issues of our time: racial and gender preferences in hiring, control of entitlement programs for the elderly, stricter surveillance of workplace conduct to enforce the intensely politicized definition of sexual harassment that began with the Clarence Thomas hearings and fueled the "Year of the Woman," and the like.

In practice, economic issues bleed into other issues. Clinton's hope to get a smooth start by concentrating exclusively on economic questions and on foreign policy only to the extent that it involves the economy seems naïve. It will take extraordinary political skills of maneuvering and conciliation for him to put together coalitions and forge workable compromises in Congress. To do so may well put him on a collision course with one or more of the Democratic party's most uncompromising constituencies. As Thomas Edsall points out,

> Insofar as liberal programs create real or perceived conflicts between essential Democratic constituencies—pitting against each other black and white civil service workers seeking promotion, for example, or black parents against Hispanic parents—the losers in each conflict may be recruited by the opposition party. Insofar as liberal programs involve affirmative action or programs to support the nonworking parents of illegitimate children, the conflicts they arouse become all the more intense.[14]

Questions of affirmative action and quotas are murky and unresolved. Clinton won the election by drawing together constituencies—notably Reagan Democrats and African Americans—that are deeply divided by such questions. Can he, as seems to have been his favored modus operandi as governor of Arkansas, finesse the matter—giving just enough to each constituency to keep it in the fold? Single parents, whether divorced or never married mothers on welfare, gave Clinton a margin of twenty points. Can Clinton continue to insist, as he did during the campaign, on "responsibility" and not be construed by welfare mothers and their leaders as "punishing the poor"? All of this remains to be seen. The most salient point, for the purpose of this essay, is that economic questions are not reducible to charts and graphs on housing starts, unemployment figures, and inflation rates; instead, these questions involve most of the inflammatory wedge issues of this country's cultural wars. To be sure, 43 percent of the voters may have named the economy as their paramount concern on election day—twice the percentage identifying any other issue as most determinative of how they voted.[15] But this datum alone doesn't give us very much specific information.

The exit polls also revealed that 54 percent of those who, when asked on election day whether a Clinton victory would make them feel excited, optimistic, concerned, or scared, said they would be apprehensive.[16] In light of that uneasiness, how Clinton and his forces parse the economy and sort out the seething mass of hopes, dreams, and fears infused within that single generic category will not only determine his political fate in 1996 but will also reveal something more fundamental—that is, whether the United States will enter the next century with the spiral of delegitimation whirling ever downward into a cynicism and hopelessness that may get translated into calls for a political savior (if not Perot then a comparable figure) or, alternatively, whether the civic bleeding will, at least partially, have been staunched. It is premature, to say the least, to sign on to Democratic chairman Ronald H. Brown's postelection euphoria: "It's a new day . . . a watershed election." [17]

The Issue That Was Not:
America and the World

One of the themes that stayed deeply in the background of the 1992 elections, despite Republican attempts to put it on the front burner, was foreign policy. Foreign policy was dead last on the list of voter concerns and, among those 8 percent to whom it was a vital issue, President Bush received 87 percent of the vote. Does this lack of interest in nondomestic affairs represent a salutary focus on the issues that plague American society or an isolationist insouciance that ill suits us in an ever more interdependent and fragile world? The answer is probably a muddy admixture of both. Bush was out of the loop for too long on domestic matters. What should have been two sure-fire political winners for him—the victory in the Persian Gulf war and the end of the Cold War—faded into the background of economic gloom, and with them went any sustained discussion during the campaign of the world beyond our shores.

It is undeniably the case, however, that although we may not be interested in foreign policy, foreign policy is interested in us. As I write this essay, the United States has committed some 28,000 troops to a U.N. effort to guarantee the delivery of humanitarian food relief in Somalia, Middle East peace talks are stalled, apprehension about nuclear stockpiles in the former Soviet Union grows, and the situation in Bosnia and Herzegovina goes from grave to desperate. Five days after the election, in an article headlined "Problems Abroad May Force Clinton to Alter Agenda," the *New York Times* described how "a series of problems abroad could force [Clinton] to devote much more time than he had planned to foreign policy." [18] To avoid being hoist by his own campaign petard, Clinton moved immediately to modify his previously harsh stance toward China, presumably to avoid a nasty confrontation with Beijing when China's favored-nation trade status comes up for review in June 1993. He is, in other words, seeking continuity and stability in foreign affairs and quickly moving to depoliticize the very issues he himself had politicized during the campaign. Scaling back the rhetoric is the easy part. Far more difficult will be figuring out what shape the "new world order" ought to take in the post-Cold War era.

Why did foreign policy recede as a public concern during the election, and what does this say about campaign 1992? For foreign leaders it sent troubling signals about a possible American retreat from the world. In the Middle East there was widespread anxiety about the fate of the peace talks. NATO leaders feared that Clinton might make good on his campaign promise to reduce American troop strength with dramatic rapidity and by half again as much as was proposed by Bush. In Eastern Europe, where the Reagan-Bush foreign policies are widely credited with having brought about the breakup of the Soviet Union, consternation over Bush's defeat was widespread: Poland's president, Lech Walesa, had gone so far as to endorse Bush's reelection. The Russians are worried that the amount of American assistance they are receiving will be cut, even though their situation is desperate, with President Boris Yeltsin's hold on power ever more precarious.

There is little doubt that Clinton's resolve will be tested by one or more international crises in the early years of his administration. There is little doubt, as well, that he will try to make good on his pledge of continuity in American foreign policy. But can he convince his fellow Americans of their need to stay involved and to bear a continuing burden for world affairs? Convincing them will be tricky in light of his own preparedness to play to protectionist and isolationist sentiment during the campaign. But he only played to it—he did not make it a centerpiece of his efforts. He can back off rather easily, but how can Americans stay in the arena if, in fact, they think the situation in the United States is as dire as the Democrats portrayed it in 1992? Are there real trade-offs to be made between foreign policy and domestic concerns, or is the conflict more apparent than real? To this question there is no definitive response. But it does seem clear that Americans are groping for a sense of how best to be engaged internationally now that communism is no more.

All the postwar presidents framed and justified U.S. international commitments by reminding people of the threat from the Soviet Union, whether as a "revisionist power," an "evil empire," or a superpower with which the United States was forced to butt heads. They did so to make sure that the Soviet way of life did not prevail beyond the areas it currently dominated, to guarantee Americans' safety, and to promote the spread of freedom abroad. That direct menace has passed. In forging the coalition that defeated Saddam Hussein, Bush showed one way to move—under the rubric of collective security with other countries. But collective security does not have the ring to it that freedom versus tyranny did. Nor do Americans know much about the cultures and people that are struggling to create viable democratic, free-market societies, especially in Central and Eastern Europe. Do we care? Yes, but in a rather anemic and abstract way—unless we are made to care by our leaders. The struggles of the post-Cold War democratic successor states must somehow get yoked in the public mind to our own future and fate. This is hard to accomplish when people are legitimately preoccupied with their own affairs. At such points, the isolationist temptation so many observers of the American republic have noted over the years sets in, justified by our concern with domestic justice.

A number of political analysts who have traveled in recent years to Central and Eastern Europe (myself among them) have come back filled with admiration for what has been accomplished and with dread about what may happen next. A member of the Hungarian parliament (the leader of the liberal opposition) told me in October 1992 that Europe was "in a more dangerous position than at any time since the end of World War II." He added, "Why can't Americans *see* this? Why is Clinton ignoring international affairs?" I had a hard time explaining, and the explanation afforded little comfort. For it does seem that Americans have a low tolerance for foreign involvement unless it is quick, splashy, and tied to opposing a demonic foe or supporting a moral venture. It seems clear, for example, that Bush would not have garnered such overwhelming domestic support for the Gulf war had Saddam and his regime not been unalloyed "bad guys" who did brutal, repressive things. Bush may have forged, through classic diplomatic means, a twenty-seven-nation coalition. But his primary focus in appealing to the American people was the need for a "just war" against "the dictator Saddam Hussein," not the necessity for slow, patient, behind-the-scenes diplomatic maneuvering of the kind for which Americans show little patience and even less tolerance.

Ironically, we may have arrived at a point in world affairs where patient and unglamorous diplomacy is what is needed most. The global ideological struggle is over, at least for the time being; freedom and markets have won. What remains are a series of highly dangerous local situations that could at any time spill over into wider conflagrations. Secretary of State James Baker's tireless Middle East diplomacy during the Bush administration is precisely what is required now, only more of it and more boldly and effectively pursued than at any time in the past, if the great changes in the world are to be consolidated and brighter democratic futures assured. Such diplomacy can take the form of offering up the United States as the honest broker in complex negotiations or of engaging active emissaries to work closely with the fledgling democracies so that we can jointly determine what the most effective course of U.S. assistance would be. It would be a bad signal indeed were the Clinton administration to downplay foreign policy as the campaign did. Americans must learn that we are in and of the world and cannot retreat from it even if we try. Moreover, whatever the United States "invests" in the democracies abroad will yield enormous benefits, including greater global peace of mind in the future. Convincing Americans of these things will be a tough political sell for the new president in light of the nigh total interdiction on foreign policy in the 1992 campaign.

The Year of the Woman, the Talk Show, and a New Social Covenant

Nineteen ninety-two was widely proclaimed to be the Year of the Woman. The election of 1988, some may recall, was supposed to be the year women "delivered the president" by handing George Bush a resounding defeat. As things turned out, more women voted for Bush than for Dukakis and, most important, large numbers of men deserted the Democrats in favor of the Republicans. In 1992 men returned to the Democratic fold and helped to hand Clinton his victory. Women supported Clinton by 46 percent to 37 percent over Bush, with Perot garnering a healthy 17 percent.[19] But the Year of the Woman was primarily about women running for Congress. A preelection poll showed that 61 percent of the electorate, when asked, said that the government would be better if more women held office.[20] On election day forty-seven women were elected to the House of Representatives, up from twenty-eight, and four new women were elected to the Senate, tripling their numbers there from two to six.

The voters' view of women's political superiority suggests that feminist ideology has taken hold. I refer to the belief, of historic lineage, that women care more about the quality of life, especially in the domestic arena, than do men.[21] This characteristic has always been a double-edged sword for feminists. On the one hand, many assert that women will do better because they somehow *are* better. On the other hand, it is important for feminists to defeat all stereotypes about gender, including the view that women are morally superior to men. Needless to say, these two positions cannot be squared with one another. Feminists tend to play either card, depending upon the context. When the issue is hiring women for traditionally male jobs, they claim that gender is irrelevant. During the election, however, we heard a lot about how women would do things better because of qualities they possess *as women.*

Although hot-button issues such as abortion and sexual harassment tended to predominate as the central concerns of feminist rhetoric during the campaign, when women were surveyed a different set of priorities emerged. Exit polls found that guaranteed health care was the runaway top issue for 86 percent of those surveyed; jobs and family issues followed in close order. (Of course, health care is a family matter first and foremost.) Only 2 to 3 percent worried about rape or sexual violence; far more (68 percent) were concerned about violent crime in their neighborhoods, in large part because of the danger crime poses for their children, who in the besieged inner cities are likely to become either recruits to gangs or victims of gang warfare.[22] All of this suggests a rather wide perception gap between the most visible feminist leaders and the majority of women.

What accounts for this perception gap? With all the data indicating enormous strides for women in the workplace, as the median pay of women as a percentage of that of men jumped sharply in the 1980s, women clearly want to cover those areas of greatest vulnerability—such as health care—for themselves and their children.[23] This may indicate that women in the general population, in contrast to feminist leaders, have a far more realistic assessment of what the growing number of women in elective offices can accomplish. Let us hope so. For the danger in proclaiming deliverance if women gain power is that the spiral of delegitimation is deepened when the deliverance fails to materialize. Moreover, the view that women *qua* women are to effect miracles overpersonalizes politics.

What actually happened in the 1992 congressional elections? As noted earlier, a record number of women were elected; the same was true for minorities. But the voters' supposed outrage at politicians did not materialize: 93 percent of the incumbents running for reelection won, and only 31 of the 110 House freshmen had never held elective office. What can we expect from this new crop? It would be a mistake to presume that some dramatic ideological shift lies just over the horizon. Most of the gains made by black and Latino candidates, for example, derived from court orders that required legislative districts to be redrawn after the 1990 census in ways that favored minority candidates. More important over the long run is that one in six incumbents, disgusted with the system, did not stand for reelection even when success seemed assured. Furthermore, if one considers the overwhelming public support for term limits—with limits on congressional terms prevailing in all fourteen states that had ballot initiatives in 1992—one finds more evidence for voter volatility. In most term limit referenda, the vote was not close—term limits won by large margins.

The Democratic leaders of the House and Senate oppose term limits, and court challenges to the constitutionality of term limits loom. But the more important issue is the mood of the electorate that term limit victories signify. As if American politics were not anti-institutional, personalistic, and single-issue-oriented enough, the voters seem to be suggesting that we need more of what ails us. As Alan Rosenthal, director of the Eagleton Institute of Politics at Rutgers University, put it, "We can expect a higher and higher turnover in the membership and leadership of state legislatures, and that means a loss of continuity, institutional memory and, to some extent, expertise. And that is likely to mean more confrontation and more conflict over the issues." [24] Term limits, endorsed by many voters out of anger and frustration, will stymie the slow and patient building of coalitions and compromise politics. They will favor flashy, showboating, single-issue efforts with a "take no prisoners" approach: What is there to lose when the cast of legislators is about to change anyway? Ironically, the Year of the Woman rhetoric plays to similar impatience with its own overblown hopes about what might be if only we elect more women or limit terms or take some other relatively simple step compared with the gradual reinstitutionalization of parties, the restoration of authentic civic discourse, and the taming of a whole range of issues from their present ideological and intemperate forms.

The Year of the Woman and the term limits movement can be variously interpreted, of course, and some may suggest that my analysis is too pessimistic. But few serious political analysts will disagree that the trend toward "teledemocracy" and talk show psychobabble is of dubious value over the long run for political parties, candidates, ideas, or voters. The election of 1992 witnessed a surge in the use of pop politics. Candidate Clinton promised to return as President Clinton to "Larry King Live" and dangled the prospect of reappearing on "Donahue"—and even on MTV and "The Arsenio Hall Show." Perhaps he will reconsider, keeping in mind the dignity of his office and his position as the leader of the free world; perhaps not. For the move to instant gratification through interactive television appears to have taken hold.

Unfortunately, the talk show approach is the television equivalent of the *National Enquirer*—pandering, mushy, hysterical, playing to the lowest common denominator. One cannot assume that the vast majority of voters are ignorant. But one can, perhaps, assume that, in their conviction that the established news media and the parties and their elected officials have all let them down, their guard is down where teledemocracy is concerned.

Take, for example, Perot's idea of the "electronic town hall." (It is well to remember that Perot declared his candidacy on a talk show and that as a man with deep pockets he could buy all the TV time he wanted—unpestered by tough questions from professional journalists—to promote his form of populist democracy.) What Perot promoted was a form of plebiscitary democracy through instant "telepolling." The problem is that plebiscitary majoritarianism is quite different from democratic debate sustained by reasoned discussion and judgment. Plebiscites have been used routinely to shore up antidemocratic majoritarian movements and regimes—Argentina under the populist dictator Juan Perón comes to mind.

The distinction between a democratic and a plebiscitary system is no idle one. In a plebiscitary system, the views of the majority can more easily swamp minority or unpopular views and trample the rights of those who hold them. Plebiscitism is compatible with an authoritarian politics that is carried out under the guise of, or with the connivance of, majority opinion. That opinion can be registered ritualistically, absent sustained debate with one's fellow citizens about substantive questions.

On the surface, being asked your opinion and being given a chance to register it instantly may seem democratic—one gets to make one's opinion known "without a lot of boring rhetoric." But the "one" in this formulation is the private viewer rather than the public citizen, and he or she would be giving an offhand opinion rather than concurring in or dissenting from a position that has been hammered out through debate. A compilation of individual opinions does not make a civic culture; such a culture emerges only from a deliberative process. Teledemocracy means that once again the political world is fragmented and the "stabilizing role of the two major parties—the Democrats and the Republicans—[is] in peril. Elections in the future may see Ross Perot-like candidates raiding the primaries of both parties, and sometimes winning nominations or taking control of whole party organizations." This "very hot kind of TV . . . will just end up pushing people from one firestorm to another." [25] In other words, the ailment is offered as the cure. Where the countervailing pressure to instant majorities will come from seems desperately uncertain.

Perhaps it will come from a new social covenant, or so we were given reason to hope in the early days of Clinton's presidential campaign. Oddly, the theme waned as the election drew near, and Clinton instead upped the ante of campaign promises to more and more groups. But the idea of a new social covenant is a vital one. Unless Americans once again can be convinced that we are all in this together; unless Americans remember that being an American is in some sense a civic, chosen identity, not an unchosen birthright; unless government can find a way to respond to people's deepest concerns, whatever various movement leaders and entrenched interests may think, the new social covenant has precious little chance of taking hold. But take hold it must if we are to stem the tide of divisive wedge issues that pit citizen against citizen in a zero-sum game.

How might a new social covenant work in practice? Consider the matter of crime in the streets and neighborhoods. Extreme libertarians argue that individual freedom can never be curtailed by government, even in the interest of public safety. Conservatives of a certain stripe disdain arguments based on individual freedom. Politicians of both left and right, playing the race card, either stoke white fear of black crime—unreasonably, for the primary victims of black crime themselves are black—or, alternatively, deny altogether the tragedy of skyrocketing crimes of violence in minority neighborhoods. The result, ideological stalemate and a deepening of social mistrust, further contributes to the spiral of delegitimation.

A new social covenant would try to draw whites and blacks together around their shared concern for safe streets and neighborhoods, in part by altering the terms of the public debate. Let us move away from hysteria and accusation and think hard about feasible public policy, a social covenant advocate might argue. He or she would tell liberals who espouse untrammeled life-style "options" that they must forgo their disdain for the values most people cherish and the concerns most people express. The interviews I have conducted with mothers and grandmothers who are active in antigang and antidrug politics show clearly how much at odds their views are with liberal dogma. They want more police, more control, stiffer penalties enforced. They want less freedom for armed teenagers to gun down innocent children on their way to school.[26] The social covenanteer would also say to conservatives that tax cuts and market strategies are ill-designed to speak directly to what concerns people the most in the worst of our inner-city neighborhoods. He or she would tell gun advocates that, yes, murderers do kill people, but they use guns to do it. Surely you would favor removing guns from the hands of dangerous people. Can you not assume that a fourteen-year-old drug-using dropout is dangerous, or potentially so? Would his freedom be unjustly hampered if we made certain that he did not carry a gun into a school, a schoolyard, or a supermarket? Government can, in fact, be effective in lowering the homicide rate and the terror rate in inner-city neighborhoods.[27] We do not need to abolish any of the Bill of Rights to accomplish these goals. But we do need a working conviction that government can and should take the steps necessary to give the neighborhoods back to the people who live, work, and go to school in them.

The new social covenant is an effort to break through ideological gridlock and reverse the spiral of delegitimation. It rests on the presumption that most Americans are people of good will who are tired of naysaying and yearn for the opportunity to work together from a stance of good will rather than to continue glaring at one another across racial, class, and ideological divides, assuming ill will on the part of others. To accomplish this reversal, we must rebuild mediating institutions such as families, volunteer associations, schools, neighborhoods, and towns. We must try to restore both citizenship and competence. These are enormous tasks.

Perhaps it might be said that the great unstated theme of the elections of 1992—unstated but animating all the rest—was frustration with what is and a yearning for something better. Unless the new social covenant, or something like it, takes hold over the next four years, the election of 1996 will be even more perplexing and perturbing in its implications than that of 1992. I refer, of course, not to the actual outcomes of various races, including the presidential contest, but to the way the campaigns were conducted and the spiral of delegitimation they exposed. I began this essay by quoting Lincoln's reference to America as "the last best hope on earth." We will know all too soon whether Lincoln's expression was an epitaph or a harbinger of a brighter democratic future for America and hence for the world. For if this great republic falters it will be the crash heard 'round the world. Our many friends in other countries, especially in the young and fragile democracies, will tremble, falter, and perhaps fail without the ballast this country and this country alone can provide. That is the glorious burden of American democracy in the next century.

Notes

1. Suzanne Garment, *Scandal* (New York: Times Books, 1991).
2. E. J. Dionne, *Why Americans Hate Politics* (New York: Simon and Schuster, 1991).
3. Thomas Byrne Edsall with Mary D. Edsall, *Chain Reaction* (New York: Norton, 1991).
4. Hugh Davis Graham, "The Origins of Affirmative Action: Civil Rights and the Regulatory State," *Annals* 523 (September 1992): 50-62.
5. Edsall and Edsall, *Chain Reaction,* 288.
6. James Q. Wilson, "The Government Gap," *New Republic,* June 3, 1991, 38.
7. Ibid.
8. A quick glance at the abortion planks of both major parties gives depressing evidence of a determination to play to absolutists on both sides of the issue rather than working effectively toward a compromise. Such a compromise would build in a strong dispensation against abortion as an untrammeled right while making provision for its availability, appropriately regulated as abortion is regulated in every Western society. But to each side compromise looks like defeat, so much has the issue been polarized. Clinton did not help matters by promising the prochoice absolutists that he would use abortion as a "litmus test" in judicial appointments, something Reagan and Bush, never explicitly promised prolife forces, although the two Republican presidents indicated that appointees' views on abortion would be a strong consideration.
9. Thomas L. Friedman, "Aides Say Clinton Will Swiftly Void G.O.P. Initiatives," *New York Times,* Nov. 6, 1992, 1.
10. See Jean Bethke Elshtain, "Issues and Themes in the 1988 Campaign," in *The Elections of 1988,* ed. Michael Nelson (Washington, D.C.: CQ Press, 1989), esp. 114-115.
11. Catherine S. Manegold, "Jackson Leads Group to Push Social Agenda," *New York Times,* Nov. 8, 1992, 17.
12. "Where Perot Ran Strongest," *New York Times,* Nov. 5, 1992, B1; Adam Clymer,

"Turnout on Election Day '92 Was the Largest in 24 Years," *New York Times*, Dec. 17, 1992, A13.
13. Friedman, "Aides Say," 10.
14. Thomas Byrne Edsall, "Willie Horton's Message," *New York Review of Books*, Feb. 13, 1992, 11.
15. Lawrence I. Barrett "A New Coalition for the 1990s," *Time*, Nov. 16, 1992, 47-48.
16. Ibid.
17. Robin Toner, "Watershed Is Seen," *New York Times*, Nov. 4, 1992, 1.
18. Thomas L. Friedman, "Problems Abroad May Force Clinton to Alter Agenda," *New York Times*, Nov. 8, 1992, 1.
19. Paul J. Quirk, "The Election," in *Elections of 1988*, 82.
20. "Exit Poll," *USA Today*, Nov. 4, 1992, 6A.
21. This is a position associated with the work of Carol Gilligan, especially her book, *In a Different Voice* (Cambridge: Harvard University Press, 1982).
22. Gail McNight, "Poll: Jobs 1st Worry for Women," *Nashville Tennessean*, Sept. 13, 1, 2A.
23. On women as the "big economic winners in the 1980s expansion," see Sylvia Nasar, "Women's Progress Stalled? Just Say No," *New York Times*, Oct. 18, 1998, Sec. 3, 1.
24. Quoted in Michael deCourcy Hinds, "Elections Change Face of Lawmaking Bodies," *New York Times*, Nov. 5, 1992, B9.
25. James M. Perry, "Party May Be Over for Democrats, Republicans as Candidates Use 'Teledemocracy,' New Media," *Wall Street Journal*, Nov. 4, 1992, A16.
26. This is the overwhelming view of all the mothers I have interviewed for a forthcoming book, *Antigone's Daughter: Mothers in Opposition*.
27. Wilson suggests this example and others, though in somewhat different language from mine, in "Government Gap," 38.

6

The Presidency: Clinton and the
Cycle of Politics and Policy

Michael Nelson

*What sort of term can Bill Clinton expect to have as president?
One common way to answer a question like this is to assess the
leadership skills that the new president brings to office. Another
approach is to look closely at the ideas that constituted his campaign
appeals and form his plans for office. Yet another concentrates on the
political environment created by the elections that brought the president and Congress to power.*

*In this chapter, Michael Nelson integrates all three lines of
analysis—skills, ideas, and elections—into a cycle theory of presidential politics and domestic policy. Using this theory, which he developed with Erwin C. Hargrove in their book* Presidents, Politics,
and Policy *(1984), Nelson predicts that Clinton—at least during
the first term—will be a President of Preparation who raises important new ideas to the top of the national political agenda rather than
a President of Achievement who can enact his program of reform.
Nelson combines historical research, current political analysis, and
political forecasting in reaching this conclusion.*

Political commentary in the wake of the elections of 1992 brought to
mind nothing so much as the cartoonist Saul Steinberg's celebrated
depiction of the typical New Yorker's mental map of the United States. New
York (especially Ninth Avenue in Manhattan) dominates the landscape, of
course, with passing attention given to the Hudson River and the neighboring state of New Jersey. Beyond that, the map grows smaller and vaguer—a
mountain or two, a handful of cities (Los Angeles, Las Vegas), a pair of
states (Texas and Nebraska).[1]

As geographically provincial as Steinberg's New Yorkers may be, modern political analysts are no better when it comes to history. In seeking
guidance about what sort of president Bill Clinton would be, postelection
commentators seldom ventured further back from the present moment than
to the presidencies of Ronald Reagan (who, it was said, knew how to concentrate his message effectively), Jimmy Carter (who did not), and John F.
Kennedy (Clinton's boyhood hero). Political scientists, one hastens to add,
have not always done much better.[2]

In truth, history has much to tell us about the prospects for the Clinton administration. Indeed, the experiences of, say, Theodore Roosevelt, Woodrow Wilson, and Warren G. Harding are as illuminating in this regard as those of Reagan, Carter, and Kennedy.

The Cycle of Politics and Policy

As Erwin C. Hargrove and I have argued elsewhere, the history of American politics and domestic policy making in the twentieth century can be told in terms of a recurring cycle of electoral politics and governmental response.[3] The focus of this cycle has been the presidency. The cycle has undergone four complete turns. With the advent of the Clinton administration, it is about to begin a fifth.

At the heart of the cycle of politics and policy is a *Presidency of Achievement*—parts, but not all, of the administrations of Woodrow Wilson, Franklin D. Roosevelt, Lyndon B. Johnson, and Ronald Reagan—during which great bursts of presidentially inspired legislation are enacted that significantly alter the role of the federal government in American society. (See Table 6-1.) These changes are grounded in American political culture, the nation's widespread and deeply rooted beliefs about how the political system ought to work and the ends it ought to serve. Presidencies of Achievement manifest new, intensely felt definitions of liberty and equality, which are the culture's two primary values concerning the ultimate purposes of government. Optimism—the sense that it is within the country's power to solve any problem—runs high. The public's usual ambivalence toward political authority resolves temporarily into faith in government, especially the president, to act as the embodiment of national purpose.

Presidencies of Achievement constitute only part of the cycle, and the period of achievement within such a presidency constitutes only a part of it, usually the first two to four years. Achievement ends when administrative difficulties arise from the attempt to attain social change through governmental action so quickly, when older meanings of cultural values are reasserted, and when the antigovernment strain in popular political thinking reemerges. The end of the achievement stage poses a problem for the political system. The grateful citizenry, voting "retrospectively," [4] is likely to reward such presidents with reelection, but it may no longer support their basic temperamental and philosophical ambition, which is to continue to make a mark on government through legislative action.

The common strategy of the second-term President of Achievement who wants to keep on achieving is to emphasize foreign policy. On the world stage, the constraints that ended the brief period of domestic legislative success are weaker: the public is more consistent in its support of strong presidential action in foreign policy and the problems of implementation are less severe. Although one cannot help but note the coincidence between Presidencies of Achievement and war—Wilson and World War I,

Table 6-1 Twentieth-Century Presidents and the Cycle of Politics and Policy

	Stages of the cycle of politics and policy	
Preparation	Achievement	Consolidation
Theodore Roosevelt	Woodrow Wilson	Warren G. Harding Calvin Coolidge Herbert Hoover
	Franklin D. Roosevelt	Dwight D. Eisenhower
John F. Kennedy	Lyndon B. Johnson	Richard Nixon Gerald R. Ford
Jimmy Carter	Ronald Reagan	George Bush
Bill Clinton (predicted)		

Note: Presidents William Howard Taft and Harry S. Truman were Presidents of Stalemate.

Roosevelt and World War II, Johnson and Vietnam—one need not draw a deterministic connection.[5] The same impulse to remake the system, at home or abroad, that led these three presidents into war prompted Reagan, the most recent President of Achievement, to forge his own brand of dramatic foreign policy reform during his second term, namely, substantial nuclear disarmament.

Each Presidency of Achievement has been followed by a *Presidency of Consolidation*, in which the reforms of the achievement stage were not rejected but rather were woven into the administrative fabric of government and retired from the roster of divisive political issues. The 1920s' presidencies of Warren G. Harding, Calvin Coolidge, and Herbert Hoover were of this kind, as were those of Dwight D. Eisenhower, Richard Nixon and Gerald Ford,[6] and George Bush. A Presidency of Consolidation concludes each turn of the cycle of politics and policy, but it also overlaps with the period in which the seeds of the next turn are planted. New social discontents arise—as they inevitably will in a dynamic society—and intellectuals in the universities and think tanks, interest group leaders, journalists, legislators, bureaucrats, and others on the fringes of power begin developing policy ideas to address them. Presidents of Consolidation, empowered only with an electoral mandate not to push aggressively for change (and in any event preoccupied with the agenda of their own turn of the cycle) are likely to be unresponsive to these new forces and uninterested in the new ideas.

Eventually, some of the social discontents become strong enough to dominate presidential politics. A president is elected because of the ability to articulate the new problems and to offer new ideas to meet them, but the victory is far from overwhelming. Thus the main task during a *Presidency of Preparation* is for the president to lay the groundwork for the Presidency of Achievement that will follow. Theodore Roosevelt, John F. Kennedy, and Jimmy Carter were the country's first three Presidents of Preparation. Bill Clinton is likely to be the next.

Although the cycle of Preparation, Achievement, and Consolidation is rooted in American political culture, Hargrove and I derive it more from empirical observation than from any theory of historical determinism. The cycle has been recurring but is not inevitable. A system-threatening political crisis can break the cyclic flow: the abruptness and severity of the Great Depression catapulted Franklin Roosevelt's New Deal into existence without a preceding Presidency of Preparation. So can a mismatch between presidential purpose and the public mood. The presidency of William Howard Taft foundered because Taft, who had been elected to carry on Theodore Roosevelt's agenda of reform, turned out to be temperamentally and philosophically unsuited to the task. Taft's administration, like that of Harry S. Truman, was a *Presidency of Stalemate* in domestic policy, one in which the president's agenda bore little resemblance to what the public was willing to accept. Taft sought consolidation when the public wanted achievement; Truman pursued achievement when the public, frazzled by years of rapid change under Franklin Roosevelt, sought consolidation.

Still, presidencies that have not fulfilled their function in the cycle of politics and policy have been rare. Presidential politics and domestic policy making have flowed along a fairly regular course for nearly a century. After a discussion of the dynamics of the cycle, that course is described in this essay, turn by turn. Finally, Clinton's election and the prospects for his first term as president are assessed in light of the theory.

Dynamics of the Cycle

The cycle of Preparation, Achievement, and Consolidation in electoral politics and domestic policy making can be thought of as a kind of machine. This image will be used to explain how the cycle works, but it also is meant to suggest how subject it is to breakdown if any of its components fail. The engine that drives each turn of the cycle from one stage to the next is *elections*. The fuel on which the engine runs is *ideas*. Presidential *leadership skill* is the carburetor that activates the fuel in response to the engine's requirements.

Elections

Many political scientists would argue that there is little relationship between the distribution of citizen preferences on issues and the actions of government. This is certainly true if the test is how fully the federal government acts to mirror the positions of a majority of citizens on a wide range of policy issues. But one needs to supplement this test with a sense of a historical process in which changes in political attitudes over time by large groups of voters either make it politically possible for government to act in new ways or preclude such action. Not all issues are equally important. The concerns that social discontent and intellectual ferment have brought to the fore at any particular time are the ones that presidential candidates must respond to and, if elected, must deal with in some manner. Seldom are popular demands clear. In 1932, for example, Americans were disenchanted with limited government and ready for new ideas, but it is unlikely that a majority of them would have endorsed the specifics of the New Deal if Franklin Roosevelt had described (or even known) what they were during the campaign. What the voters offered Roosevelt instead was a "permissive consensus" to experiment and, if successful, be rewarded with approval and reelection.[7]

Presidencies of Achievement, which form the heart of the cycle, are the most direct products of the election process. They become possible only when three conditions are met: (1) A candidate campaigns for the presidency with promises, however general, of significant reform; (2) the candidate is elected by a large majority; and (3) the president-elect's victory is accompanied by large gains for the party in Congress.

The first two conditions are obvious; the third, less so. The reason that the size of the gains, more than the size of the party's contingent in Congress, matters is because the gains invariably are attributed, accurately or not, to the president-elect's "coattails." [8] Such gains create a heightened disposition among legislators of both congressional parties to support the president's legislative initiatives: copartisans because they want to ride the bandwagon, members of the opposition because they want to avoid being flattened by it. A president whose election is not accompanied by large gains is more likely to be regarded by legislators as tangential to their own political fortunes. Franklin Roosevelt had an easier time with the Congress that was elected in 1932, which contained many new Democrats, than with the Congress that was chosen in the 1936 elections, in which the Democrats made only small gains. This was so even though the total Democratic membership in the latter Congress was larger. More recently, Carter had very little success with his first Congress, which the Democrats controlled 61-38 in the Senate and 292-143 in the House, in part because the 1976 elections added only one member to the House Democratic ranks and no new senators. Reagan, who faced a narrowly Republican Senate (53-46) and a Democratic House (192-243), did very well with Congress because his election in 1980 was joined to a net gain of twelve Republican senators, enough to take control of the Senate, and thirty-three Republicans in the House. The governing coalitions that Presidents of Achievement construct are personal as much as party coalitions.

Table 6-2   Initial Elections of Presidents of Preparation,
Achievement, and Consolidation

| President | Victory margin over nearest opponent | | Gains for president-elect's party in Congress | |
	Popular vote (%)	Electoral vote	House	Senate
Preparation				
T. Roosevelt (1904)	18.8%	196	43	0
Kennedy (1960)	0.3	84	−21	0
Carter (1976)	2.1	57	0	1
Clinton (1992)	5.5	202	−10	0
Achievement				
Wilson (1912)	14.4	347	62	9 [a]
F. Roosevelt (1932)	17.7	413	97[a]	12 [a]
Johnson (1964)	22.6	434	37	1
Reagan (1980)	9.7	440	33	12 [a]
Consolidation				
Harding (1920)	26.4	277	63	11 [a]
Coolidge (1924)	25.3	246	22	3
Hoover (1928)	17.4	357	30	8
Eisenhower (1952)	10.7	353	22[a]	1 [a]
Nixon (1968)	0.7	110	5	6
Bush (1988)	7.8	325	−3	0

[a] President's party took control of the house of Congress.

Presidents of Preparation can be distinguished from Presidents of Achievement by the size of their electoral mandates: they run change-oriented campaigns but win by smaller margins or with shorter coattails than do Presidents of Achievement. (See Table 6-2.) Presidencies of Consolidation often are ushered in by enormous landslides. Such victories can be easily misinterpreted. Eisenhower, a landslide winner with long coattails in 1952, was variously criticized by both liberals and conservatives for not using his popularity to try to transform the government in behalf of their respective causes in the manner of a President of Achievement. In truth, the mandate of the President of Consolidation comes as a result of the campaign promise *not* to push for substantial domestic policy changes. Presidents of Consolidation are empowered by their elections but only to consolidate.

Leadership Skill

Even in fulfilling their historic function as Presidents of Preparation, Achievement, or Consolidation, not all presidents enjoy personal political suc-

Table 6-3   Primary Leadership Skill Requirements and the Cycle of
Politics and Policy

Skill	President of Preparation	President of Achievement	President of Consolidation
Strategic sense	X	X	X
Presentation of self	X	X	
Tactical skills		X	
Management			
Lieutenants	X	X	
Bureaucracy			X

cess in office. The problem may arise (as it did in the case of Johnson and Vietnam) in the realm of foreign affairs. Or, as with Nixon and Watergate, the president's weakness may be moral. More often, however, presidents succeed because of their leadership skills or fail because of their lack of them.

What leadership skills do presidents require? The skill that all presidents need most is a strong strategic sense of the grain of history—an ability to understand the public mood and to shape and fulfill the historical possibilities of the time.[9] Presidents also must be able to present themselves and their policies to the general public through rhetoric and symbolic action and to deal in a tactically skillful way with the Washington community (especially Congress) through negotiation, persuasion, and other forms of political gamesmanship. Finally, presidents need skills of management, both of lieutenants (White House staff members and political appointees in the departments) who can help them form their public policies and of the large organizations in the bureaucracy that are charged to implement those policies.

Presidents at different stages of the cycle require these abilities in different combinations. (See Table 6-3.) Presidents of Preparation, who are change-oriented but lack a sufficient electoral mandate to enact most of their more substantial proposals, need a strong strategic sense, an ability to develop sound and appealing policy ideas through the management of their lieutenants, and (to sell these ideas) a well-developed aptitude for self-presentation to the American people. Because Presidents of Achievement do have a mandate, they need all of these skills and one more: the tactical ability to persuade members of Congress to enact their policies. The more status-quo-oriented Presidents of Consolidation, in partial contrast, require a strategic sense and a special ability to manage the bureaucracy more than they need the skills whose value is in enacting new policies.

Ideas

Presidents of Preparation and Presidents of Achievement cannot assume that a deep inventory of policy ideas that are suitable to their purposes will be available when they take office. The reason is that successful ideas are more than just substantively sound, although that standard alone is a high one. They also must be politically appealing.

To be sure, expert knowledge is important. Theories based on evidence and analysis may permit the problems they address to be managed and alleviated, if not solved. Such theories also may supply the president with a confident sense of purpose and direction that can be communicated to others as a basis of political support.

But even when accurate expert theories are available, they are insufficient to the president's purposes. Successful ideas are syntheses of expert knowledge, values grounded in the political culture, and short-term political reality. They not only are accepted by policy experts and political elites as workable, but they also respond in culturally acceptable terms to the social discontents of the times.[10]

Three Turns of the Cycle: 1901-1977

The cycle of politics and policy is a twentieth-century phenomenon, but its seeds were planted by the Constitutional Convention in 1787 and generally lay dormant for more than a century thereafter. Intentionally or not, the Framers' design of the executive assured that, to the extent the federal government ever became the main object of public demands for political action, the presidency would become the center (although not necessarily the master) of the American political system.[11] No other component of the constitutional system was institutionally capable of providing what *The Federalist* refers to as "energy"—that is, leadership. In the nineteenth century, national—and thus presidency-centered—politics and policy were the exception. In the twentieth century, they have been the rule.

From Theodore Roosevelt to Herbert Hoover

Theodore Roosevelt succeeded to the presidency when William L. McKinley was assassinated in 1901 and was elected to a term in his own right in 1904. He took office just as the dominant trend of late nineteenth-century American society—its rapid transformation from a congeries of regional economies and small businesses into a mostly national economy dominated by large corporations—was cresting. The implications of the newly nationalized economy for a more active federal government and, especially, for a strengthened presidency, were significant: it is no coincidence that the cycle of politics and policy first appears in this period.[12] As Elihu Root described the new political challenges of the era:

The relations between the employer and the employed, between the owners of aggregated capital and the units of organized labor, between the small producer, the small trader, the consumer, and the great transporting and manufacturing and distribution agencies all present new questions for the solution of which the old reliance upon the free action of individual wills appears quite inadequate. And in many directions the intervention of that organized control which we call government seems necessary to produce the same result of justice and right conduct which obtained through the attrition of individuals before the new conditions arose.

Roosevelt believed that the federal government's response to the transformation Root described should be to "recognize the inevitableness of combinations in business and meet it by a corresponding increase in governmental power over big business." He drew his broad philosophy and specific policy ideas from the Herbert Croly wing of the urban, middle-class Progressive movement of the 1890s. The Square Deal was Roosevelt's legislative effort, first, to ease the task of breaking up the trusts, holding companies, and other "combinations" whose purpose was to stifle competition and keep prices high, and second, to empower the federal government to regulate the behavior of all corporations engaged in interstate commerce.

Roosevelt fully achieved neither of these goals. His election victory in 1904, although substantial, was not sufficient to convince Congress that his platform had overwhelming public support. But Roosevelt's vigorous use of the White House as a "bully pulpit" placed his progressive ideas at the top of the national political agenda and set the stage for their later enactment, albeit in somewhat different form. The historian Arthur Link's judgment that Roosevelt's "chief contribution to the reform cause was the publicity he gave it" may sound condescending, but it defines a successful Presidency of Preparation.[13]

Woodrow Wilson, whose bias was toward the Louis Brandeis-led wing of the Progressive movement, which advocated corporate smallness, nonetheless inherited and built upon Roosevelt's efforts. (As noted earlier, Roosevelt's handpicked successor, William Howard Taft, who had been elected in 1908 with a mandate for legislative achievement, suffered a Presidency of Stalemate when he did not pursue it.) Wilson's election in 1912 was not only impressive in its own right but was accompanied by what were then the largest gains in history for a president's party in the House of Representatives (sixty-three seats) and by a ten-seat gain in the Senate, which gave the Democrats control of that body for the first time in twenty years. Wilson used this mandate to persuade Congress to enact his New Freedom agenda: the Clayton Act, which strengthened the federal government's antitrust powers; the Federal Trade Commission Act, which created the FTC and gave it authority to punish unfair business competition; the Underwood-Simmons Tariff Act, which lowered tariffs and provided for an income tax; and the Federal Reserve Act, which created the Federal Reserve Board and assigned it control over the nation's credit system.

Taken as a whole, Wilson's Presidency of Achievement inaugurated a role for the federal government as a national "umpire" that would regulate the excesses of private economic power in defense of personal liberty. During the 1920s, for all Warren Harding's talk during the 1920 presidential campaign about a return to the "normalcy" of the McKinley years, neither he, Calvin Coolidge, nor Herbert Hoover did much to roll back the Roosevelt-inspired, Wilson-enacted changes. The acquiescence of these three Presidents of Consolidation effectively wove the New Freedom into the fabric of government. They did, however, try their best to prevent Congress from extending the federal role from umpire to "player," or active promoter of the general welfare. Harding vetoed a soldier's bonus bill and Coolidge the McNary-Haugen farm relief bill. Hoover resisted for as long as possible various efforts to create public works projects for unemployed workers in the face of the Great Depression, which struck the nation in 1929. Ideas such as these formed the substance of the next turn of the cycle.

From Franklin D. Roosevelt to Dwight D. Eisenhower

Because of the suddenness and severity of the depression, the second turn of the cycle of politics and policy had no Presidency of Preparation. Hoover was, in most ways, part of the previous era. "Economic depression," he told Congress in 1930, "cannot be cured by legislative action or executive pronouncement," only by "self-reliance." But neither was a preparation stage needed. Franklin D. Roosevelt's overwhelming victory in 1932 (at the time the largest ever against an incumbent president) was accompanied by a ninety-seat gain for his party in the House (far exceeding Wilson's previous record) and a change in the Senate from a one-seat Democratic deficit to a twenty-five-seat Democratic majority. The results of the elections were evidence enough that the public was anxious for new and dramatic policies.

Roosevelt's inauguration on March 4, 1933, was followed by the celebrated "first hundred days." An emergency banking bill, completed by the president and his advisers at 2:00 a.m. on March 9, was passed unanimously by the House that same day after thirty-eight minutes of debate; it became law within hours when the Senate followed suit. Other bills followed in rapid succession and were rushed through after testimonials such as that of House Democratic leader Joseph Byrns ("This . . . is a time to get behind our great leader and follow him and be guided by his judgment, rather than our own") and this one from Bertrand Snell, the House Republican leader: "If you are going to accomplish this purpose you must put it up to the President of the United States and hold him responsible." The spring calendar of legislative achievement included the following:

March	9:	Emergency Banking Act
March	26:	Economy Act
March	31:	Civilian Conservation Corps

April 19:	Gold standard abandoned (ratified by Congress on June 5)
May 12:	Federal Emergency Relief Act
	Agricultural Adjustment Act (AAA)
	Emergency Farm Mortgage Act
May 18:	Tennessee Valley Authority (TVA) Act
May 27:	Truth-in-Securities Act
June 13:	Home Owner's Loan Act
June 16:	National Industrial Recovery Act
	Glass-Steagall Banking Act
	Farm Credit Act

A "second hundred days" followed the 1934 congressional elections, in which the president's party, contrary to precedent, gained seats: nine in the House, ten in the Senate. In early 1935 Congress passed the National Labor Relations Act, the Social Security Act, acts to strengthen the previous banking and TVA laws, and a tax act that increased the responsibility of the wealthy.

The legislation of the second hundred days was aimed more at restructuring the economy than was the legislation of the first hundred days, which was preoccupied with the need to salvage it. But the public philosophy of the New Deal was fairly consistent throughout: the federal government is ultimately responsible for securing welfare, security, and employment, the foundations of the people's liberty. Roosevelt's intellectual debt to ideas that had been propounded in the 1920s and before was varied. As the political scientist James MacGregor Burns notes, Roosevelt "had grasped the standard of Wilsonian reform in his measures for federal supervision of securities, friendliness to labor, business regulation. He had trod Cousin Theodore's old path in conservation and in the elements of planning in the AAA. He had filched a plank from American socialism in the public ownership features of TVA," and later, in the Social Security and tax bills.[14]

Roosevelt was reelected in 1936 by the largest electoral-vote majority in history (523-8), which he took to be a mandate to continue the reform process to whatever ends he chose and through whatever obstacles he faced. But his party's gains in the 1936 congressional elections were relatively modest. As a result, legislators in 1937 were less likely than in the preceding four years to attribute their present or future political success to obedience to Roosevelt. Congress resisted his plan to pack the Supreme Court, and voters in 1938 refused Roosevelt's pleas to defeat anti-New Deal Democrats in primary elections. What one author calls "deadlock on the Potomac" ensued.[15] In 1941 America's intervention in World War II rendered domestic politics and policy less important.

Roosevelt died in April 1945. Harry S. Truman succeeded to the presidency with domestic policy achievement high on his list of goals. (He was determined, he later wrote, not to allow "the progress of the New Deal to be halted in the aftermath of the war as decisively as the progress of Woodrow Wilson's New Freedom had been halted after the first World War.") Before the year was out Truman had called on Congress to enact legislation for full employment, public housing, farm price supports, national health insurance, and civil rights, among other new and dramatic causes. Congress's response was tepid; the reaction of voters in the 1946 midterm elections was to send Truman a Congress controlled by the opposition party. With the notable exception of civil rights, Truman downplayed his reform agenda during the 80th Congress of 1947-1949 and won a surprising and substantial election victory in 1948. But when he revived his efforts under the Fair Deal banner during the second term, his popularity again dwindled. Truman's domestic policy proposals were to make up much of the agenda of the next turn of the cycle, but it brought him only a Presidency of Stalemate during his own tenure.

Dwight D. Eisenhower, elected in 1952, was the quintessential President of Consolidation. Ignoring pleas from the conservative wing of his own party to abolish TVA, severely reduce federal spending, and generally undo "twenty years of treason," Eisenhower pursued a course that was responsive to the public desire for a slowdown but not a reversal of course in domestic policy. Eisenhower called his program "dynamic conservatism," but "passive liberalism" was more like it. Few steps were taken to roll back the New Deal. Eisenhower's conservatism was confined mostly to bringing fiscal and administrative order to the Roosevelt-induced reforms.

From John F. Kennedy to Gerald Ford

The consolidation stage of one turn of the cycle is the incubation stage of the next. The Progressive movement developed as a force in national politics in the 1890s, laying the intellectual groundwork for Theodore Roosevelt and Woodrow Wilson. Much of what eventually became the New Deal was germinating among intellectuals and progressives in Congress during the 1920s.

In the late 1950s some congressional Democrats, especially in the Senate, advanced a number of policy initiatives that were designed to extend the active concern of the federal government to racial and economic minorities whom the New Deal really had not helped and to "quality-of-life" issues such as education and the environment. Their style of policy entrepreneurship embodied the nexus between advocacy groups, intellectuals, and legislators on the fringes of congressional power.[16]

As a representative and senator in the 1950s, John F. Kennedy had not been a particularly liberal or crusading legislator. As a candidate for president in 1960, however, he consciously adopted the increasingly popular issue positions that had been developed by liberal Democratic legislators and intellectuals. In a campaign dominated by his call to "get this country moving again," Kennedy won against the Republican nominee, Vice President Richard Nixon, but only by three-tenths of a percentage point in the popular vote. His party actually lost twenty seats in the House.

Even some liberal Democrats said at the time that they sensed neither a great public imperative that new programs be passed nor a willingness to pay for them with higher taxes. Public opinion, although supportive, was not solid.

The legislative measures that Kennedy flagged as most important failed to pass during his brief presidency: federal aid to education, medical care for the aged, a department of urban affairs, a civil rights bill, and a tax cut. These failures, however, were part of a coherent presidential strategy, which was to submit controversial legislation to Congress with accompanying presidential messages as a form of public education. Kennedy's eyes were on 1964 and the creation of a large reelection majority that also would give him the increase in congressional support that he needed. In effect, he saw his first term Presidency of Preparation becoming a second-term Presidency of Achievement.

Ironically, it was Kennedy's death and the accompanying sense of crisis and catharsis that, more than anything else, hastened public support for his programs. Lyndon B. Johnson, who succeeded to the presidency on November 22, 1963, pleaded for passage of the civil rights bill and tax cut in the name of the fallen leader ("Let us continue") and in 1964 accomplished the victories. In the fall Johnson ran an essentially nonpartisan, "president of all the people" campaign against Sen. Barry Goldwater of Arizona, an extreme conservative who violently opposed the new liberal platform. Johnson portrayed Kennedy's New Frontier and his own Great Society programs as moderate and broadly acceptable, in contrast to the alleged desire of Goldwater to dismantle Social Security and abolish the TVA. Johnson's astonishing landslide victory, which brought thirty-seven new liberal Democrats into the House with him, triggered the next burst of presidential achievement. As the political scientist Roger Davidson writes, "The legislative record of the 89th Congress (1965-1967) reads like a roll call of contemporary government programs: Medicare/Medicaid, Voting Rights Act of 1965, Older Americans Act, Freedom of Information Act, National Foundation on the Arts and the Humanities, highway beautification, urban mass transit, clean water, and the Departments of Transportation and Housing and Urban Development, among others." [17]

The New Deal had committed the federal government to assuring the economic security of the vast majority of Americans; the Great Society added quality-of-life concerns to that commitment and extended its coverage to racially and economically deprived minorities in the name of equality. But the new center could not hold. Popular support for civil rights and antipoverty programs had never been as unambiguous as the 1964 elections seemed to suggest. Voters were defending the New Deal against Goldwater as much as they were affirming the Great Society. As long as three-fourths of the American people held to the belief that any able-bodied person could find a job and earn a living, there simply was no solid support for a "war on poverty." [18]

Cultural values aside, many of the achievements of the 1960s somehow went sour. Civil rights and antipoverty measures, although not radical, created such turmoil in their implementation that large numbers of Americans sought a period of respite. It was painfully clear, even to adherents of the Great Society, that many of its programs had been designed badly and were not meeting early hopes. These issues, in addition to the Vietnam War, broke the Johnson coalition wide open, roughly dividing white southerners and northern blue-collar workers against blacks and professionals. Nixon's victory in 1968 over Vice President Hubert H. Humphrey, combined with the large vote for former Alabama governor George C. Wallace's independent candidacy, affirmed increasing public distress about the war, social unrest, and racial conflict.

Presidents of Consolidation seldom are elected on the basis of positive policy proposals. They can, however, play a constructive role in rationalizing and legitimizing the programs of Presidents of Achievement. Nixon and a number of his appointees brought a managerial style to government. They did not formally reject the purposes of the Great Society (nor did Gerald Ford, who succeeded to the presidency when Nixon resigned in 1974) but instead sought for ways to change the way the programs worked. Their efforts eventually generated plans for general and special revenue sharing with state and local governments, a self-styled New Federalism. The idea was to consolidate numerous narrow categorical grant programs for education and poverty into broad block grants to lower levels of government, which would have discretion about how to spend the funds according to local needs. Thus, in the realm of domestic policy, the Nixon and Ford administrations served as typical Presidencies of Consolidation.

The Fourth Turn of the Cycle
Jimmy Carter, Ronald Reagan, George Bush

The fourth turn of the cycle of politics and policy was marked not only by a new round of presidents but also by a change from liberalism to conservatism and, in cultural terms, from equality to liberty. These changes were neither accidental nor easy. Their origin lay in the last years of the Nixon and Ford administrations. The early and mid-1970s were unusual for several reasons,[19] including one that sometimes is overlooked: the intellectual ferment and social discontent that was occurring outside government. New problems seemed less tractable than older ones had been: in the economy, "stagflation," a condition of simultaneous high inflation and high unemployment; in social policy, the development of a seemingly permanent underclass; in foreign policy, disorientation about the U.S. role in world affairs. Many liberals lost confidence in their ability to define the direction of policy change and to develop appropriate programs to achieve progress. Some of them joined ranks with ideologically aggressive neoconservatives and New Right intellectuals, whose ideas on supply-side economics, corporate deregulation, administrative decentralization, traditional morality, and nuclear strategy were percolating in conservative think tanks such as the Heritage Foundation and the American Enterprise Institute and in journals of opinion such as *Commentary* and *The Public Interest.*

Preparation: Jimmy Carter

Although the fourth turn of the cycle began with the election of a new Democratic president, the results of the 1976 elections allowed for virtually no claim of a mandate from the voters. Carter's margin of victory over Ford was tiny, and his party gained only one additional seat in Congress. Worse, Carter was the first Democratic president in this century to be forced to confront policy problems that were not amenable to the traditional programmatic impulses of his party's coalition. Stagflation seemed chronic, with the "misery index" of inflation plus unemployment at 12 percent in January 1977; the federal budget deficit was growing rapidly, largely because of sharp increases in the costs of Great Society entitlement programs such as Medicare, Medicaid, and food stamps; industrial productivity was declining; and the continuing rise in international oil prices seemed to require severe conservation measures. To complicate matters, Carter had played to the public's disenchantment with government during the election campaign, with special attention to bureaucratic inefficiency and the moral laxity of Watergate. This was not a strong platform from which to launch an activist administration.

Carter came to the presidency with a coherent philosophy of domestic policy, one grounded in an approach of comprehensive solutions based on sound and dispassionate analysis. He was a fiscal conservative and social liberal who thought it was possible to pursue humane social goals through restrained budgetary policies and efficient management.[20] Conservative but tolerant on moral issues, Carter preached conscience and traditional values while eschewing the demands of the Religious Right to enact into law its positions on school prayer and abortion.

Unfortunately, Carter found that there was no organized political constituency for his centrist approach. For example, his welfare reform proposal, which sought to provide the poor with greater security at no additional cost through more efficient design and administration, incurred the opposition of liberals because it was fiscally austere and of conservatives because it did not carry austerity far enough. Ultimately, the public became convinced that a president who could not lead his own party must be ineffectual.

Carter's problems were complicated by his limited repertoire of leadership skills. As one who felt that, once elected, his main task was to make "correct" decisions and simply explain them, Carter gave little attention to the persuasive presentation of his policies and of himself as leader to the nation. In dealing with other Washington politicians, he showed himself even less interested in appealing to their political incentives as a means of tactical leadership. As for Carter's management of authority for policy formation, it oscillated between drowning himself in the technical details of some policies, often losing sight of larger political realities in the process, and freely delegating responsibility for the remaining issues to others, usually with little guidance about what he desired. Finally, Carter's strategic sense of the historical possibilities of his time was limited. Unlike Kennedy, Carter did not see the need for a preparation stage in which he would select a few crucial goals, nurture political support for them, and tie their enactment to a clear sense of policy direction. Bucking the tide in his own party and with no other base of support to substitute for it, Carter tried unsuccessfully to be a President of Achievement during his first term.

Still, despite his woes in office and his humiliating defeat in the 1980 election, Carter served as a President of Preparation for Ronald Reagan and his policies. The themes of Carter's administration, the most conservative of any twentieth-century Democrat, foreshadowed Reagan: moral conservatism, by example and exhortation if not by law; a preoccupation with inflation, growth, and deregulation in economic policy (Carter's success in securing legislative deregulation of the airline and trucking industries was unparalleled); and an antibureaucratic, anti-Washington posture that more than anything else accounted for his rise from the obscure status of a former southern governor to that of the presidential nominee of the Democratic party.

Achievement: Ronald Reagan

Carter's actions as president reflected his rhetoric but were unable to fulfill it. In 1980 the voters' concerns about inflation, high interest rates, slow economic growth, excessive regulation, and big government created a climate in which a candidate who promised great and sudden change in the role of the federal government in American society could thrive. Ronald Reagan's election clearly set the stage for a Presidency of Achievement: he pledged enormous tax cuts, serious reductions in social spending, and an unprecedented peacetime defense buildup during the campaign; won by the largest electoral vote in history against an incumbent president (489-49); and secured substantial gains for his party in Congress. The Republicans even took control of the Senate for the first time since 1955. Public confidence in government rose.[21]

Seizing the moment, Reagan moved simultaneously on almost all political fronts during his first months in office. For domestic policy ideas, he drew from the ranks of supply-side economists and other conservative intellectuals, including his own Office of Management and Budget (OMB) director, former representative David Stockman. Reagan's initial budget included eighty-four proposals to reduce or eliminate federal programs. A *New York Times* survey later found that he had won on 60 percent of them, including assaults on political "untouchables" such as housing assistance, public service employment, food stamps, child nutrition, and aid to working welfare mothers. (Most important, these victories involved "85 to 90 percent of the dollar savings he wanted.") [22] Reagan also was able to reduce the number of federal categorical grant programs from 361 to 259 by eliminating some and consolidating others into block grants. (At the same time, the money for these programs was substantially reduced.) His Task Force on Regulatory Relief, with Vice President George Bush as chair, checked the historical increase in new federal regulations, and his reductions in the enforcement divisions of agencies such as the FTC and the Occupational Safety and Health Administration diminished the effectiveness of existing ones. Reagan secured the enactment of a 25 percent cut in the federal income tax on individuals, with the permanent indexing of the tax brackets to the cost of living to start soon afterward. Corporations benefited from the new tax law even more. Defense spending soared.

Congress's acquiescence in all this was nearly complete. In 1981 Republican senators and representatives gave Reagan the highest "index of loyalty" of any party to its president since Congressional Quarterly began keeping score in 1953. The conservative coalition also had its best year ever, winning 92 percent of the votes on which it was active, as Republican legislators were joined by conservative "Boll Weevil" Democrats, who represented districts in which Reagan and his policies were popular.[23] Even the House Democratic leadership initially bowed to Reagan's power, handing over virtual control of the legislative agenda to the president. An aide to Speaker Thomas P. O'Neill, Jr., said:

> What the Democrats did, in extraordinary fashion, was to recognize the cataclysmic nature of the 1980 election results. The American public wanted this new president to be given a chance to try out his programs. We weren't going to come across as being obstructionists.

Reagan saw himself from the start as a president in the mold of Franklin Roosevelt. Like his Democratic predecessor, Reagan wished to bring a new deal to the nation that would form the basis for a new political era. He had all the rhetorical abilities required of a President of Achievement: having spent most of his adult life either as a public speaker or before the camera as an actor, he was particularly adept at clarifying complex issues through a simple, smoothly delivered message. Reagan's presentational skills supplemented his strategic sense that voters wanted root-and-branch, not incremental approaches to the problems that concerned them. He also realized that, both as an overall strategy and as a tactical ploy with members of Congress and other Washington politicians, he should set his policy course and stay with it, even in the face of short-term adversity, such as the recession of 1981-1982. Reagan's "stay the course" approach conveyed a strong sense of purpose and self-confidence that reinforced his image as a leader. This belief carried over into his management of authority within the executive branch; there he reserved fundamental choices to himself and delegated almost everything else to lieutenants who had been appointed to the White House staff, OMB, and the departments primarily because of their political loyalty and ideological purity.

Like previous Presidents of Achievement, Reagan ran a reelection campaign in 1984 that pointed with pride to his first-term successes but said very little about his plans for the second term. Like them, too, he won an overwhelming personal landslide from the grateful voters (his opponent, former vice president Walter F. Mondale, carried only one state) but with minimal coattails for his party's congressional candidates. Bereft therefore of both a mandate and a domestic agenda for the second term, Reagan turned to foreign affairs. One secret and partially illegal venture, to sell arms to Iran and divert the proceeds of the sales to the anticommunist contra rebels in Nicaragua, blew up in the president's face when it became public in 1986 as the notorious Iran-contra scandal. A second venture, however, was considerably more successful. Reagan held out the olive branch to his age-old nemesis, the Soviet Union. He and the new Soviet leader, Mikhail Gorbachev, negotiated the Intermediate-range Nuclear Force (INF) Treaty in 1987, the first treaty in history to bring about the destruction of an entire class of nuclear weapons. The same optimism about his ability to roll back communism through accelerated defense spending that had characterized the first term marked Reagan's equally successful steps toward nuclear disarmament during the second term.

Consolidation: George Bush

Because of the Twenty-second Amendment, which entered the Constitution in 1951, Reagan's second term as president was by definition his last term. (He would have liked to run again.) In 1988, for the first time in twenty years, both major-party candidates for president, Vice President Bush and Gov. Michael S. Dukakis of Massachusetts, the Democratic nominee, were nonincumbents. Both, too, presented themselves to the voters as would-be Presidents of Consolidation who were less interested in rolling back the Reagan achievements than in dealing with some of their unpleasant political and administrative side effects, especially the enormous annual budget deficits that, taken together, had tripled the national debt from $1 billion to $3 billion during Reagan's eight years as president. In his acceptance speech to the Democratic convention, Dukakis described the election as being "about competence, not ideology" and claimed that his experience as the two-term governor of a large industrial state had equipped him to run the federal government effectively and economically. Bush, for his part, portrayed himself as the true heir to Reagan, albeit a "kinder and gentler" version. His famous "read my lips: no new taxes" pledge was joined to a promise to be the "education president" and the "environmental president."

Politically, Bush's argument was the more persuasive. On election day he won the support of 83 percent of those voters who approved the highly popular Reagan's performance as president.[24] His victory margin was convincing: 53 percent to 46 percent in the popular vote, 426 to 111 in the electoral college. Bush's pollster and political strategist, Robert Teeter, set the election into historical context:

> We've only had fundamental changes five or six times in our two-hundred-year history. In 1980 there was this fundamental change [with Reagan]. In 1984, people said, "We like the change." So by 1988 there was no desire to make a 180-degree turn. They said, "What is needed to be done is modify it, build on it." [25]

Bush carried the theme of continuity and consolidation past the election. His inaugural address not only thanked Reagan "for the wonderful things that you have done for America" but was laden with repeated invocations of words such as *continuity, continuance,* and *continuum.* In April 1989 Bush reaffirmed his status as Reagan's heir by telling reporters, "We didn't come in here throwing the rascals out." His chief of staff, John Sununu, described the Bush administration as a "friendly takeover" of its predecessor.[26]

In contrast to Reagan, however, Bush gave almost all of his attention as president to his constitutional roles as chief diplomat and commander in chief. Although foreign policy had not been a prominent theme of Bush's presidential campaign, it was in a sense the theme of his life: before becoming vice president, Bush had served as U.S. ambassador to the United Nations, director of the Central Intelligence Agency, and emissary to China. Nor was his foreign preoccupation surprising in view of the events that dominated the first part of the Bush administration, especially the collapse of communism in Eastern Europe and the Soviet Union in 1989 and Iraq's invasion of Kuwait in 1990. Bush handled both sets of developments with consummate skill. He was encouraging but not intrusive when first Poland, East Germany, and the other Soviet-dominated governments in Eastern Europe and then the Soviet Union itself collapsed. A more assertive policy may well have provoked a defensive, even military response from the Soviets; a less supportive one may have turned the newly free and democratic governments against the United States. Later, in the Middle East, Bush assembled an unprecedentedly large and diverse multinational coalition to support and finance his Desert Storm campaign against Iraq. The Allies' military offensive drove the Iraqi forces out of Kuwait with dazzling dispatch in early 1991 and severely weakened the military capacity of Iraq's leader, Saddam Hussein, to threaten neighboring nations and dominate the world's petroleum markets.

Bush's international triumphs notwithstanding, it is, as we have seen, domestic rather than foreign policy that drives the electoral cycle.[27] On election day 1992 only 8 percent of the voters said that foreign policy had been an important consideration in their choice of a presidential candidate. Eighty-seven percent of this group voted for Bush, but many more voters resented what they regarded as his concern for the world's problems at the expense of their own.[28] To be sure, Bush could have done differently. Riding high in the polls after the triumph of Desert Storm in March 1991, he had enjoyed a rare opportunity to mobilize Congress in support of a domestic agenda of consolidation. But Bush had no such agenda. As Sununu had told a conservative audience the previous November, "There's not another single piece of legislation that needs to be passed in the next two years for this president. In fact, if Congress wants to come together, adjourn, and leave, it's all right with us." [29]

To the extent that Bush dealt with domestic affairs, he was generally unsuccessful. His main challenge as a President of Consolidation was to smooth the rough edges of Reagan's achievements, notably the budget deficit. Both politically and substantively, Bush failed miserably in this effort. In September 1990 he abandoned his "no new taxes" pledge in return for Congress's agreement to reduce federal spending over a five-year period. Announcing the budget deal at the White House, Bush proclaimed, "It is balanced, it is fair, and in my view, it is what the United States of America needs." A month later, inundated by criticism from conservative, antitax Republicans and from voters who were outraged that he had violated his main campaign promise, Bush told reporters that the agreement made him "gag," a line he maintained through the end of the 1992 election campaign.[30]

Meanwhile, the deficit actually continued to rise: the accumulated shortfalls of Bush's four years as president added another trillion dollars to the national debt. The reason was that, although inflation remained low and the Federal Reserve Board pushed down interest rates, the economy was suffering in other ways that had budgetary side effects. Despite an uptick in late 1992, real economic growth averaged less than 1 percent per year during the Bush administration, the lowest rate in any four-year period since before World War II and about one-fourth the average annual rate of growth. Americans' real per capita income fell. Unemployment rose. Because of the weak economy, tax revenues from the stagnant national income decreased even as government expenditures increased to meet the rising demand for unemployment insurance, food stamps, and other forms of public assistance.[31]

If Bush failed to smooth the Reagan administration's rough edges, his record was at best mixed in his second major challenge as a President of Consolidation: to soften its hard edges. Reagan's neglect of the environment and civil rights had been unpopular even when he was president.[32] Bush acted to remedy this neglect, signing the Clean Air Act of 1990 and the Civil Rights Act of 1991. But in each case, his commitment was less than total. The Civil Rights Act became law only after a long and acrimonious squabble with Congress over the issue of racial quotas. The Clean Air Act soon was undermined by the antienvironmental Council on Competitiveness, a regulatory review board chaired by Vice President Dan Quayle that became business's court of last resort in the Bush administration.

During any Presidency of Consolidation, new social discontents and policy ideas to meet them arise to form the ingredients of the next turn of the cycle of politics and policy. The Bush administration was rich in creative conservative thinkers, such as Secretary of Housing and Urban Development Jack Kemp, Secretary of Education William J. Bennett, vice presidential chief of staff William Kristol, and White House domestic policy adviser James Pinkerton. These "New Paradigm" intellectuals offered innovative, antibureaucratic solutions in education, poverty, and housing. But, like most Presidents of Consolidation, Bush's domestic policy gaze was backward rather than forward. He was encouraged in this tendency by other, more cautious aides, such as Sununu, Secretary of the Treasury Nicholas Brady, and OMB director Richard Darman. When Bush's advisers could not agree on a course of action (which, not surprisingly, was often the case) the president's inclination was to do nothing. "Do no harm" and "I don't want to do anything dumb" were the oft-repeated watchwords of the Bush presidency.[33]

President (of Preparation) Bill Clinton

Bill Clinton would like nothing better than to be a President of Achievement in the mold of Woodrow Wilson, Franklin Roosevelt, Lyndon Johnson, and Ronald Reagan. But he probably is fated (at least during his first term) to be a President of Preparation like Theodore Roosevelt, John Kennedy, and Jimmy Carter.

Why is Clinton unlikely to join the ranks of Presidents of Achievement during the next four years? Simply put, the confluence of conditions required for a Presidency of Achievement—an empowering election, leadership skill, and ideas—has not yet occurred for Clinton.

Election

The main reason that Clinton probably will be a first-term President of Preparation rather than a President of Achievement is the nature of the elections that brought him to power. To be sure, Clinton was a change-oriented candidate. As he declared frequently during the campaign, the theme of his domestic agenda was neither "trickle-down economics" (the standard Republican approach) nor "tax-and-spend government" (the traditional Democratic solution) but rather "invest and grow"—that is, channel federal money into new education, training, and infrastructure development programs designed to enhance U.S. competitiveness in an increasingly international economy. Policy proposals aside, nothing embodied Clinton's innovating campaign theme more tangibly than did his selection of Sen. Albert Gore, Jr., of Tennessee as his vice presidential running mate. Defying the canons of old-style ticket balancing, Clinton chose as his running mate someone who resembles him in several politically significant ways: like Clinton, Gore is southern, politically moderate, Baptist, and a baby boomer.[34] In contrast, Bush, running with Quayle again on the ticket, appealed to the voters on the issueless basis of trust—trust in him to handle foreign policy crises and distrust of an opponent who, Bush charged, had dodged the draft as a young man and had led Arkansas poorly as governor.

But Clinton's victory on election day, although substantial, was not overwhelming. His 43 percent of the popular vote was noticeably short of a majority—short, even, of the 46 percent that Dukakis received as the Democratic nominee in 1988. Although supporters of Ross Perot's independent candidacy helped to raise voter turnout from 50.1 percent in 1988 to 55.2 percent in 1992, Clinton was elected with the endorsement of only 24 percent of the voting-age population, the smallest share for any president since John Quincy Adams in 1824.[35] Equally important, Clinton's 370 electoral votes compared unfavorably with the initial victories of all the century's other Presidents of Achievement: 435 for Wilson in 1912, 472 for Roosevelt in 1932, 486 for Johnson in 1964, and 489 for Reagan in 1980.

In the congressional elections, Clinton's party made no gains in the Senate and actually lost ten seats to the Republicans in the House of Representatives. Virtually every member of Congress received a higher share of the vote than did Clinton. On the day after the election, Senate Republican leader Robert Dole claimed half-facetiously that he had as much of a mandate from the voters as did Clinton because his party's 43 percent share of the Senate matched exactly the new president's 43 percent of the popular vote.

Exit polls revealed a strong desire in the electorate for economic improvement—on this, Clinton and the country were of one mind. But voters apparently were not yet ready for the sort of dramatic legislative change that marks a Presidency of Achievement. By a margin of 55 percent to 36 percent, they professed to prefer a government that would "cost less in taxes but provide fewer services" to one that would "provide more services but cost more in taxes." By 54 percent to 22 percent, they said that "the highest priority for the next President" should be "reducing the budget deficit" rather than "expanding domestic programs." [36] Nor have most Americans regained their cultural optimism about the ability of the federal government to make things better. On the eve of the election, only 22 percent—the historic low—said that they "could trust the government in Washington to do what was right" always or even most of the time.[37]

Leadership Skill

Clinton is well endowed with the skills of presidential leadership. His strategic sense developed rapidly after his defeat for reelection as governor of Arkansas in 1980. Clinton lost because he tried to impose his ideas on the people of his state; after learning to listen carefully to the voters before trying to lead them, he was elected four times. Substantively, although Clinton's career in state government leaves him with much to discover about foreign affairs, he is widely regarded (along with Gore) as one of the most serious students of domestic public policy on the current political scene.

Clinton's style of presenting himself to the general public is well suited to recent developments in the mass media. He is not an especially gifted orator, but he is sharp and persuasive in question-and-answer formats. Some of those formats, such as televised press conferences, are long established. Others became prominent during the 1992 election campaign, notably phone-in talk shows and "town meetings" in which voters ask questions directly. Two of the most prominent landmarks in Clinton's march to the presidency—an April 1 "Donahue" appearance on the eve of the New York primary and the second presidential debate on October 15—were programs of this sort. He almost certainly will rely on them heavily as president, along with bus tours, "drop-ins" at malls and McDonald's, televised issues conferences, and other symbolic actions of the kind that were effective during the campaign and the transition period.

Skills of self-presentation are especially important for Presidents of Preparation: their major challenge is to raise to the top of the national political agenda the dramatic proposals for change that they espouse, then gradually build a public constituency in support of them. So is the ability to manage presidential lieutenants, both in the White House and in the executive departments and agencies, whose assistance is essential to the development of specific legislative proposals. Here, too, Clinton has a demonstrated record of success, not just in Arkansas but on a national stage. As chair of the Democratic Leadership Council during the 1980s, he organized and worked with a coterie of academic and political advisers to draft a number of innovative, centrist approaches to public policy.[38] The new burden, however, will be to manage lieutenants on the grander scale of the presidency. Clinton's choice of an inexperienced chief of staff, childhood friend Thomas F. "Mack" McLarty, may not serve him well in this regard.[39]

The greatest challenge of political skill that the new president will face will be tactical, as he tries to lead Congress. After twelve years of "gridlock" with the Republican presidents Reagan and Bush, Democrats in Congress say they want to cooperate with the new Democratic president. But their experience is in opposing presidents, not supporting them; only a small minority were in Congress during the Carter administration. They also have a backlog of Bush-vetoed legislation in areas such as family and medical leave, abortion, campaign finance, and gun control that, in their eagerness to make up for lost time, may dilute Clinton's ability to concentrate congressional and public attention on his economic agenda. Finally, although the 103d Congress has fewer Democrats than the previous one, many more of them are women, African Americans, and Latinos, most of whom will be inclined to push Clinton in a much more liberal direction than he would like to take.[40]

Difficult circumstances aside, Clinton is a master of political argument, cajolery, and bargaining, all of them tactical skills that will stand him in good stead with Congress. His only apparent weakness is a strong desire to please everyone, a tendency that he traces to the experience of growing up in a troubled home. His conciliatory approach to opponents in Arkansas sometimes proved to be the basis for legislative success when he was governor, but at other times this approach led him to side-step difficult issues or to make unnecessary concessions that diluted the effectiveness of his policy proposals. In any event, tactical skills, along with the ability to manage the large organizations of the executive branch, are not the essential leadership skills of a President of Preparation.

Ideas

Clinton has never lacked for ideas about what the government should do differently and better. During the 1980s, in contrast to almost all other modern presidents, Clinton was actually a central figure among those working on the fringes of power to develop the ideas that later would form the central themes of his campaign and his presidential agenda.[41] His invest-and-grow approach to the economy is the product of a long colleagueship with economic analysts such as Robert Reich, David Aschauer, Ira Magaziner, and Derek Shearer. Many of the ideas that constitute this approach were hammered out, at least in general terms, before Clinton launched his bid for the presidency in discussions sponsored by the Progressive Policy Institute, the research component of the Democratic Leadership Council.

The essence of invest-and-grow is outlined in Reich's 1991 book, *The Work of Nations*.[42] Reich argues that in an increasingly international economy, in which jobs and capital flow easily from one country to another, a nation's only viable strategy for long-term prosperity is to enhance the value of its fixed assets, namely, the quality of the work force and the soundness of the infrastructure. To Clinton and his advisers, the policy implications of this analysis are clear: invest public funds both to improve the productivity of workers through education and training programs and to improve the infrastructure, the latter by keeping roads, bridges, railways, and the like in good repair and by building a national information network that links colleges, businesses, and government agencies. Not only will such spending enhance economic growth, they argue, but it eventually will yield dividends in the form of higher tax receipts. Aschauer estimates that every $10 billion that is wisely invested in enhancing the infrastructure brings an annual return of $7 billion in improved worker productivity, about a quarter of which is returned to the federal treasury in taxes.[43] To spur private investment, Clinton favors measures such as an investment tax credit for business and a limited capital-gains tax cut to reward those who support new business ventures.

During the campaign, Clinton also advanced a number of other important domestic goals, such as a national health insurance program that would somehow reduce the cost of health care while making insurance coverage universal, a thoroughly reformed welfare system that would foster responsibility and job seeking on the part of welfare recipients, and a national service program in which young people would receive stipends to attend college in return for their full-time participation in public service activities.

These ideas and others like them—a middle-class tax cut, a one-hundred-thousand-person reduction in the size of the federal civil service (matched by a one-hundred-thousand-person increase in the number of police officers), a lifting of the ban on homosexuals in the military, an end to adult illiteracy "in five years," and so on—had less to do with a coherent economic strategy than with the exigencies of electioneering.

Unfortunately for Clinton, the same economic problems that made possible his election also promise to constrain the expansiveness of his policy ideas. Foremost among these problems is the budget deficit, which both the voters and, perhaps more significantly, the financial markets insist must be reduced lest inflation and interest rates rise and the economy be strangled by debt. Clinton's programs carry a high price tag: $220 billion in new spending over four years, by his own cautious estimate. Because the financial yield from his invest-and-grow strategy would come only in the long term, the money to pay for the new programs and to reduce the deficit would have to be raised or saved in the short term. Clinton's proposals to acquire the $220 billion for new spending and an additional $75 billion or so for deficit reduction include some realistic elements—a 5 percent tax increase on those earning $200,000 or more and accelerated reductions in defense spending, for example—but also some fanciful ones, notably his wildly inflated estimates of what can be saved by strictly enforcing the tax laws on foreign corporations and by eliminating waste from government. In truth, it simply will be impossible for Clinton to have his new programs and deficit reduction simultaneously, much less a middle-class tax cut.

The problems with Clinton's agenda of reform are political as well as intellectual. Obviously, he will face the loyal opposition of congressional Republicans—that is the nature of two-party politics. But Clinton's more serious frustrations may be with his fellow Democrats and the constituency groups they represent. In addition to their pent-up legislative agenda from the Reagan-Bush years, congressional Democrats have political concerns of a kind that could easily transform sound infrastructure investment into wasteful pork-barrel spending. The list of possible conflicts is long: Clinton basically supports the North American Free Trade Agreement with Mexico and Canada, which Democratic-affiliated labor unions and environmentalists oppose; Clinton wants to trim the federal work force, which Democratic civil servants and legislators want to expand; Clinton wants national educational standards and teacher testing, which are anathema to teacher associations; and so on. With a weak electoral mandate, Clinton is unlikely to be able to persuade either the Republicans or a sufficient number of the Democrats in Congress of the wisdom of his more dramatic ideas.

Conclusion

In sum, Clinton is unlikely to be a President of Achievement during his first term. Instead, he almost certainly will be a President of Preparation. As such, he will encounter periods of great frustration. Some even have drawn a historical analogy between Clinton and Carter. As was the former Georgia governor, they predict, so will the former governor of Arkansas be whipsawed by the Scylla of rising budget deficits and the Charybdis of Democratic special-interest groups clamoring for new and expensive government programs. As with Carter, too, the inexperienced Clinton will be weak and uncertain in foreign affairs. The analogy ends with Clinton's defeat in 1996 by a Republican party whose dominance in presidential elections will prove not to have been ended by his 1992 victory (any more than by Carter's in 1976) but merely interrupted.

Other scenarios are equally plausible. The fate of the President of Preparation need not be unhappy, even on its own terms. Two of Clinton's three predecessors in this role, Theodore Roosevelt and John F. Kennedy, have been judged by historians as successful presidents: Roosevelt was ranked as "near great" and Kennedy as "above average" in the most recent round of ratings, and even Carter scored as an "average" president.[44] The President of Preparation performs a vital function in the cycle of politics and policy: to raise important new social concerns to the top of the national political agenda and to propose new solutions to address those concerns. It takes strong leadership skills and a wealth of innovative policy ideas to perform this function well.

Nor is a Presidency of Preparation necessarily the end of the story for a president. The history of such presidencies is riddled with lost opportunities for achievement status. Roosevelt almost certainly would have been his own President of Achievement if he had run for reelection in 1908, but, even though he had served only one full term and part of William McKinley's, he withdrew in deference to the two-term tradition. (In 1912, too late, Roosevelt forsook the tradition and ran again as a third-party candidate. That he had declined a "third cup of coffee" in 1908, he said, did not mean he never wanted to drink coffee again.) Kennedy, as noted earlier, was consciously preparing for a second-term Presidency of Achievement at the time of his assassination, a year in advance of the 1964 elections.

The bad news for Clinton, then, is that his Presidency of Preparation may fail; the good news is that it may succeed. The best news, however, is that with the right combination of leadership skills, policy ideas, and, most important, a landslide reelection with long congressional coattails in 1996, Clinton could become a President of Achievement during his second term.

Notes

1. Saul Steinberg, *Saul Steinberg* (New York: Knopf, 1978), 79.
2. For a critique of political scientists' generally ahistorical approach to the presidency, see Michael Nelson, "Is There a Postmodern Presidency?" *Congress and the Presidency* 16 (Autumn 1989): 155-162.
3. See, for example, Erwin C. Hargrove and Michael Nelson, *Presidents, Politics, and*

Policy (Baltimore: Johns Hopkins University Press, 1984); Hargrove and Nelson, "The Presidency: Reagan and the Cycle of Politics and Policy," in *The Elections of 1984*, ed. Michael Nelson (Washington, D.C.: CQ Press, 1985), 189-214; and Hargrove, *The Power of the Modern Presidency* (New York: Knopf, 1974), chap. 6.

4. Morris P. Fiorina, *Retrospective Voting in American National Elections* (New Haven: Yale University Press, 1981).

5. It is tempting to add Truman—a would-be President of Achievement who entered the United States into the Korean War—to the list.

6. In classifying the Ford administration as a continuation of Nixon's Presidency of Consolidation, Hargrove and I have departed from our earlier interpretation. Compare Hargrove and Nelson, *Presidents, Politics, and Policy*, with Hargrove, "The Presidency: George Bush and the Cycle of Politics and Policy," in *The Elections of 1988*, ed. Michael Nelson (Washington, D.C.: CQ Press, 1989), 153-180.

7. The term is the political scientist V. O. Key's, from his book *Public Opinion and American Democracy* (New York: Knopf, 1961).

8. A great deal of academic research suggests that the "coattail effect" is lesser in magnitude and greater in subtlety than most politicians believe. But, as Gary C. Jacobson has pointed out, as long as politicians—especially members of Congress—believe in it, the coattail effect will matter as much as if it were real. See Jacobson, *The Politics of Congressional Elections*, 3d ed. (New York: HarperCollins, 1992), chap. 8.

9. "Strategic sense" strongly resembles Woodrow Wilson's idea of "interpretation." See Jeffrey K. Tulis, "The Two Constitutional Presidencies," in *The Presidency and the Political System*, 3d ed., ed. Michael Nelson (Washington, D.C.: CQ Press, 1990), 85-115. For a fuller discussion of presidential leadership skill, see Hargrove and Nelson, *Presidents, Politics, and Policy*, chap. 4.

10. For an interesting elaboration of Hargrove's and my propositions about ideas in the cycle of politics and policy, see Thomas S. Langston, *Ideologues and Presidents: From the New Deal to the Reagan Revolution* (Baltimore: Johns Hopkins University Press, 1992).

11. For a fuller discussion of this point, see Hargrove and Nelson, *Presidents, Politics, and Policy*, chap. 2.

12. For a full discussion of these implications, see Sidney M. Milkis and Michael Nelson, *The American Presidency: Origins and Development, 1776-1990* (Washington, D.C.: CQ Press, 1990), chaps. 8-9.

13. Arthur S. Link, *Woodrow Wilson and the Progressive Era, 1900-1917* (New York: Harper, 1954), 2.

14. James MacGregor Burns, *Roosevelt: The Lion and the Fox* (New York: Harcourt, Brace, Harvest ed., 1956), 179.

15. Ibid., 337. On the Court-packing issue, see Michael Nelson, "The President and the Court: Reinterpreting the Court-Packing Episode of 1937," *Political Science Quarterly* 103 (Summer 1988): 267-293.

16. James L. Sundquist, *Politics and Policy: The Eisenhower, Kennedy, and Johnson Years* (Washington, D.C.: Brookings Institution, 1968), chaps. 9-10.

17. Roger Davidson, "The Presidency and Congress," in *The Presidency and the Political System*, ed. Michael Nelson (Washington, D.C.: CQ Press, 1984), 385.

18. Lloyd A. Free and Hadley Cantril, *The Political Beliefs of Americans* (New York: Simon and Schuster, 1968), 5-40.

19. For example, the unprecedented resignation of President Nixon and ascension to the presidency of Gerald Ford, who had never been elected to any national office.

20. Erwin C. Hargrove, *Jimmy Carter as President: Leadership and the Politics of the Public Good* (Baton Rouge: Louisiana State University Press, 1988).

21. Seymour Martin Lipset and William Schneider, *The Confidence Gap: Business, Labor, and Government* (New York: Free Press, 1983), 21-22.

22. Robert Pear, "The Reagan Revolution," *New York Times*, Jan. 31, 1984.

23. Bill Keller, "Voting Record of '81 Shows the Romance and Fidelity of Reagan Honeymoon on Hill," *Congressional Quarterly Weekly Report*, Jan. 2, 1982, 19; and Irwin P. Arieff, "Conservatives Hit New High in Showdown Vote Victories," *Congressional Quarterly Weekly Report*, Jan. 9, 1982, 50.

24. William Schneider, "Solidarity's Not Enough," *National Journal*, Nov. 12, 1988, 2853-2855.

25. Quoted in Michael Duffy and Dan Goodgame, *Marching in Place: The Status Quo Presidency of George Bush* (New York: Simon and Schuster, 1992), 19.

26. Ibid., 37.

27. See Stephen Hess and Michael Nelson, "Foreign Policy: Dominance and Decisiveness in Presidential Elections," in *Elections of 1984*, ed. Nelson, 129-154.

28. Laurence I. Barrett, "A New Coalition for the 1990s," *Time*, Nov. 16, 1992, 47-48.

29. Duffy and Goodgame, *Marching in Place*, 82

30. Ibid., 83, 285.

31. Benjamin M. Friedman, "Clinton's Opportunity," *New York Review of Books*, Dec. 3, 1992, 44.

32. Hargrove and Nelson, "The Presidency," 201-202.

33. Duffy and Goodgame, *Marching in Place*, 70-71, 283.

34. As I note in Chapter 8, Gore's nomination balanced the ticket in ways more subtle than age, religion, ideology, and geography.

35. Exit polls indicated that the number of Perot supporters who said they would not have voted if Perot had not been on the ballot amount to 3 percent of the electorate. "Where Perot Ran Strongest," *New York Times*, Nov. 5, 1992. The comparison with John Quincy Adams is in Adam Clymer, "Turnout on Election Day Was the Largest in 24 Years," *New York Times*, Dec. 17, 1992.

36. William Schneider, "A Loud Vote for Change," *National Journal*, Nov. 7, 1992, 2542-2544. In state elections, conservatives dominated the initiative and referendum process, and the Republicans gained more than seventy seats in the legislatures. Thomas B. Edsall, "Coattails? There Were None," *Washington Post National Weekly Edition*, Jan. 4-10, 1993, 15. The exit poll was conducted by Voter Research and Surveys, General Election, Nov. 3, 1992.

37. Adam Clymer, "GOP, Hopeful of Big Gains, Sees Its Chances Fade," *New York Times*, Nov. 2, 1992.

38. See, for example, Julie Rovner, "When It Comes to Finding His Way, Clinton Won't Need a Map of Hill," *Congressional Quarterly Weekly Report*, Nov. 14, 1992, 3622-3623.

39. On the need for a strong chief of staff, see John P. Burke, "The Institutional Presidency," in *Presidency and the Political System*, 3d ed., ed. Nelson, 383-408.

40. As a result of the 1992 congressional elections, the number of women in Congress rose from thirty to fifty-three, the number of African Americans rose from twenty-five to thirty-nine, and the number of Latinos rose from eleven to seventeen.

41. See Rovner, "When It Comes to Finding His Way."

42. Robert B. Reich, *The Work of Nations: Preparing Ourselves for 21st-Century Capitalism* (New York: Knopf, 1991). See also Bill Clinton and Al Gore, *Putting People First: How We Can All Change America* (New York: Times Books, 1992).

43. David Aschauer, "Is Public Expenditure Productive?" *Journal of Monetary Economics* 23 (March 1989): 177-200.

44. Robert K. Murray and Tim H. Blessing, "The Presidential Performance Study: A Progress Report," *Journal of American History* 70 (December 1983): 535-555.

7

Congress: Unusual Year, Unusual Election

Gary C. Jacobson

Historically, congressional elections have been marked by great regularities. Overwhelmingly, the winning candidates are "white men in blue suits." Incumbent members of Congress, especially in the House of Representatives, almost always are reelected. The victorious party in the presidential election usually gains seats in Congress.

As Gary C. Jacobson demonstrates in this chapter, the congressional elections of 1992 did not follow the historical pattern. In demographic terms, women, most of them Democrats, tripled their number in the Senate (from two to six) and substantially increased it in the House (from twenty-eight to forty-seven). Latinos increased the size of their ranks in the House from eleven to seventeen, and the number of African Americans rose from twenty-five to thirty-eight. Politically, incumbents were defeated in record numbers in primary elections; many more retired in anticipation of a defeat. Little partisan turnover occurred (none in the Senate); to the extent that it did, President-elect Bill Clinton's Democratic party actually lost ten seats in the House.

Jacobson describes the unusual results of the congressional elections and explains them in terms of several characteristics of 1992 that made it an unusual political year, such as the legacy of the Clarence Thomas hearings and the House banking scandal.

Like the presidential race, the 1992 congressional elections departed dramatically from recent historical patterns. For one thing, they were unusually competitive. The elections produced the largest turnover of membership in the House of Representatives in more than forty years; 110 new members took office in January 1993.[1] The influx of new members sharply altered the House's *demographic* makeup. The number of women representatives rose from twenty-eight to forty-seven; of African Americans, from twenty-five to thirty-eight; of Latinos, from eleven to seventeen. Twelve new senators also took office, four of them women, one of the women (Carol Moseley-Braun of Illinois) an African American; in all, the election tripled the number of women senators from two to six. Another of the entering

Table 7-1   Membership Changes in the House, 102d to 103d
Congresses

Members	102d Congress (elected 1990)	103d Congress (elected 1992)	Change
Democrats	268	258	−10
Republicans	166	176	+10
Independent	1	1	0
Women	28	47	+19
African Americans	25	38	+13
Latinos	11	17	+ 6
Freshmen	45	110	+65
Democrats			
Incumbents reelected	195		
Incumbents defeated	16		
Freshmen	63		
Republicans			
Incumbents reelected	129		
Incumbents defeated	8		
Freshmen	47		

senators, Ben Nighthorse Campbell of Colorado, is a member of the Northern Cheyenne Council of 44 Chiefs and sports a ponytail.

Despite all of this turnover, *partisan* change in Congress was exceedingly modest. Republicans, although losing the presidency, picked up ten seats in the House, leaving the Democrats with a reduced (but still comfortable) 258-176 majority. The Senate elections produced no net partisan change at all, leaving the Democrats with the same 57-43 majority they enjoyed before election day. Tables 7-1, 7-2, and 7-3 summarize the results.

The coincidence of a large turnover in membership with a small partisan swing in the House is a historical oddity. In other postwar elections, a large turnover of House seats has been accompanied by a large partisan swing. This is clear from Figure 7-1, which plots the net partisan swing against the number of new members in elections since 1942. The 1992 result is uniquely off the diagonal—a very large turnover with a very small net partisan shift. Had 1992 matched the historical average, the House would have undergone a net partisan swing of about fifty-four seats; the actual swing fell short of the expected one by nearly five standard deviations.[2]

The year 1992, then, provided a most peculiar set of congressional elections. Why was turnover so high? Why were its partisan consequences so small? Why did the Republicans pick up House seats while losing the White House? Why the abrupt increase in the representation of women and minorities? What are the prospects for the 103d Congress?

Table 7-2   Membership Changes in the Senate, 102d to 103d Congresses

Members	102d Congress	103d Congress	Change
Democrats	57	57	0
Republicans	43	43	0
Women	2	6	+4
African Americans	0	1	+1
Freshmen	4	12	+8
Democrats			
Incumbents reelected	13		
Incumbents defeated	2		
Freshmen	7		
Republicans			
Incumbents reelected	10		
Incumbents defeated	2		
Freshmen	5		

An Unusual Year

The peculiarities of the 1992 congressional election reflect the converging effects of three basic environmental forces—divided government, a stagnant economy, and reapportionment—refracted through such signal events as the Anita Hill-Clarence Thomas dispute, the House banking scandal, and a Democratic presidential victory. The most consequential of the forces that produced this complex chain of events was divided government.

The Setting: Divided Government

The 1992 elections were preceded by twelve years of divided government, with Republicans Ronald Reagan and then George Bush in the White House and the House of Representatives and the Senate (after 1986) controlled by Democratic majorities. Both the forces that produced divided government and the politics divided government engendered had profound effects on electoral politics in 1992.

Divided government in the Reagan-Bush years emerged from the electorate's unwitting attempt to have its cake and eat it too. Poll after poll taken during the 1980s and early 1990s found solid majorities in favor of an impossible combination of low taxes, generous social spending, and a balanced budget.[3] It is hardly surprising that, given a choice, people would declare themselves for benefits and against costs. The surprise is that electoral politics in this era gave them the option of voting simultaneously for Democratic

Table 7-3   Senate Election Results by State, 1992

State	Vote total	Percent of two-party vote
Alabama		
Richard C. Shelby (D)*	1,017,332	66.3
Richard Sellers (R)	517,644	33.7
Alaska		
Frank H. Murkowski (R)*	107,026	58.0
Tony Smith (D)	77,654	42.0
Arizona		
John McCain (R)*	740,578	63.7
Claire Sargent (D)	421,405	36.3
Arkansas		
Dale Bumpers (D)*	545,325	59.8
Mike Huckabee (R)	362,203	40.2
California		
Barbara Boxer (D)	4,859,119	53.1
Bruce Herschensohn (R)	4,292,237	46.9
Dianne Feinstein (D)	5,496,905	59.2
John Seymour (R)*	3,780,880	40.8
Colorado		
Ben Nighthorse Campbell (D)	798,864	54.9
Terry Considine (R)	656,426	45.1
Connecticut		
Christopher J. Dodd (D)*	887,734	61.0
Brook Johnson (R)	568,269	39.0
Florida		
Bob Graham (D)*	3,214,708	66.3
Bill Grant (R)	1,688,522	33.7
Georgia [a]		
Paul Coverdell (R)	633,182	50.6
Wyche Fowler (D)*	618,190	49.4
Hawaii		
Daniel K. Inouye (D)*	207,794	68.0
Rick Reed (R)	97,653	32.0
Idaho		
Dirk Kempthorne (R)	269,209	56.5
Richard Stallings (D)	207,124	43.5
Illinois		
Carol Moseley-Braun (D)	2,555,304	54.8
Richard S. Williamson (R)	2,107,955	45.2
Indiana		
Daniel R. Coats (R)*	1,249,724	60.2
Joseph H. Hogsett (D)	887,549	39.8
Iowa		
Charles E. Grassley (R)*	894,235	71.9
Jean Lloyd-Jones (D)	349,461	28.1
Kansas		
Bob Dole (R)*	700,534	66.7
Gloria O'Dell (D)	349,379	33.3

continued

Table 7-3 *Continued*

State	Vote total	Percent of two-party vote
Kentucky		
Wendell H. Ford (D)*	835,883	63.7
David L. Williams (R)	477,040	36.3
Louisiana		
John B. Breaux (D)*	unopposed	
Maryland		
Barbara A. Mikulski (D)*	1,247,386	71.2
Alan L. Keyes (R)	503,956	28.8
Missouri		
Christopher S. Bond (R)*	1,221,453	53.6
Geri Rothman-Serot (D)	1,057,357	46.4
Nevada		
Harry Reid (D)*	247,732	56.0
Demar Dahl (R)	194,527	44.0
New Hampshire		
Judd Gregg (R)	247,215	51.5
John Rauh (D)	232,846	48.5
New York		
Alfonse M. D'Amato (R)*	3,007,882	50.9
Robert Abrams (D)	2,899,888	49.1
North Carolina		
Lauch Faircloth (R)	1,276,831	52.0
Terry Sanford (D)*	1,176,939	48.0
North Dakota		
Byron L. Dorgan (D)	178,443	60.2
Steve Sydness (R)	117,832	39.8
Kent Conrad (D)[b]	102,887	65.3
Jack Dalrymple (R)	54,726	34.7
Ohio		
John Glenn (D)*	2,418,464	54.8
Mike DeWine (R)	1,992,793	45.2
Oklahoma		
Don Nickles (R)*	757,876	60.5
Steve Lewis (D)	494,350	39.5
Oregon		
Bob Packwood (R)*	612,238	52.3
Les AuCoin (D)	558,015	47.7
Pennsylvania		
Arlen Specter (R)*	2,344,397	51.4
Lynn Yeakel (D)	2,215,472	48.6
South Carolina		
Ernest F. Hollings (D)*	578,749	51.2
Thomas F. Hartnett (R)	550,900	48.8
South Dakota		
Tom Daschle (D)*	216,869	66.6
Charlene Haar (R)	108,573	33.4
Utah		
Robert F. Bennett (R)	418,309	58.2
Wayne Owens (D)	300,404	41.8

continued

Table 7-3   *Continued*

State	Vote total	Percent of two-party vote
Vermont		
Patrick J. Leahy (D)*	143,286	55.5
James H. Douglas (R)	114,835	44.5
Washington		
Patty Murray (D)	1,035,909	54.7
Rod Chandler(R)	856,595	45.3
Wisconsin		
Russell D. Feingold (D)	1,284,285	53.3
Bob Kasten (R)*	1,123,715	46.7

Note: Asterisks indicate incumbents.

[a] Fowler won the most votes on November 4, but he did not win the absolute majority necessary for victory under Georgia law; the listed vote is for the November 20 runoff, which Coverdell won.

[b] Conrad, who had retired from the other North Dakota Senate seat, won the special election held December 4 to replace Quentin Burdick, who died September 8.

Congresses so they could receive the benefits they enjoyed and Republican presidents so they would not have to pay for them.

During the 1980 Reagan campaign, Republicans had discovered the political magic in supply-side economics. The magic lay in its claim that the government could reduce taxes without reducing spending or borrowing money because lower taxes would stimulate so much economic growth that tax revenues would not actually decline. Republicans thus could promise to reduce taxes without having to concede that programs would also have to be slashed lest the red ink flow.

Upon taking office, the Reagan administration duly proposed large supply-side tax cuts. Congressional Democrats quickly surrendered to the political appeal of reducing taxes and even raised the ante by adding tax breaks of their own. The administration also attracted enough Democratic votes to impose cuts in domestic social programs, but these reductions were more than offset by increases in defense spending. When a sharp recession hit in late 1981 and the supply-side dividend fell far short of the administration's optimistic projections, large budget deficits began to accumulate. Widespread economic hardship led Congress to resist further reductions in domestic spending. The recession encouraged Democrats to attack the equity and effectiveness of Republican economic policies, and attacks on Reaganomics became the main theme of their 1982 congressional campaigns. The 1982 election enlarged the Democratic House majority by twenty-six seats, stiffening congressional opposition to further domestic cutbacks.

The experience of the early 1980s taught Republicans that opposing taxes was good politics but that attacking popular domestic programs was not. Democrats learned that most large domestic programs were indeed pop-

Figure 7-1   Turnover and Partisan Change in U.S. House Elections, 1942-1992

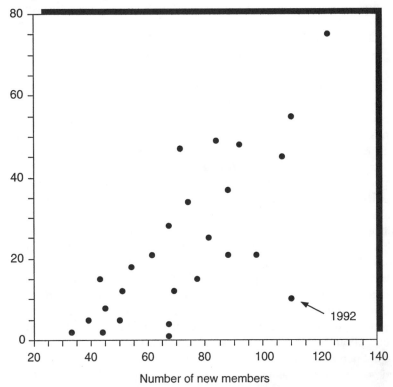

Net partisan change

Number of new members

ular but that people did not like paying for them. In subsequent campaigns, voters were thus offered the opportunity to declare themselves simultaneously in favor of low taxes and generous domestic spending. They could—and did—elect Republican presidents on a promise of "no new taxes" and Democratic majorities in Congress committed to maintaining or increasing their favorite domestic programs.[4] Neither side was candid about the price. Republicans insisted that economic growth would provide sufficient tax revenues to maintain popular programs and shrink the deficit without additional taxes. And, taking Democratic presidential nominee Walter F. Mondale's fate in 1984 after he promised to raise taxes as an object lesson, Democrats continued to champion popular programs and initiatives without acknowledging that the money to pay for them would have to be borrowed or raised through higher taxes.

Budget action that was faithful to these electoral stances guaranteed continued deficits. Republican administrations accepted large deficits rather than raising taxes to pay for government programs that Democratic Congresses refused to cut; and Democratic Congresses accepted large deficits rather than reducing government programs when Republican presidents refused to pay for them by initiating tax increases. There is nothing mysterious about the continuing budget deficits; they were the product of a compelling political logic. But the deficits also represented Congress and the president's failure to deliver the public's third economic desideratum: a balanced budget. The political problem this failure posed for both sides became more acute as the growing mountain of government debt threatened the economy's long-term vitality.

The principal effort to attack the deficit during the 1980s was the Gramm-Rudman-Hollings scheme, enacted in 1985, which required Congress and the White House to achieve a balanced budget by meeting a series of progressively lower yearly deficit targets. If Congress and the president did not agree on how to make the required cuts, reductions were to occur automatically and across the board on all programs that were not explicitly exempted. The initial deadline for reaching a balanced budget was 1991. When Gramm-Rudman-Hollings was revised in 1987, the deadline was extended to 1993. Each year it became more difficult to reach the deficit targets, as the easy moves—changes in accounting procedures and other tricks commonly dismissed as "blue smoke and mirrors"—were exhausted. But because the electoral stakes were so high, both sides nonetheless remained strongly disposed to resist spending cuts or tax increases that violated the promises they had made to their core supporters. Republicans had made opposition to taxes the centerpiece of their strategy for becoming the majority party. Democrats, although seeking to avoid the "tax and spend" brand, had prospered as the defenders of domestic programs serving old people, poor people, farmers, workers, the environment, education, and so on. As long as both sides saw smaller political damage in deficits than in what they would have to give up to reduce the deficit, no solution was possible, and most of the energy went into avoiding partisan blame for failing to reach agreement.

This maneuvering put all participants in a serious bind when the leaders on both sides finally decided that large, permanent deficits were too dangerous to be ignored. The only feasible outcome was a compromise that included both spending cuts and tax increases. But such a compromise required not only that both parties abandon positions that were central to the images they sought to project but that many members of Congress betray their own campaign promises. If either side balked, however, it could be branded as irresponsible and unfit to govern. Budget politics under divided government had become a no-win game.

In May 1990 President Bush sought to break the stalemate by inviting congressional leaders to a budget summit with "no preconditions," implying that tax increases were on the table. Democratic negotiators suspected a trap, and little progress was made until the president explicitly agreed that "tax revenue increases" would be part of the agreement. In late October, after much additional haggling, the negotiators cut a deal to reduce the projected deficit by nearly $500 billion over the next five years through a combination of tax and fee increases and caps on benefits.

Both the unedifying process (which included months of unproductive closed-door negotiations, numerous leaks, trial balloons, and false starts, and a brief shutdown of some federal agencies when a deadline was not met) and the unpalatable product (an agreement that raised taxes and cut back on some popular social programs) angered large segments of the public. With the economy in recession, tolerance for bickering politicians was at a low ebb, and self-sacrifice was a tough sell. Reviews of both Congress's and the president's budget performances were decisively negative; two-thirds of the people polled opposed the budget deal and disapproved of both sides' handling of the issue.[5]

Voters carried their anger into the polls on election day. The average vote for House incumbents dropped sharply in 1990, reaching its lowest point since 1974. Punishment was bipartisan. In contrast to every other postwar election, the average vote for incumbents of *both* parties fell. (Normally, one rises and the other falls, reflecting the dominant partisan tide.) Still, turnover was modest; only 15 of the 406 House incumbents, and one Senate incumbent, were voted out of office.

Why did so many incumbents survive the voters' wrath? Many otherwise vulnerable members escaped defeat because they faced such feeble opposition. Three things are necessary for voters to oust an incumbent: (1) a good reason, (2) an acceptable replacement (roughly defined as an experienced officeholder), and (3) a campaign with sufficient financial resources to let voters know about the first two. In 1990 voters had a good reason—anger over the budget deal—to reject incumbents, but acceptable replacements and money for their campaigns were in exceedingly scarce supply.[6]

With so few strong challengers poised to exploit the windfall the budget deal had suddenly handed them, most incumbents were spared, although more than a few got their worst electoral scare in years. More by accident than by design, the events that so angered voters in 1990 had taken place too late in the election cycle to mobilize potential challengers and campaign contributors. House incumbents were also helped by the calendar in another way, namely, the prospect of redistricting after 1990. With all the uncertainties associated with new district maps, ambitious, experienced potential challengers of both parties had reason in 1990 to be patient for a couple more years, when new boundaries would be in place and the new districts, along with anticipated retirements, would produce a bumper crop of open seats.[7]

The surviving incumbents no doubt hoped they had put the deficit on the back burner, and for a while budget politics was forgotten as everyone's attention turned to the Gulf war. The dramatic diplomatic and military successes that drove Saddam Hussein's Iraqi forces from Kuwait in early 1991 raised George Bush's performance ratings to unprecedented heights. Congress's public standing also improved markedly, but the war issue threatened political problems for the members in both houses—almost all of them Democrats—who had voted against authorizing the president to use military force against Iraq. By the war's end, George Bush looked unbeatable for 1992, and Republicans were relishing the prospect of recruiting Gulf war heroes to challenge Democratic doves. The war, Bush's popularity, and the prospect of reapportionment promised a banner Republican year.

The Economy

The Republicans' high expectations foundered on the economy. The 1990 midterm elections had coincided with a recession; but so had midterms in five of the previous six postwar Republican administrations. (The Reagan administration in 1986 is the exception.) Bush's problem was that, although the economy had rebounded strongly from these earlier midterm recessions, only a feeble, fitful recovery followed the 1990 recession. The economy's annual growth rate from the bottom of the recession in the first quarter of 1991 through the third quarter of 1992 was less than 2 percent, not enough to make a dent in the high unemployment figures. Indeed, the economy's annual growth rate for the entire Bush presidency was less than 1 percent, the lowest for any administration since the Great Depression.

Divided government exacerbated the president's economic troubles. The huge budget deficit—a creature of divided government—made it nearly impossible to stimulate the economy in the customary way, through tax cuts or deficit spending, without upsetting financial markets so much that the move would create more economic difficulties than it solved. Nonetheless, in late 1991 the president's chief economic adviser, Michael Boskin, had proposed to prod the sluggish economy by cutting taxes. This would have required the president to declare an economic emergency, because only then could he ignore the 1990 budget agreement's requirement that any revenue loss be offset by an equivalent spending cut. In order to reassure financial markets, the stimulus package would also have had to include future spending cuts and caps on entitlement programs such as Medicaid and Medicare.

The president decided against adopting the Boskin plan on the advice of other administration officials, who argued that the economy would take care of itself in time for the election. (They were nearly right—good economic news began appearing in late October 1992, just in time to be too late to help Bush.) But they also feared that Congress would not enact the package without exacting too high a price. The political wounds the administration had suffered in getting the 1990 budget agreement were still fresh— Bush's breaking of the "no new taxes" pledge haunted him until the end— and they were reluctant to return to that battlefield. Divided government thus helped to deter timely action to get the economy in shape for the 1992 election.[8]

The economy's continuing weakness steadily sapped the support the president had acquired by bringing the Gulf war to a successful conclusion.

Figure 7-2 Public Opinion on the Economy, Congress's Perform-
mance, and President Bush's Economic Performance,
August 1990-July 1992

Percent of respondents

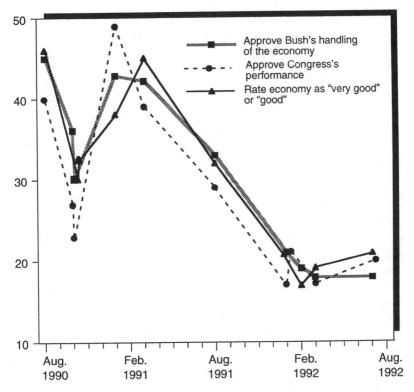

Public attention turned from foreign affairs, a venue where Republicans have
enjoyed an advantage for years, to domestic economic issues, where the
faltering economy played to the Democrats' strength.[9] But the Democrats
controlled Congress, and the economy formed the basis of the public's disaffection with Congress as well as with the president. This is evident from
Figure 7-2, which displays the trends in the public's opinion on three issues
that were addressed together at irregular intervals in a subset of the CBS
News/*New York Times* polls conducted during the two years leading up to the
election: the condition of the economy, President Bush's handling of the
economy, and Congress's job performance.

Figure 7-2 shows that the public's ratings of Congress's performance and
the president's handling of the economy moved in lockstep with its assessment
of the economy.[10] Public anger over the budget compromise in October 1990
hit the president and Congress equally hard; so did the growing economic
discontent that later replaced the euphoria briefly engendered by the Gulf war.

The three trends hit the bottom together in late winter 1992.

Congress and the president suffered from bad economic news at the same time and to the same degree. This pattern makes it easy to understand why President Bush's attempts during the 1992 campaign to blame the Democrats in Congress for the economy fell flat. The public was not disposed to make distinctions when it came to allocating blame; when reminded of why they were fed up with Congress, people were also reminded of why they were fed up with the president. But the pattern also meant that the weak economy was not an unalloyed Democratic advantage. To the extent that voters blamed Democrats in Congress as well as the president for failing to address economic problems effectively, the issue could cut both ways. Still, as discussed later, the economy did ultimately help congressional Democrats because it contributed so much to Bill Clinton's victory.

Obviously, Americans in 1992 had no dearth of reasons for disdaining Congress: overdrafts, pay raise subterfuges, ethical lapses, the savings and loan debacle. But as the data in Figure 7-2 show, what gave these issues their potency was something more basic: the government's apparent inability to address a host of economic problems that had driven public confidence in the economy to a seventeen-year low.[11] In good economic times, Americans have shown themselves to be remarkably tolerant of their politicians' perks and peccadillos; but bad times bring out a resentful streak of puritanism that expresses itself in demands for probity and reform.

The twelve years of divided government also had made the assignment of blame for economic and other troubles problematic. When one party controls both Congress and the White House, the public has an obvious target for its wrath: the party running the show. Whether or not the ruling party is actually to blame for bad times is beside the point; for better or worse, responsibility comes with power. Divided government invites each party to blame the other, and the public ends up agreeing with, and blaming, both. Under divided government, the impulse to "throw the rascals out" is harder to obey because the rascals are harder to identify. The simplest solution is to blame everyone, and so ill-considered "reforms" such as legislative term limits become the popular rage.

Redistricting

The electoral consequences of a sour economy under divided government were complicated by an accident of the calendar. In obedience to the Constitution, House seats were reapportioned and district boundaries redrawn for 1992 to reflect the population shifts recorded by the 1990 census. Nineteen seats were redistributed from slow-growing to fast-growing states; twenty-one states either gained or lost seats in the House. Most of the states that kept the same number of seats had to redraw districts to meet the equal-population requirement.

Election years that end in "2" typically produce higher turnover in the

House than do other years; members whose districts disappear or are changed in politically damaging ways are more likely than usual to retire—and more likely than usual to be defeated if they do not. Still, in recent decades, re-apportionment has added, on average, only about ten new members to the House beyond the normal turnover. An additional circumstance exaggerated the effect of redistricting for 1992 and the rest of the decade. The Supreme Court had, in a 1986 decision *(Thornburg v. Gingles)*, construed the Voting Rights Act to require that House district lines not discriminate, even uninten-tionally, against minorities. The decision was widely interpreted to require mapmakers to design districts in which racial and ethnic minorities were in the majority wherever residence patterns made this possible.[12]

Furthermore, districts in several of the largest states were redrawn for 1992 by mapmakers who, in contrast to past practices, studiously ignored the interests of incumbents. In California, three "special masters"—retired judges appointed by the state supreme court—drew a map that paired in-cumbents in six districts even though California had *gained* seven seats. (The court took over when the Republican governor and Democratic legislature could not agree on a map.) The court-appointed expert who drew Florida's new map did so without knowing where the incumbents lived. The New York legislature adopted a map based on a state court plan that was chosen only because the alternative federal court plan was even more disruptive. In Michigan, a three-judge panel deemed the plans submitted by both parties to be "excessively partisan" and drew a radically different map of its own.[13] In previous reapportionment cycles, state legislatures did more of the work and routinely sought to protect the incumbents of one or both parties (de-pending on whether one or both controlled the state government and thus had any say in the matter). Courts, largely indifferent to the fate of incum-bents and parties, did far more to shape districts for the 1990s.

Both the pressure for "minority-majority" districts and court interven-tion worked, in principle, to the advantage of Republicans. Most black and Latino voters favor Democrats, so ethnic gerrymanders concentrate Demo-cratic votes in districts where they are "wasted" because the party wins by many more votes than it needs—precisely what a partisan Republican gerry-mander would accomplish. Courts also drew maps more congenial to Repub-licans than the predominantly Democratic state legislatures would have de-vised on their own. (In Texas and North Carolina, where Democrats controlled the legislature and the statehouse, the new maps carefully pro-tected Democratic incumbents.) The partisan thrust of reapportionment clearly favored Republicans.

By itself, redistricting would have inspired an unusually large number of House retirements and produced a bumper crop of vulnerable incumbents in 1992. But the effects of redistricting were strongly reinforced by two other circumstances: the public's overwhelming contempt for Congress and the House banking scandal, which gave an individual focus to many voters' dif-fuse disdain for its members.

Overdrafts

Until its abolition in 1991, the House bank had existed in one form or another since 1830. The paychecks of members who used its services were automatically deposited in their accounts, which they could draw on by writing personal checks. For as long as anyone could remember, the bank gave members free "overdraft protection"—that is, the bank honored a check even when a member's account held insufficient funds to cover it. The bank refused to cover the checks of only the most flagrant abusers of this privilege. On more than one occasion, the system had come under scrutiny and criticism—if only as a political disaster waiting to happen—but not until the public became fed up with Congress for failing to take action against pressing national problems did the disaster occur. Auditors' reports of hundreds of members writing thousands of overdrafts became public knowledge in 1991. Coming at a time when the public was already primed to think the worst of Congress, and Republicans were desperate for any issue that might unlock the Democrats' almost half-century grip on the House, damage control proved impossible. Pressure from constituents, the media, the White House, hungry junior House Republicans, and, finally, innocent members who wanted to be absolved of suspicion made it impossible for the House leadership to sidetrack the issue. Members were left with no alternative but to vote to disclose all the names of the bad-check writers and the numbers of overdrafts they had written.

The Clarence Thomas Hearings

The Senate does not have a bank, but its Judiciary Committee did hold the October 1991 hearings in which Anita Hill accused Supreme Court nominee Clarence Thomas of sexual harassment. The all-male committee's treatment of Hill and her accusations infuriated many women, provoking the startling upsurge in political activity among women that was a unique feature of the 1992 elections. Thomas would not have been nominated had the Senate not been controlled by Democrats. Bush chose Thomas to divide the opposition party; Senate Democrats might have balked at elevating yet another conservative Republican to the Court but not at the risk of offending some of their own core supporters by rejecting an African American nominee. Thus the "Year of the Woman" was another legacy of divided government.

An Unusual Election

Divided government, the economy, redistricting, the House banking scandal, and the Clarence Thomas hearings set in motion the remarkable events of 1992. This section traces their complex effects on the 1992 congressional elections.

Table 7-4   Competition and Turnover in House Elections, 1982-1992

House seats	1982	1984	1986	1988	1990	1992
Congressional candidates	2,240	2,036	2,036	1,873	1,792	2,950
Uncontested seats[a]	56	67	71	78	85	34
Open seats	58	27	44	27	30	91
Experienced challengers[b]	26.7%	15.9%	13.8%	12.3%	10.4%	22.1%
Incumbents' vote[c]	65.0%	66.2%	68.4%	68.3%	64.0%	63.6%
Marginal incumbents[d]	28.6%	23.0%	15.3%	12.7%	23.5%	33.4%
Retiring incumbents	40	22	38	23	27	66
Defeated incumbents						
Primary election	10	3	2	1	1	19
General election	29	16	6	6	15	24
Total	39	17	8	7	16	43
Freshmen	81	45	50	34	45	110

[a] Only one major-party candidate on the general election ballot.

[b] Percentages of challengers who previously have held elective public office.

[c] Mean percentages of the two-party vote won by incumbents in contested elections.

[d] Percentages of incumbents elected with less than 60 percent of the two-party vote.

Competition and Turnover

The combination of redistricting, widespread disgust with Congress, and the individual vulnerability of members with significant overdrafts combined to produce a complete reversal of recent historical trends in congressional elections. There was a dramatic increase in the overall level of competition. Electoral competition depends largely on the availability, quality, and resources of nonincumbent candidates. Because the strongest potential candidates pursue rational career strategies, they take the field only when the prospects of winning (and of attracting resources) are higher than usual. Open seats consistently attract ambitious, career-oriented aspirants. Experienced and savvy challengers also emerge in greater numbers to take on incumbents when national conditions render the attempt less quixotic.[14]

In sharp contrast to the 1990 elections, the public's anger at Congress rose in plenty of time to shape the career decisions of potential candidates in 1992. Among incumbents, individual targets could be identified according to their vulnerability on the overdraft issue by mid-April 1992 at the latest. (The troubles of some were known even earlier.) The upheavals expected from redistricting, which had justified patience in 1990, dictated boldness in 1992. Some of the consequences for competition in House elections are documented in Table 7-4.

First, 1992 saw an astonishing jump in the sheer number of people seeking major-party nominations for Congress. The Federal Election Commission received filings from one thousand more candidates in 1992 than the

1982-1990 average. Not surprisingly, this surge was reflected in a precipitous drop in the number of seats won without major-party opposition in the general election. Only 34 seats went uncontested by one of the major parties in 1992, compared with 85 such seats in 1990 and an average of 71 for the previous decade. Indeed, fewer House seats went uncontested in 1992 than in any other postwar election. One reason was the unusually large number of seats with no incumbent running; open seats almost always attract candidates from both parties. But most of the difference is accounted for by occupied seats. Only 26 of 349 incumbents (7.4 percent) were spared a major-party opponent. Both the number and percentage of uncontested incumbents reached their lowest levels for the entire postwar period, falling more than 2.5 standard deviations below their 1946-1990 averages (67 and 17.3 percent, respectively). On the Senate side, only a single senator was unopposed in 1992, compared with five in 1990.

The 91 open seats that were up for grabs in the general election also set a postwar record; the previous high was 65, the 1946-1990 average, about 44. This record was created out of two others: postwar highs in the numbers of voluntary departures from the House (66) and of incumbents defeated in primary elections (19).[15]

The quality of challengers in 1992 was also considerably improved over recent elections. A simple but functional measure of quality is previous experience; candidates who have won lower elective offices are, on average, more effective and successful when they run for Congress than those who have not.[16] In 1992, 22 percent of both parties' challengers previously had held elective office, up from a postwar low of 10 percent for both parties in 1990. Still, this percentage was lower than in other recent election years in which the incumbents of at least one party fared poorly, such as 1974 and 1982. The politically ambitious professionals had a wider selection of opportunities in 1992 because an unusual number of seats lacked an incumbent, and, as always, experienced candidates flocked to compete for open seats. Although the percentage of experienced candidates for open seats in 1992 was typical for recent elections—59 percent—the number of open seats was so great that the number of experienced candidates running for them, 101, far exceeded the previous postwar record of 60 (not to mention the average of 41).

Heightened competition led to closer contests. The average share of the two-party vote won by incumbents in 1992 (63.6 percent) was the lowest since 1966, and the proportion of marginal incumbents (those who won with less than 60 percent of the two-party vote) was the highest since 1964: 33.4 percent. These figures are all the more impressive because they were recorded after many of the most vulnerable incumbents had already retired from the House or been defeated in primary elections.

Reapportionment and the general disdain for Congress, which was given individual focus by the House banking scandal, share principal responsibility for high turnover. Reapportionment threw a record number of House incum-

Table 7-5   House Bank Overdrafts and Membership Attrition
(in percentages)

Fate of representative	Number of overdrafts			
	None	1-99	100-199	200 or more
Retired from politics [a]	8.9	11.9	15.0	33.3
$X^2=13.09$, p<.005	(168)	(219)	(20)	(27)
Defeated in primary [b]	2.0	2.2	18.8	27.8
$X^2=37.91$, p<.001	(146)	(181)	(15)	(18)
Defeated in general election [c]	2.8	5.6	23.1	15.4
$X^2=11.83$, p<.01	(140)	(172)	(13)	(13)
Not in 103d Congress [d]	17.3	24.7	50.0	59.3
$X^2=28.86$, p<.001	(168)	(219)	(20)	(27)

Source: Gary C. Jacobson and Michael Dimock, "Checking Out: The Effect of Bank Overdrafts on the 1992 House Elections" (Paper delivered at the annual meeting of the Midwest Political Science Association, Chicago, April 15-17, 1993).

Note: Ted Weiss, D-N.Y., who died Sept. 14, 1992, is not included; Walter B. Jones, D-N.C., who died Sept. 15, 1992, but had already announced his retirement, is included. The number of cases from which the percentages were calculated are in parentheses.

[a] Left the House but did not run for another public office.

[b] Based on members seeking reelection; excludes the four pairs of incumbents competing with one another because of redistricting.

[c] Based on members winning renomination; excludes the five pairs of incumbents competing with one another because of redistricting.

[d] Not in 103d Congress for any reason.

bents into districts with other incumbents; some retired, some moved, and some (a total of nine in the primary and general elections) lost contests to other incumbents in redrawn districts. But the consequences of redistricting were greatly amplified by the publication of each member's record with the House bank.

Table 7-5 displays the consequences of these disclosures. The likelihood of exit from Congress by every route—retirement, defeat in the primary, and defeat in the general election—increased significantly with the number of bank overdrafts. When the 103d Congress convened in 1993, more than half the members of the 102d whose overdrafts had reached triple digits were gone, while 83 percent of those with a completely clean record resumed their seats. Had members with overdrafts been returned to Congress at the same rate as those without any, the 103d would have 78 newcomers rather than 110, and turnover would have been about average for a year ending in "2."

As high as it was, House turnover was lower than many observers anticipated; predictions had ranged from 120 to as many as 150 newcomers. Table 7-5 helps to explain why only twenty-four incumbents lost in November:

many of the most vulnerable members were already gone. Most of those who survived despite a large number of overdrafts came from districts in which their party enjoyed an overwhelming advantage.

The House banking scandal and its consequences are profoundly ironic. Contrary to the view initially spread by the media and accepted by the public, the overdrafts violated no laws and cost the taxpayers no money.[17] Yet the scandal ended many more congressional careers than policy disasters such as the savings and loan debacle, which left taxpayers holding the bag for hundreds of billions of dollars, or the quadrupling of the national debt from $1 billion to $4 billion in little more than a decade. Members of Congress routinely escape individual blame for major policy failures because the legislative process diffuses responsibility; the action is so complex, the details of policy so arcane, each individual's responsibility so obscure that it is impossible to figure out who is culpable and who is not. Everyone with a checking account understands what it means to balance a checkbook, however, and each House member's culpability was precisely measured in the count of unfunded checks. People may not have known who was to blame for gridlock, but they did know who wrote overdrafts. Like the drunkard in the old joke who searches for his car keys under the street light, not because he dropped them there, but because that's where the light is, voters used irrelevant information that was available and comprehensible as a substitute for relevant information that was not.[18]

High turnover always changes the face of Congress in some way; usually, the change is partisan and generational. In 1992 the major changes were instead demographic; 40 of the 110 newly elected members were ethnic minorities, women, or both. The increase of more than 50 percent in the number of African Americans and Latinos serving in the House is a direct result of the ethnic gerrymanders carried out at the behest of the courts. The plans worked; only one white candidate (Gene Green, D-Texas) was elected to a designated minority-majority district. The Year of the Woman, on the other hand, although helped along by redistricting, was primarily an artifact of divided government.

The Year of the Woman

The proximate reason for the abrupt increase in the number of women elected to the House and Senate in 1992 was the abrupt increase in the number of politically talented and experienced women who sought and won nominations for congressional seats in competitive states and districts. The surge of experienced, well-financed women candidates was in turn a direct consequence of the widespread outrage that was generated by the Thomas hearings.

The Year of the Woman—more precisely, the year of the Democratic woman—was forged in the primaries. The success rate of women candidates in general elections for the House (44 percent of those running) was not

Table 7-6   Gender and Success in the 1992 House Elections

Candidates	Women	Men	Percent women	Net change
Incumbents				
Democrats	17	181	8.6	
Winners	14	168	7.7	−3
Percent winners	82.3	92.8		
Republicans	9	119	7.0	
Winners	9	111	8.3	0
Percent winners	100.0	93.3		
Challengers				
Democrats	27	93	22.5	
Winners	2	4	33.3	2
Percent winners	6.9	4.3		
Republicans	13	182	6.7	
Winners	0	13	0.0	0
Percent winners	0.0	7.1		
Open seats				
Democrats	26	63	29.2	
Winners	19	38	33.3	18 [a]
Percent winners	73.0	60.3		
Republicans	13	75	14.8	
Winners	3	31	8.8	3
Percent winners	23.1	41.3		

[a] One of the Democratic women who won an open seat replaced another female Democrat.

dramatically higher than it had been over the previous two decades (39 percent), but the number of women running, 106, was far above the previous high of 69 in 1990. More important, half the nonincumbent women were running for open seats.

The data in Table 7-6 pinpoint the source of women's gains in the House. Contests involving incumbents contributed nothing. Republican women neither gained nor lost seats in such races; three Democratic congresswomen lost, and two Democratic women challengers won, for a net *loss* of one seat. Women's gains were concentrated entirely in the open House seats, with most of the action on the Democratic side. Twenty-nine percent of the Democrats running for open seats were women, and 73 percent of them won. Because their success rate was a bit higher than that of Democratic men seeking open seats, fully one-third of the Democrats elected to open House seats were women. Among Republican candidates for open seats, women did not fare so well as men; only three won. Thus nearly all the gains made by women in the 1992 House elections were the consequence of Democratic women taking open seats.

Table 7-7   Experience, Gender, and Success of Nonincumbent
House Candidates, 1992 (in percentages)

Candidates	Prior elective office	Winners	
		Prior office	No prior office
Challengers			
Democrats			
Men	24.7	8.7	2.9
	(93)	(23)	(70)
Women	18.5	40.0	0.0
	(27)	(5)	(22)
Republicans			
Men	24.3	13.6	5.1
	(181)	(44)	(137)
Women	21.4	0.0	0.0
	(14)	(3)	(11)
Open seats			
Democrats			
Men	66.7	71.4	38.2
	(66)	(42)	(21)
Women	69.2	83.3	50.0
	(26)	(18)	(8)
Republicans			
Men	53.3	52.5	28.6
	(75)	(40)	(35)
Women	30.8	50.0	11.1
	(13)	(4)	(9)

Note: The number of cases from which the percentages were calculated are in parentheses.

Democratic women did unusually well in 1992, then, because they won an uncommonly large share of the nominations for seats that their party's candidates would have had a serious chance of winning regardless of gender—specifically, seats not defended by an incumbent. They also did well because they were, by the standard of experience, high-quality candidates. This is evident from Table 7-7, which lists the proportion of nonincumbent candidates (by gender, party, and type of race) who had previously held some elective public office, along with their electoral fates. The Democratic women running for open seats were the most experienced of any subgroup, and their success rate was the highest of any. Observe, however, that prior elective office is strongly related to electoral success in all categories; winning is far more closely linked to experience than to gender. Women hold a lot more House seats in the 103d Congress, not because being female was such a great advantage in the general election, but because so many of the high-quality candidates in competitive districts were women.

The advances made by women in the Senate were also rooted in the

Table 7-8 Women Senate Candidates, 1992

Candidate	Party and state	Status	Previous office	Outcome
Barbara Mikulski	D-Md.	incumbent	U.S. Senate	won
Barbara Boxer	D-Calif.	open seat	U.S. House	won
Carol Moseley-Braun	D-Ill.	open seat	county recorder	won
Patty Murray	D-Wash.	open seat	state senate	won
Dianne Feinstein	D-Calif.	challenger	mayor	won
Claire Sargent	D-Ariz.	challenger	none	lost
Jean Lloyd-Jones	D-Iowa	challenger	state senate	lost
Gloria O'Dell	D-Kan.	challenger	none	lost
Geri Rothman-Serot	D-Mo.	challenger	city council	lost
Lynn Yeakel	D-Pa.	challenger	none	lost
Charlene Haar	R-S.D.	challenger	none	lost

primaries. Three of the four newly elected women—all Democrats—won open Senate seats; the fourth, Dianne Feinstein of California, defeated an appointed senator, John Seymour, who was an incumbent in name only. In contrast, the six women (five Democrats, one Republican) who faced elected incumbent senators in the general election lost. (The lone incumbent woman, Barbara Mikulski of Maryland, won reelection.) All the victors previously had held elective office, whereas four of the six losers were pursuing their first. The experience of Lynn Yeakel, a first-time candidate whose challenge to Sen. Arlen Specter, R-Pa., was fueled almost entirely by women's anger at his grilling of Anita Hill during the Thomas hearings, is instructive. The issue got Yeakel the nomination and formed the foundation of a strong challenge, but her inexperience led to mistakes during the campaign, and she ultimately came up short. The summary data on women Senate candidates are in Table 7-8.

Only one of the new women senators—Feinstein, who had narrowly lost a race to be California's governor in 1990—would have been a sure bet to win nomination without the special stimulus of the Anita Hill-Clarence Thomas confrontation. Carol Moseley Braun defeated incumbent Democrat Alan Dixon, who had voted to confirm Thomas, in the Illinois primary and then held on to win the general election against a relatively obscure first-time candidate. Patty Murray's self-described status as "a mom in tennis shoes" helped her to emerge on top in Washington State's "jungle" primary (in which candidates from all parties run on a single ballot, with the top Democratic and Republican vote getters winning each party's nomination). Barbara Boxer took the California nomination despite having 143 overdrafts at the House bank in large part because of the attention and support her gender attracted in the primary.

Apart from putting a record number of women into the upper house,

the 1992 Senate elections were not unusual. The average level of competition is always higher in Senate than in House elections—stronger challengers, closer elections, incumbents defeated more frequently—and 1992 was
no exception. But neither was it special. The numbers of newcomers
(twelve) and successful challengers (four) were about average. The inci-
dence of marginal incumbents—56 percent received less than 60 percent of
the vote—was about 10 percentage points higher than it was in the 1980-
1990 period, but that is the only sign of unusually intense competition. The
strange part of the 1992 Senate elections was the absence of net partisan
change.

Partisan Change in the House

Although the 1992 elections brought high turnover and sharp changes
in the House's demography, they registered little partisan change. The forces
that generated turnover did not have a consistent partisan thrust. Conditions
that favored Republicans—reapportionment, the House banking scandal, the
low repute of a Congress run by Democrats, perhaps the Gulf war—were
offset by conditions that favored Democrats—the stagnant economy, George
Bush's unpopularity, and Bill Clinton's vigorous and successful presidential
campaign.

Reapportionment, along with public disdain for Congress in general and
for check kiters in particular, should in theory have helped the Republicans
gain House seats. Most incumbents were Democrats, and a larger share of
Democrats had problems with overdrafts. Only 32.7 percent of the Democrats in the 102d Congress had no recorded overdrafts, and 13.4 percent had
one hundred or more. Among Republicans, 47.9 percent had no overdrafts,
and only 6.6 percent had one hundred or more. The damage to the Democratic party was limited, however, because some of its most vulnerable incumbents departed before Republicans could get a shot at them in the general election; fifteen of the thirty-six Democrats who wrote one hundred or
more unfunded checks were not on the November ballot. The new Democratic candidates won the seats of eight of the ten Democrats with one
hundred or more overdrafts who retired or lost the primary (and whose
districts did not disappear through redistricting). Moreover, by election day
the overdraft issue faced competition for public attention from issues that
had been at the center of the presidential campaigns—the economy, health
care, taxes—which were more central to voters' lives and on which Democrats had an overall edge.

Despite their modest gain of ten seats, reapportionment clearly helped
Republicans, because they would have done even worse under the old district maps. Redistricting allowed them to pick up a few seats even though
their presidential candidate got less support than any Republican since
Alfred Landon in 1936. But the Republicans fell far short of gaining the
twenty-five to thirty seats considered possible as late as September, and their

even headier dream of taking majority control of the House was again deferred indefinitely.[19] Even though voters in the states that had gained seats were considerably more Republican than voters in the states that had lost seats, Republicans enjoyed a net gain of only 2 seats among the 310 at stake in the affected states.[20] Eight of the 10 seats that Republicans added were in states that did not gain or lose seats. In 4 of these 8 cases, redistricting gave the Republican candidate a major boost by adding Republican voters to what already were heavily Republican districts.

The Gulf war, which had loomed so large only eighteen months before the 1992 House elections, played only a minor role in the outcome. It may have had some effect on the fates of those Democrats who represented districts where Bush was popular and had voted against authorizing the use of military force. In districts held by Democrats but won by Bush in 1988 with greater than his national average of 54 percent, 30.4 percent of the Democrats who voted against the war were opposed by experienced challengers, compared with 18.1 percent among those who voted for the war ($X^2 = 3.44$, p<.07). The antiwar Democrats were also the more likely to lose (16.7 percent, compared with 3.3 percent; $X^2 = 8.63$, p<.004). Of course, where Bush was strong, Democrats tended to vote for the war; only 30 of the 172 Democrats from strong Bush districts voted against the president. All told, the Gulf war vote may have lost the Democrats a handful of seats, but all of these losers had other troubles that might easily have cost them their seats anyway.

The Republicans' redistricting and other advantages were largely offset by the weakness at the top of the ticket. The drag of a presidential candidate who could attract only 38 percent of the vote made it harder to exploit electoral opportunities, particularly because Bush's decline from 1988 was steeper in the states that had gained seats in the House than in the states that had lost them. On the other hand, redistricting certainly protected Republican House candidates from the full effect of the Clinton victory.

California provides the starkest example of the standoff between the conditions that favored Republicans and those that favored Democrats. Throughout the 1980s Republican party officials had complained that Democratic state legislatures had deprived them of their rightful share of House seats by flagrant partisan gerrymandering. California was their main case in point, and rightly so: the Democrats in the California legislature had indeed done all they could to help their party's House candidates when redrawing the map after the 1980 census. The Democrats held a 26-19 majority in California's delegation to the 102d Congress. In 1992 the Republican governor, Pete Wilson, was able to move redistricting out of the Democratic legislature and into the state supreme court, which supervised the drawing of a map that delighted Republicans. Nonetheless, the Democrats won thirty of the fifty-two newly drawn seats in November—precisely the same proportion (58 percent) they won in 1990.

The presidential campaigns helped dash Republican hopes in California and elsewhere in 1992. Although Clinton's victory was no landslide, presidential campaign strategies helped Democrats in a number of states. Organizational coattails, at least, came into play. Clinton's wide lead in so many state polls forced Bush to campaign for states his party usually took for granted and to ignore other states where his cause appeared hopeless. In some large states, such as New York, Illinois, and California, the Republican presidential campaign was nearly invisible, leaving the other candidates on the Republican ticket to fend for themselves against united, energized statewide Democratic organizations. The result was an electoral debacle for Republicans up and down the ticket.

Clinton's campaign and victory probably was most helpful to Democrats running for open seats.[21] Party line voting is typically higher in these elections, and, as nonincumbents, the Democratic candidates did not carry the negative baggage associated with Congress. For this reason, the payoff Republicans expected from the new open seats that were created by redistricting and the preelection departure of Democratic incumbents did not materialize. Republicans managed a net gain of only two seats in open districts.

Partisan Change in the Senate

The absence of partisan change in the Senate is somewhat more surprising. Redistricting was not, of course, a factor. The seats at stake in 1992 were the same that had given control of the Senate to the Republicans with a twelve-seat swing in 1980 and to the Democrats with an eight-seat swing in 1986. But this time, they produced no net partisan change at all. The balance of national partisan forces had something to do with this stasis, but the customary idiosyncrasy of Senate elections had more to do with it.

Republicans initially had expected to cash in on both the Gulf war and the fact that the Democrats had more seats to defend (twenty-one of thirty-six), nine of which had been won only narrowly in 1986. Later in the campaign, Democrats anticipated picking up some seats with the help of anger over the Thomas hearings, the faltering economy, and Clinton's coattails. In the end, both parties were probably helped a little by their particular issues, and the net result was a wash. The two Democratic senators who lost (Terry Sanford of North Carolina and Wyche Fowler of Georgia) were among the three southern Democrats who had opposed authorizing the president to use military force against Iraq (Ernest Hollings of South Carolina, the third, won with just 52 percent of the vote). How much this vote contributed to their defeats is uncertain because both Sanford and Fowler had been narrow victors in 1986 and had other serious electoral problems. Still, if not decisive, their vote against going to war was certainly a. political liability.

On the Democratic side, the economy and Clinton's strength probably helped Russ Feingold to defeat Bob Kasten, the Republican incumbent, in Wisconsin. Some of Dianne Feinstein's landslide margin over John Seymour

Table 7-9   Correlation Between Senate and Presidential Election
Results, 1988 and 1992

Senate winner	States won by presidential candidate	
1988	Bush	Dukakis
Republican	11	3
Democrat	14	5
$X^2 = .10$, n.s.		
1992	Bush	Clinton
Republican	9	5
Democrat	5	15
$X^2 = 5.25$, $p < .05$.		

in California is attributable to her gender and Clinton's appeal in California, but she was the stronger candidate by almost any standard and would have won in 1992 without any help from national forces. If there was any helpful Democratic trend in 1992, it showed up mainly in the narrowness of some Republican incumbents' escapes and the relative ease with which most of the Democrats who had once seemed vulnerable won reelection. Six of the Republican winners got no more than 52 percent of the two-party vote; all but one of the Democratic winners (Ernest Hollings) enjoyed wider margins of victory. Democrats were aided by the departure of two scandal-ridden incumbents (Alan Cranston of California and Brock Evans of Washington) and their replacement by stronger Democratic nominees. Both parties held on to all of their open Senate seats.

As always, local matchups go far to explain the results of the Senate elections in 1992. Nonetheless, the election results for senator and president were not completely independent, as they had been in 1988 (see Table 7-9). The partisan outcomes matched in twenty-four of thirty-four states; the state-wide two-party vote shares for president and senator were correlated at .47 ($p < .01$), compared with an insignificant .16 in 1988. These results are consistent with the idea that by November the same considerations that were shaping presidential voting were influencing voters' choices lower on the ballot. The question of coattails aside—we can begin to measure them only when more detailed information is available—the outcomes of the November Senate elections suggest that fundamental concerns about the economy, taxes, and the future direction of the country had come to overshadow the issues of gender and congressional malfeasance that had dominated the primary election season.

The House results are also consistent with this interpretation. The voters' expression of anti-incumbent sentiment turned out to be considerably milder in the general election than most observers had expected. By November more basic considerations had come to the fore. Voters faced a choice between two parties (made more relevant and distinct by the presidential campaign) and two individuals as well as between a newcomer and an incumbent, and everything we know about voting behavior in congressional elections tells us that the first two dimensions would dominate the decision.[22] Of the 348 House incumbents still on the ballot in November, 324 (93 percent) were reelected.

There is also considerable evidence that voters had become disillusioned with divided government. According to an NBC News/*Wall Street Journal* poll, the public, which had supported having the presidency controlled by one party and Congress by the other by 2-1 margins during the first three years of the Bush presidency, was evenly divided on the question by August 1992; in an exit poll taken on election day, voters said that unified government was "better for the country" than divided government by a 62-28 margin.[23] Despite the Republicans' fondness for attacking the Democratic Congress for its contribution to gridlock, this change in sentiment did not bode well for them. Practically speaking, the likelihood of ending divided government by electing Bill Clinton was certainly far greater than of ending it by electing a Republican Congress, and anyone who paid attention to politics would know that. In this light, it is worth noting that ten of the nineteen successful House challengers (eight Republicans, two Democrats) took districts where the incumbent did not, in terms of the district's partisan coloration, belong in the first place. A move toward greater partisan consistency in voting would be expected from an electorate disenchanted with divided government.

The Perot Effect

Ross Perot's remarkable showing in the presidential election naturally raises the question of whether his candidacy had any effect on the congressional contests. None is discernable in the aggregate results. Perot voters were by definition opposed to politics as usual and might have been expected to vote en masse against incumbents. There is no evidence that they did so. Incumbents' electoral fates were totally unrelated to Perot's level of support in their states. Perot's temporary withdrawal in July, when he was running even with the major-party candidates in some polls, probably made him an irrelevancy in congressional campaigns. Had he stayed in and remained popular, congressional candidates of both parties would have faced the complex tactical problem of how to position themselves to appeal to both their own partisans and Perot's followers. The action would have been fascinating, the consequences hard to predict.

Term Limits

If Perot's candidacy had any effect, it probably helped to ensure the passage of congressional term limit initiatives in the fourteen states where they were on the ballot. Voters who turned out only because Perot was on the ballot certainly added to the margins by which these measures won. Showing some confusion about what it was they wanted, the same voters who supported term limits by 2-1 margins reelected 110 of 116 incumbents running in the states with term limits on the ballot, including 70 whose service exceeded the proposed limit (which varied from six to twelve years for representatives, depending on the state).[24]

Limiting congressional terms is an idea that rests more on emotion than analysis.[25] It provides a focus for public outrage against elected officials at a time when responsibility for political failure has been blurred by divided government. People who continue to approve of and vote for their own representative can support term limits to express their disdain for Congress as an institution. Indeed, citizens appear to be quite willing to sacrifice their own esteemed representatives and senators if, by doing so, they can prevent electorates in other states and districts from continuing to elect *their* own favorites. Members of Congress should be grateful that state-imposed term limits are almost certainly unconstitutional and that the Constitution provides no mechanism for a national referendum.[26]

The 103d Congress

After a tumultuous election year in which the voters were supposed to be united in their disgust with politics as usual, it is ironic to discover that most of the newly elected members of Congress are experienced professional politicians. More than 70 percent of the new House members, and ten of the twelve new senators, are veterans of lower elective offices. The new class of representatives and senators looks far more like astute professionals who have made successful career moves than like outsiders crashing the gates. This is not to say that they disdained to adopt outsider stances for their campaigns; shrewd candidates know that they have no choice but to be opportunists, using whatever issues the times offer to attract voters. But a great majority of the true outsiders who sought to ride into Congress solely on an antigovernment tide were left outside on election day.[27]

For this reason, the new Congress is not likely to be the hotbed of internal reform that had been expected when the talk was of 150 newcomers. For a time, it seemed that the only mandate the new class would share was to make its members' own lives more miserable by cutting back on perks and privileges. To do so would have been to mistake effect for cause, however. Public ire at the likes of overdrafts, pay raises, and the House gym is fueled primarily by unhappiness about the nation's economy and the general state of American public life. The fundamental source of public disaffection with Congress as well as with President Bush was the widespread sense that the country was moving in the wrong direction and no one was doing anything about it. Most of the newly elected members—and those who remain—seem politically savvy enough to realize that they will be judged far more by how effectively they and the new president address pressing economic and social problems than by any internal reforms they may adopt. What ultimately matters to voters is not how their representatives run Congress but how they run the country.

If this analysis is accurate, congressional Democrats have a large stake in the success of the Clinton administration and a powerful incentive to help it succeed. If Clinton fails to deliver on the economy, health care, and other major problems, and especially if congressional obstruction is to blame, Democrats in the House and Senate are likely to find themselves in deep political trouble. They are smart enough to realize this, so the prognosis for a period of cooperation between Congress and the president of the sort not seen since the Johnson administration is good.

The newly elected members of Congress—at least on the Democratic side—should be inclined to work with the president. Many campaigned on themes similar to Clinton's, promising to do something about jobs, health care, and education, but without behaving like traditional tax-and-spend liberals. The newly elected African American and Latino members are not, by earlier standards, particularly radical.[28] Many of them are from the South (ten of the eleven states of the old Confederacy sent at least one African American representative to the 103d Congress), reinforcing the trends that have made southern Democrats a less and less distinct wing of the congressional party.[29] As southern Democrats have come to represent constituencies that look increasingly like those represented by Democrats elsewhere, party unity in Congress has become easier for the Democrats to achieve. This should give Clinton an edge that his Democratic predecessors in the White House have not had.

Toward 1994

Clinton will need all the help—and luck—he can get, because the main legacy of divided government is a national agenda long on problems and short on solutions. Economic issues remain a political mine field. Democratic constituencies are itching to have Clinton and Congress deliver on the promises of new programs and initiatives; Republicans are poised to jump on any tax increase; Ross Perot stands ready to excoriate deficit spending. Even if Clinton's administration is reasonably successful, Republicans can look forward to picking up seats in Congress in 1994; Republican congressional candidates have always done well at midterm when a Democrat sits in the White House. And if the Clinton administration proves incapable of delivering on campaign promises to move the country forward, Republicans will be in a position to reap all of the deferred dividends from redistricting, and then some.

Notes

1. The 110 new House members are more than 2.5 standard deviations above the average of 64 over the past four decades.

2. This is calculated from the following regression estimates:

   Partisan seat swing $= -27.7 + (.745 *$ number of new members)
   (-3.66) (7.09)
   $R^2 = .69$; $SEE = 11.2$; $N = 23$ (1946-1990); t-ratios are in parentheses

3. Gary C. Jacobson, *The Electoral Origins of Divided Government: Competition in U.S. House Elections, 1946-1988* (Boulder: Westview Press, 1990), 106-109.

4. Gary C. Jacobson, "The Persistence of Democratic House Majorities," in *The Politics of Divided Government*, ed. Gary W. Cox and Samuel Kernell (Boulder: Westview Press, 1991), 57-84.

5. CBS News/*New York Times* poll, Oct. 28-31, 1990.

6. Eighty-four House incumbents and five senators had no major-party opponent in the general election. Those House incumbents who were challenged were blessed with the most unpromising group of challengers in any postwar election. Only 10 percent faced challengers who had ever won an elective public office, a proportion falling more than two standard deviations below the postwar mean. Little money flowed into the coffers of such an unpromising lot; they raised and spent less in real terms than any class of challengers since 1974. See Gary C. Jacobson, "Divided Government, Strategic Politicians, and the 1990 Congressional Election" (Paper delivered at the annual meeting of the Midwest Political Science Association, Chicago, April 18-20, 1991), 7-8.

7. Ibid., 3-4.

8. James Risen, "Bush Bypassed Last Chance to Spur Economy," *Los Angeles Times*, Nov. 2, 1992, D1.

9. John Petrocik, "Divided Government: Is It All in the Campaigns?" in *Politics of Divided Government*, 20-30.

10. The correlation between assessments of the economy and of Congress across the surveys used in Figure 7-2 $(N=10)$ is .85; between the economy and Bush's handling of the economy, .96; and between Congress and Bush's handling of the economy, .91. The president's rating on the economy is correlated with his overall performance rating at .96 as well—though his overall rating averages about 26 percentage points higher.

11. *Los Angeles Times*, Sept. 25, 1992, A22.

12. Rhodes Cook, "Map-Drawers Must Toe the Line in Upcoming Redistricting," *Congressional Quarterly Weekly Report*, Sept. 1, 1990, 2786-2793.

13. Ronald D. Elving, "GOP Gets a Better Shot at California Seats," *Congressional Quarterly Weekly Report*, Feb. 1, 1992, 260-262; Jeffrey L. Katz, "Turnover Is Only Certainty for Florida's Delegation," *Congressional Quarterly Weekly Report*, Aug. 15, 1992, 2475-2476; Bob Benenson and Ines Pinto Alicea, "State Legislators in New York Near Compromise on Map," *Congressional Quarterly Weekly Report*, June 6, 1992, 1641-1642; Charles Mahtesian and Ines Pinto Alicea, "Redone District Lines Nudge Dwyer, Pursell from House," *Congressional Quarterly Weekly Report*, March 28, 1992, 825-828.

14. Gary C. Jacobson and Samuel Kernell, *Strategy and Choice in Congressional Elections*, 2d ed. (New Haven: Yale University Press, 1983), 29-34.

15. Also contributing to the total number of open seats was the death of one incumbent and redistricting plans that left five pairs of incumbents squaring off in the general election.

16. Gary C. Jacobson, "Strategic Politicians and the Dynamics of U.S. House Elections, 1946-86," *American Political Science Review* 83 (1989): 781-784.

17. Adam Clymer, "Public Believes the Worst on Bank Scandal," *New York Times*, April 2, 1992.
18. Samuel Popkin, *The Reasoning Voter* (Chicago: University of Chicago Press, 1991), 92-95.
19. William J. Eaton, "Angry Electorate Has House Incumbents Feeling Jittery About Campaign," *Los Angeles Times*, Sept. 18, 1992, A18; Dave Kaplan and Charles Mahtesian, "Election's Wave of Diversity Spares Many Incumbents," *Congressional Quarterly Weekly Report*, Nov. 7, 1992, 3570.
20. George Bush had won 55.9 percent of the votes cast in 1988 in the states gaining seats, 51.8 percent in the states losing seats.
21. Kaplan and Mahtesian, "Diversity Spares Incumbents."
22. Gary C. Jacobson, *The Politics of Congressional Elections*, 3d ed. (New York: HarperCollins, 1992), chap. 6.
23. David Shribman, "Public Is Turning Against Divided Government, and Bush's 'Gridlock' Speech May Turn on Him," *Wall Street Journal*, Sept. 9, 1992, A16; *New York Times*, Nov. 4, 1991, B1.
24. Thomas Galvin, "Limits Score a Perfect 14-for-14, but Court Challenges Loom," *Congressional Quarterly Weekly Report*, Nov. 7, 1992, 3594.
25. Jacobson, *Politics of Congressional Elections*, 247-248.
26. Jenifer Warren and Alan C. Miller, "Wins in 14 States Fuel U.S. Term Limit Drive," *Los Angeles Times*, Nov. 5, 1992, A13.
27. Jeffrey Katz, "Candidates Move to Outside as Tactic to Win Races," *Congressional Quarterly Weekly Report*, May 2, 1992, 1176-1180.
28. William J. Eaton, "Minorities' House Gain May Help Clinton," *Los Angeles Times*, Nov. 7, 1992, A16.
29. The exception is Arkansas, which does not have a sufficient number of seats (four) and blacks (16 percent) for a workable racial gerrymander.

8

Conclusion:
Some Things Old, Some Things New

Michael Nelson

To political journalists, whose gaze is ever concentrated on the present, every election is new and important in its own right. The elections of 1992, trumpeted variously in the post-election day media for inaugurating a new generation of leadership, a new Democratic party, a new era for women in politics, and other such innovations, were no exception. Political scientists tend to take a longer view. A few "critical" elections—that is, elections that usher in an enduring realignment of the political parties, such as those of 1860, 1896, and 1932—occupy center stage in their treatment of electoral history, but most elections drift into the background.[1] By that standard, 1992 seems likely to settle into the pages of the academic journals as a rather ordinary affair.

Not surprisingly, neither profession of political analysts has it all right or all wrong. A careful reading of the preceding seven chapters of this book suggests that the truth about the elections of 1992 lies somewhere in between the journalist's "gee-whiz!" and the political scientist's "ho-hum." Some things were new about this election, some were old.

Some Things New

Among the new elements in 1992 (new, that is, to the modern political era) were these: the generational change in executive leadership, the election of a Democratic president, the improved quality of the presidential campaign, innovative roles for the media in the campaign, the independent candidacy of Ross Perot, the rapid change in the demographic makeup of Congress, and the end (or interruption) of the era of divided government.

Generational Change

The most visible, if not the most important, new aspect of the elections of 1992 was the youth of its victors. Is any image from the campaign more vivid than that of baby boomers Bill Clinton and Albert Gore dancing with their wives and children on the stage of the Democratic convention to the music of Fleetwood Mac?

Clinton was born in 1946. His recent predecessors as president were born much earlier: George Bush in 1924, Ronald Reagan in 1911, Jimmy

Carter in 1924, Gerald Ford in 1913, Richard Nixon in 1913, Lyndon B. Johnson in 1908, and John F. Kennedy in 1917. In generational terms what makes Clinton distinctive is less his age upon taking office (Kennedy, forty-three, was younger than Clinton, forty-six) than the contrasting national experiences that shaped his and the earlier presidents' lives. For each of Clinton's recent predecessors, the primary shaping experiences were the Great Depression and World War II. For Clinton, the first postwar president, the shaping experiences were the New Frontier and Great Society and the war in Vietnam. Indeed, one of the major contrasts of the 1992 campaign, as Donald E. Stokes and John J. DiIulio, Jr., point out in Chapter 1, was between Bush the gung-ho World War II pilot and Clinton the morally anguished Vietnam-era student.

The full political significance of the generational change that brought Clinton and Gore (who was forty-four on inauguration day) to office is not yet apparent. But clearly the Manichean world view that flowed from the experiences of the previous generation—Is big government good or bad? Should the United States seek to defeat or coexist with communism?— means little to the new president. Instead, Clinton has been led by his generation's morally ambiguous experiences to consider more pragmatic questions, such as—good or bad intentions aside—when and how is government intervention helpful or not helpful in solving a particular problem?

A Democratic President

A Democrat was elected president in 1992 for the first time in sixteen years and only the second time in twenty-eight years. It is hard to overstate just how completely the Republicans have dominated recent presidential politics. From 1968 to 1988 the Republican nominee won five of six elections: Nixon in 1968 and 1972, Reagan in 1980 and 1984, and Bush in 1988. All but the first of these victories was a landslide; in contrast, the Democrats' single triumph (Carter in 1976, two years after the Watergate crisis drove Nixon from office in disgrace) was narrowly won. The Democratic candidates' share of the popular vote in this period was pitifully low: 43 percent for Hubert H. Humphrey in 1968, 38 percent for George McGovern in 1972, 50 percent for Carter in 1976, 41 percent for Carter in 1980, 41 percent for Walter F. Mondale in 1984, and 46 percent for Michael S. Dukakis in 1988. Collectively, the Democratic nominees won 679 electoral votes in these elections, compared with 2,501 for the Republicans.

Clinton's victory, although cheering to Democrats, was less than triumphant. To be sure, he received more electoral votes (370) than any Democrat had won since Johnson in 1964. Twenty-one states with 191 electoral votes had supported the Republican nominee for president in all six elections of the 1968-1988 era; Clinton won these states by a 118-73 electoral vote majority. But Clinton won only 43 percent of the national popular vote— exactly the average share received by his six Democratic predecessors. The enduring question then is, Did the Democrats win the presidential election in 1992, or did the Republicans, whose candidate received 37.4 percent of the popular vote, simply lose it?

A Better Campaign

Enduring or fleeting, substantial or modest, Clinton's victory was the product of an improved political campaign, according to Paul J. Quirk and Jon K. Dalager in Chapter 3. Quirk and Dalager define a good presidential campaign as one in which the candidates compete by advancing reasonable and specific positions on the major issues facing the country and in which the voters are able to learn about these positions and about aspects of the candidates' records and character that bear on their competence to be president.

To be sure, the 1992 campaign did not fully realize this ideal of a good presidential campaign. Some pressing national issues, especially the budget deficit, race relations, and foreign policy, were ignored by the major-party candidates. The debate on some other issues was superficial (Clinton's tax proposals), narrowly short-term (Bush's economic policies), or irrelevant (Clinton's student protests against the Vietnam War).

Still, Quirk and Dalager argue, the presidential campaign was better in 1992 than in other recent elections. Bush, Clinton, and Perot debated—and the media covered—some issues in considerable detail. The candidates "largely avoided using the most blatantly deceptive or manipulative methods of persuasion," again under the watchful gaze of the media. And the voters, much more than in 1988, were satisfied that they had learned enough about the candidates and the issues to make an informed choice on election day.

New Roles for the Media

Political scientists are fond of observing that, as the political parties have become less important in determining which candidates are nominated for president and how the voters decide whom to support, the mass media, especially television, have become more important. Nothing happened in 1992 to challenge the truth of this observation. But much happened to change the means by which the media cover the candidates for the benefit of the voters and the candidates use the media to reach the voters.

As Philip Meyer notes in Chapter 4, the most obvious new roles for the media in 1992 were created by the candidates. Former governor Jerry Brown of California and independent businessman Ross Perot were innovative in their use of toll-free telephone numbers, Brown to solicit campaign donations and Perot to recruit volunteers. Brown and Perot also bought time on television to speak to the voters in thirty-minute "infomercials," a throwback to the early days of television campaigning that was so old as to seem new. Perot and, later, Bush and Clinton handled live televised call-ins from the voters on "Larry King Live," "Donahue," and the various network morning shows. In an effort to reach young voters, Clinton played the saxophone on "Arsenio Hall" and answered questions on MTV. Meanwhile, spot advertising declined.

Important as these innovations by the candidates were, Meyer argues that in less noted but perhaps more significant ways the media adopted new roles in their coverage of the candidates. On the national level, for example, all the network evening news programs reduced candidate sound bites and media events in favor of longer, more analytic stories about the issues. On the local level, newspapers in cities such as Charlotte, North Carolina, and Wichita, Kansas, actively sought to learn about their readers' concerns and directed their campaign reporting accordingly. As a result, "horse race" coverage of which candidate was gaining and which falling back on a particular day was reduced in favor of covering the issues. The improved campaign that Quirk and Dalager describe owed much to the media's new roles.

Ross Perot

Ross Perot was not the first significant independent candidate of the modern political era. George C. Wallace, the segregationist governor of Alabama, ran a strong presidential campaign in 1968, as did Rep. John B. Anderson of Illinois in 1980.[2] But the Perot candidacy of 1992 differed from its predecessors in several important ways.

For one thing, Perot was not an established political leader when he entered the race, as were Wallace, Anderson, and the other prominent independent candidates of the twentieth century: Gov. J. Strom Thurmond of South Carolina and former vice president Henry A. Wallace in 1948, Sen. Robert M. LaFollette of Wisconsin in 1924, and former president Theodore Roosevelt in 1912. Indeed, Perot explicitly assailed the unwillingness of politicians to meet the pressing national crises of the day, contrasting their failures to his own problem-solving successes in business. For another, Perot was enormously well financed. Lacking the resources of a major party, Anderson and George Wallace had run shoestring campaigns, an especially enervating disability for candidates who cannot count on the support of fellow partisans in the electorate but must build their coalitions from scratch. Perot simply opened his multi-billion dollar wallet and spent approximately $60 million of its contents. Finally, despite the peculiar hat in, hat out, hat in rhythm of his campaign, which is chronicled by Ryan J. Barilleaux and Randall E. Adkins in Chapter 2 and by Quirk and Dalager in Chapter 3, Perot amassed 19 percent of the popular vote, more than any other independent candidate had won since Roosevelt in 1912.

In the aftermath of the election, Perot's candidacy left two questions unresolved. First, will he transform his independent candidacy into a third party that will endure and nominate candidates for other offices?[3] It is far from certain that Perot will do this or that he will succeed if he tries. Typically, in the modern era, the supporters of an independent candidate have nothing more in common with each other or with their candidate than their dislike of the current Republican and Democratic nominees. As a result, there is little to unite them for a constructive long-term effort. Second, can an independent or third-party candidate who lacks a regional base be anything more than a sideshow in presidential elections? Unlike Thurmond and George Wallace, who spoke for much of the Deep South and carried several states, Perot spoke for many voters in every region but for a plurality in none. Because he carried no states, his electoral vote (constitutionally, the only vote that counts in a presidential election) was zero.[4]

A New Look for Congress

In contrast to the presidential election, the congressional elections of 1992 witnessed no departure from the partisan patterns of the modern era. In political terms what was new about 1992, according to Gary C. Jacobson in Chapter 7, was how little partisan swing there was. The Democrats have controlled the House of Representatives since 1955; they control it still. Their 258-176 majority in the 103d Congress, ten seats fewer than in the 102d as a result of modest Republican gains, is barely below their recent average. The Democrats also have controlled the Senate since 1955—except for the first six Reagan years—and continue to do so. The postelection Democratic majority in the upper house, 57-43, is the same as it was before the election, slightly higher than their recent average.

Nevertheless, the 103d Congress, especially the House of Representatives, looks different from previous Congresses in every way but its partisan makeup. More new members (110) entered the House in 1993 than in the past forty years, the result mostly of dramatic increases in the number of retirements (66, compared with 27 in 1990) and primary election defeats (19, compared with 1 in 1990). Demographically, 1992 was the "Year of the Woman," especially the Democratic woman: the number of women representatives and senators rose from 28 to 47 and from 2 to 6, respectively. Ethnic minorities (again, mostly Democrats) benefited from the election as well: the number of African Americans in Congress increased from 25 to 38 in the House and from 0 to 1 in the Senate, and the ranks of Latinos in the House rose from 11 to 17.

United Party Government

Clinton's victory in the presidential election, joined with continued Democratic success in Congress, is a departure from the modern era of divided government, in which different political parties have usually controlled the presidency and Congress. Historically, united party government has been the norm—from 1901 to 1969 the same party controlled both elected branches 79 percent of the time—but the elections of 1968 marked the beginning of a historically unprecedented pattern of Republican presidents and Democratic Congresses. From 1969 until Clinton's inauguration in 1993, united government prevailed only 18 percent of the time, during the four years of the Carter administration.

According to Jacobson, divided government "emerged from the electorate's unwitting attempt to have its cake and eat it too." Progovernment Democratic candidates for Congress promised the voters that they would protect popular but expensive social programs, antitax Republican presidential candidates promised not to make anyone pay for those programs, and both were elected. Other explanations for the phenomenon of divided government may be added to this analysis. Republican candidates for president benefited from the widespread perception that they were better able than their Democratic opponents to protect the national security, a largely executive responsibility. Furthermore, the Republican candidates represented the more homogeneous and thus the more united party, another important advantage in presidential elections.[5]

Does Clinton's election mark the end of the era of divided government or, like the Carter administration, will it only be an interlude? In 1992 the voters became concerned about the enormous budget deficits that, Jacobson argues, inevitably accompany divided government and about the economic problems to which these deficits contributed. Wanting united government (polls showed a departure from previous elections on this count) and aware that electing a Democratic president was, practically speaking, more likely to bring the two branches into partisan accord than overturning the deeply entrenched Democratic majority in Congress, the electorate chose Clinton. Again, one may expand upon this explanation of the 1992 results. The Republicans lost much of their national security-based advantage in presidential elections when the Cold War ended, reducing the public's concern about foreign affairs. In addition, the Democratic party presented a much more united front to the voters than did the Republicans, who were newly torn by the abortion issue and other questions of morality.

In sum, the foundations of divided government have eroded. But they have not crumbled. The Republicans undoubtedly will find it easier to reunite in opposition than the Democrats will to remain united in power. The national Democratic party has yet to show that it can win a majority of popular votes for its presidential nominees. The end of the Cold War does not mean that the world is no longer a dangerous place. Meanwhile, the Republicans have yet to come close to winning the House; their peak since 1956 is 192 seats, 26 short of a majority. If Clinton's performance on the economy or in foreign affairs is weak, the Republicans probably will recapture the White House in 1996 and, lacking control of Congress, will restore divided government.

Some Things Old

Not all aspects of the elections of 1992 were new. As the preceding chapters show, much about the elections was familiar, at least in terms of the modern era. Among the "some things old" were the century-long cycle of politics and domestic policy into which Clinton's election fell, the structured workings of the quarter-century-old reformed nominating process for presidential candidates, the enhanced position of the vice president, and the mix of valence politics and cultural politics that constitutes the substance of political campaigns.

The Cycle of Politics and Policy

As I indicate in Chapter 6, Clinton's election fits neatly into the cycle of politics and domestic policy that has characterized the twentieth-century presidency. Clinton ran a change-oriented campaign in the hope of becoming a President of Achievement—that is, a president who is able to persuade Congress to enact legislation that significantly alters the role of the federal government in American society. Like Woodrow Wilson, Franklin D. Roosevelt, Johnson, and Reagan—the century's previous Presidents of Achievement—Clinton seems to be endowed with the requisite leadership skills and policy ideas to succeed. Unlike them, however, his change-oriented campaign was not accompanied by the sort of personal landslide victory and long congressional coattails that a Presidency of Achievement requires.

Instead, Clinton probably will be a first-term President of Preparation in the mold of Theodore Roosevelt, Kennedy, and Carter. The historical function of such presidents is to raise new ideas (in Clinton's case, an "invest-and-grow" strategy for long-term economic prosperity) to the top of the national political agenda. Like his predecessors, Clinton took office in the wake of a President of Consolidation (Bush in his case, Dwight D. Eisenhower in Kennedy's, Nixon and Ford in Carter's) whose main business was to rationalize the legislative accomplishments of the most recent President of Achievement. Although problems await Clinton, the cycle theory predicts that if he is a successful President of Preparation he may win a sufficiently convincing reelection in 1996 to become a second-term President of Achievement.

The Nominating Process

Most political scientists still describe the presidential nominating process that emerged from the late 1960s and early 1970s as "new." As Barilleaux and Adkins suggest in Chapter 2, it is time for a different adjective. The process of selecting delegates through open primaries and caucuses that replaced the traditional convention system dominated by party leaders will mark its twenty-fifth anniversary in 1994.[6]

Not just the rules but also the rhythm of the reformed nominating process has become a settled part of the modern political era. Barilleaux and Adkins find, in both the Democratic and the Republican parties, a stable "nominating environment" with four main elements: (1) established methods and timing of delegate selection, (2) the media's role as intermediary in the process, (3) the importance of fund raising to winning the nomination, and (4) the entrepreneurial nature of presidential candidacies. Clinton and Bush each thrived in this environment in 1992. Each also navigated success-fully through the five stages of the nomination race that Barilleaux and Adkins identify: the preelection-year "exhibition season," in which the field of contenders forms; the February "winnowing" stage of early primaries and caucuses, in which the weaker candidates fall by the wayside; the delegate-rich "breakaway" stage in March, when a strong front-runner emerges; the spring "mop-up" stage, in which the front-runner consolidates the victory; and the summer "convention" stage, which is really the beginning of the general-election campaign.

The Vice Presidency

Clinton's selection of Gore as his vice presidential candidate impressed many political observers as a new tactic in presidential elections. Departing from the traditional practice of ticket balancing (that is, naming a running mate who is substantially different from the head of the ticket), Clinton chose someone who is a fellow southerner, a fellow Southern Baptist, a fellow political moderate, a fellow baby boomer, and a fellow policy "wonk."

Yet the Gore nomination was more in keeping with modern "politics as usual" than may seem apparent. It was, as Quirk and Dalager note, ticket balancing of a subtle kind: Clinton's potential vulnerabilities as a foreign policy novice, prodevelopment governor, skirt chaser, and draft avoider were buttressed by Gore's Senate experience, environmentalist credentials, stable family life, and service in the Vietnam War. More important, however, Clin-ton's selection of Gore satisfied the modern public concern that the vice president be ready and able to step into the presidency at a moment's notice, a concern born chiefly of the nuclear age, in which the harm an incompetent president can do could be cataclysmic. In recent years, the concern for vice presidential competence has led presidents to entrust their vice presidents with visible and substantial roles in their administrations and with the institu-tional resources to perform their roles well.[7] It also has led most presidential candidates to choose running mates who impress the voters as being of presi-dential caliber. (When candidates have failed to do so, as Bush did in choos-ing Dan Quayle in 1988, they have paid the price in the coin of lost votes on election day.)[8] Before selecting Gore, Clinton followed the modern practice of having a trusted adviser, Warren Christopher, direct a thorough study of the backgrounds of prospective running mates.

Issues

Elections are, by their nature, choices among individuals: the result of an election is that a person assumes an office. But elections are substantive matters as well. In no small measure, the candidates present themselves to the voters in terms of the issues of the day. The issues that made up the elections of 1992 mixed valence politics and cultural politics in the same blend that has dominated the modern political era.

Valence politics, according to Stokes and DiIulio in Chapter 1, is fought over issues on which the disagreement is about performance more than position. Every candidate, and virtually every voter, is in favor of peace and security, economic prosperity, honest government, and law and order; there is no prosurrender, prodepression, procorruption, procrime party. Candidates and parties differ strongly, however, on who is best able to satisfy these desiderata. Bush, Clinton, and Perot did not disagree at all on the need to increase economic growth, for example; what they debated furiously in their three nationally televised encounters in mid-October was which of them was most likely to secure this goal as president. Candidates also differ on which valence issue should be the most important in an election. The three candidates in 1992 had few disagreements about foreign policy, but Bush clearly thought that it should matter more in the voting than Clinton and Perot did.

Stokes and DiIulio argue that, because of the decline of political parties and the "kaleidoscopic" nature of the problems that vex modern governments, valence politics is more important in the modern era than "position politics." Position issues are those matters on which the candidates take opposing stands—for or against slavery in the Civil War era; for or against social welfare programs during the New Deal. Jean Bethke Elshtain, in Chapter 5, adds to their analysis a lively mix of cultural issues on which position politics still dominates, such as abortion and family values. She hopes, however, for a "new social covenant" between the voters and their leaders in which the clamoring voices of special-interest pleaders will be drowned out in favor of open, consensus-seeking discussion concerning the common interests of all.

Conclusion

Every election has some new elements. In 1988, for example, the country witnessed the first election of an incumbent vice president as president since 1836; it also was the first time that a new president was elected, as Bush was, while his party simultaneously was losing seats in the House, the Senate, the state legislatures, and the state governorships. Every election also has some familiar qualities: the Republican and Democratic parties dominate the race, the overwhelming majority of incumbents are reelected to Congress, and so on.

As we have seen, the elections of 1992 were no exception to the rule of "some things old, some things new." That a young Democrat was elected president against the incumbent and a serious independent candidate after a high-quality campaign in which the media played innovative roles was new, as was the election of a demographically diverse Congress that, because it too was Democratic, offered the country united party government. Clinton's place in the cycle of politics and policy, the nominating process, the vice presidency, and the issues were familiar features of the elections, at least in terms of the modern era.

To an unusual extent, the new elements in 1992 seem potentially more important than the old. Much depends on what happens between these elections and the next. A successful Clinton administration may set the stage for a new Democratic majority, a Presidency of Achievement, and an end to, not just an interruption of, the era of divided government. If Clinton is politically unsuccessful, the forecast for 1996 is much more uncertain.

Notes

1. V. O. Key, "A Theory of Critical Elections," *Journal of Politics* 17 (February 1955): 3-18.
2. Independent candidates differ from third-party candidates. Independent candidates run as individuals; third-party candidates are the nominees of established party organizations.
3. Theodore J. Lowi, "The Party Crasher," *New York Times Magazine*, Aug. 23, 1992, 28-30.
4. Thurmond won only 2 percent of the national popular vote but carried four states with thirty-nine electoral votes. George Wallace won 14 percent of the popular vote, five states, and forty-six electoral votes. Perot won 19 percent of the popular vote but no states and no electoral votes.
5. Michael Nelson, "Constitutional Aspects of the Elections," in *The Elections of 1988*, ed. Michael Nelson (Washington, D.C.: CQ Press, 1989), 181-209.
6. The McGovern-Fraser commission, known formally as the Commission on Party Structure and Delegate Selection, was created in 1969 by the Democratic National Committee to reform the party's presidential nominating process in favor of more rank-and-file participation. Its innovations, although modified over the years, have fundamentally transformed the nominating processes of both major parties. See "The McGovern-Commission Report," in *Historic Documents on Presidential Elections, 1787-1988*, ed. Michael Nelson (Washington, D.C.: Congressional Quarterly, 1991), 574-584.
7. Michael Nelson, *A Heartbeat Away* (Washington, D.C.: Brookings Institution/Priority Press, 1988). See also Nelson, "Choosing the Vice President," *PS: Political Science and Politics* 21 (Fall 1988): 858-868.
8. Nelson, "Constitutional Aspects of the Elections," 190.